REPRESENTING FEMALE ARTISTIC LABOUR, 1848–1890

Representing Female Artistic Labour, 1848–1890

Refining Work for the Middle-Class Woman

PATRICIA ZAKRESKI
University of Exeter, UK

ASHGATE

Published by
Ashgate Publishing Limited
Gower House
Croft Road
Aldershot
Hampshire GU11 3HR
England

Ashgate Publishing Company
Suite 420
101 Cherry Street
Burlington, VT 05401-4405
USA

Ashgate website: http://www.ashgate.com

British Library Cataloguing in Publication Data
Zakreski, Patricia
   Representing female artistic labour 1848–1880 : refining work for the middle-class woman
   1. Women in literature 2. English literature – 19th century – History and criticism 3. Middle class women – Great Britain – Social conditions – 19th century 4. Middle class women – Employment – Great Britain – History – 19th century 5. Women artists in literature 6. Women authors in literature
   I. Title
   820.9'9287'09034

Library of Congress Cataloging-in-Publication Data
Zakreski, Patricia.
   Representing female artistic labour, 1848–1890 : refining work for the middle-class woman / Patricia Zakreski.
      p. cm.
   Includes bibliographical references and index.
   ISBN 0-7546-5103-7 (alk. paper)
   1. Middle class women—Employment—England—History—19th century. 2. Sex role in literature. 3. Work in literature. 4. Needleworkers—England—History—19th century. 5. Women artists—England—History—19th century. 6. Women authors—England—History—19th century. 7. Actresses—England—History—19th century. 8. Women—England—History—19th century. I. Title.

   HD6136.Z25 2006
   331.40942'09034—dc22

                                                                                    2005033201

ISBN-13: 978-0-7546-5103-1
ISBN-10: 0-7546-5103-7

Printed and bound in Great Britain by MPG Books Ltd, Bodmin, Cornwall.

Contents

List of Figures

Acknowledgements

This book was written with the help of many people, both in its initial preparations as a doctoral thesis and during subsequent revision. I would especially like to thank Sally Shuttleworth, Jackie Labbe, Shirley Foster and Valerie Sanders. At various stages in the preparation of this book, their advice and careful reading has been invaluable. I would also like to thank my colleagues at the University of Exeter for their assistance during the final phase of this book.

I am very grateful to the University of Sheffield for providing the grant that made this research possible. I would like to thank the staffs of the University of Sheffield Library, the British Library, the Fawcett Library, the Sheffield City Library, and Special Collections at the University of Exeter for patiently fulfilling all my requests.

Quotations from *Aurora Leigh* by Elizabeth Barrett Browning edited by Kerry McSweeney (1993) by permission of Oxford University Press.

Introduction

Refining Work

Writing in 1861 about the need for a realistic understanding of women's lives in Victorian England, the author of 'Facts *Versus* Ideas' for the *English Woman's Journal* listed a series of 'stereotyped phrases' that she thought had become overused and meaningless:

> In speaking or writing of woman and her affairs, the public have so long been accustomed to a certain set of stereotyped phrases, (many of these now done to death, and fit only to be cast aside as useless) that when other signs are chosen to represent what is alive and not dead, alarm is taken lest some idol or household image is about to be demolished … The one most often called for, brought forward rightly or wrongly on every possible occasion, and used whenever the speaker or writer feels himself embarrassed, or in danger of arriving at other conclusions than he knows are expected, (from at least the male portion of his audience) is the word "domestic", and it invariably winds up some grand, fantastic rhodomontade about feeling and feeling alone. This peroration, so "touchingly tender", is quite conclusive to those who *listen* but do not think; the speaker or writer is applauded accordingly, and Paterfamilias is once more assured that all is right with his household gods.[1]

The word 'domestic', she notes, is used to describe the home as a sphere dedicated solely to emotion; consequently, the domestic sphere had become enshrined and deified as a realm of womanly self-sacrifice and unassailable virtue through unthinking repetition by the self-satisfied male householder. Her particular problem with this sentimental idealisation of the domestic is that in limiting the function of domesticity it restricts women to the inanity of the middle-class household existence and denies the possibility:

> that a woman may be employed in other work than household, and yet be domestic in the simple meaning of the word, in the same way that some men are called "domestic", although they have their business out of doors to attend to. Consequently, women may be full of home love, and home affections, who in like manner have an occupation requiring their presence for some many hours of the day elsewhere.[2]

Remaining in the domestic sphere, this author argues, is not a necessary constituent of a domestic identity.

---

1   A.R.L., 'Facts *Versus* Ideas', *English Woman's Journal* 7 (1861), pp. 74-75.
2   Ibid., p. 77.

Such claims, that a woman could still be domestic while working outside the home, were not often so readily admitted in the debate concerning proper occupations for middle-class Victorian women. To associate the middle-class woman with the degrading public world of the marketplace was to contradict the cherished image of her as the embodiment of private virtue and unworldly moral superiority. Indeed, the mainstream notion that her most appropriate function, whether married or not, was that of the domestic guardian – the 'angel in the house' – seemed to preclude the very notion of public work for women. 'It is a woman's *business*', a writer for the *Quarterly Review* had argued ten years earlier, 'to be beautiful'.[3] But women's 'business' could not be so easily circumscribed as this writer implies. Throughout the second half of the nineteenth century, a series of complex arguments sought to redefine and expand the notion of woman's business. In particular, many looked to artistic employment as the solution to the 'problem' of women's need and desire for work. It is the project of this book to trace these arguments as they developed both alongside and in contrast to the separate spheres ideology.

The ideology of separate spheres disavowed any connection between models of femininity and paid work. Professional, remunerative work was defined as a masculine concept, and the 'woman's sphere' of the domestic was identified as a place of leisure and a haven from the rigours of the capitalist marketplace. It is important to note that, as social historians such as Elizabeth Roberts and Andrew August have shown, there was no real expectation of such separation in the lives of working-class women.[4] The operation and manipulation of the separate spheres ideology was a definitively middle-class affair. For middle-class women, therefore, the possibility of combining 'home affections' with 'business out of doors' was problematic. The domestic ideal demanded the middle-class woman's physical and emotional devotion to the home.

In addition to the social and cultural impact of the separation of spheres, the central division in the domestic ideology between work and domesticity was, by the 1830s and 1840s, also seen to be crucially important to the preservation of the bourgeois marketplace. The separation of spheres legitimated the paternalistic industrial system by providing, in the structure of family relationships, a model of a harmonious and morally-determined system of hierarchical management in which the greatest good was achieved under the protective supervision of the bourgeois male figurehead.[5] Practically, this system contributed to the female labourer's second-class status in the industrial marketplace: she was generally either confined to less skilled work that did not demand high wages or was paid less than men for the

---

3   'Beauty Natural to Woman', *Quarterly Review* (1851), rpt. in *Eliza Cook's Journal* 6 (1852), p. 255 [italics in original].

4   Elizabeth Roberts, *Women's Work 1840-1940* (London: Macmillan Education, 1988), and Andrew August, 'How Separate a Sphere? Poor Women and Paid Work in Late-Victorian London', *Journal of Family History* 19 (1994), pp. 285-309.

5   Catherine Gallagher, *The Industrial Reformation of English Fiction 1832-1867* (Chicago: University of Chicago Press, 1985), pp. 119-20.

same work. Ideologically, however, this system sought to obscure women's actual work and to uphold instead women's detachment from the degradation of economic concerns. In their role as detached observers, women were supposed 'to act as the conscience of bourgeois society and through their influence over men mitigate the harshness of an industrial capitalist world'.[6] Any issue that challenged the sanctity of the domestic ideal, therefore, could also be seen to call into question predominant assumptions about modern industrial relations.

The plight of the surplus woman and the reduced gentlewoman, therefore, captivated the public's attention. Identified by the manufacturer W.R. Greg as 'redundant', these women, who often had to work to support themselves, were seen as a problem by writers like Greg because their very existence threatened social and economic stability.[7] While the stability of the domestic ideal required the preservation of the ideology of separate spheres, the publication of the 1851 census returns meant that it was no longer possible to deny the fact that many women were not only working but were also solely self-supporting. The census returns for 1841 for England and Wales had revealed that 21 percent of the female population of all classes, about one and a half million women, were engaged in some kind of paid employment. By 1851, that number had risen substantially to two and a half million, and for the next 30 years, the proportion of women working remained fairly stable at about 28 percent.[8] Besides revealing the increase in the number of women who were working, the results of the 1851 census also challenged fundamental tenets of domestic ideology. In showing that there was a 'surplus of 126,000 marriageable women', the 1851 census sparked wide-ranging debate about what 'was to be done about these "surplus" women'.[9] While the numbers reported by the census included working and middle-class women, the publication of the results had distinct implications for different classes.[10] Most significantly for the middle-class woman, these results made it clear that marriage and motherhood could not be the destiny of every English woman.

The revelation that a large number of middle-class women needed to work in order to support themselves caused a crisis for the image of the woman as the domestic goddess that many writers on the Woman Question raced to resolve. Motherhood was still imagined by many social commentators as the path to reaching

---

6   Judith Lowder Newton, *Women, Power, and Subversion: Social Strategies in British Fiction 1778-1860* (Athens: University of Georgia Press, 1981), p. 19.

7   W.R. Greg, 'Why Are Women Redundant?', *National Review* 14 (1862), p. 434-60.

8   These numbers are approximate and have been taken from Edward Higgs, 'Women, Occupations and Work in the Nineteenth-Century Censuses', *History Workshop* 23 (1987), pp. 59-80.

9   Charles M. Willich and E.T. Scargill, 'Tables Relating to The State of The Population of Great Britain at The Census of 1851, with a Comparative View, at the Different Ages, of the Population of France; Also a Comparative Return of Births and Deaths, 1838-1854', *Journal of the Statistical Society of London* 21, no. 3 (1858), p. 300.

10   For a discussion of the differing results see Phillippa Levine, *Victorian Feminism, 1850-1900* (London: Hutchinson, 1987), chaps 4 and 5.

womanly fulfilment, but many also argued that giving a woman 'something to do', whether necessary or not, was a better option than mourning for what they saw as an irretrievable ideal.[11] The difficulty of this position arose in confronting the question of how a woman could maintain her role as the custodian of the domestic ideal while spending 'many hours of the day elsewhere'. In response, some writers emphasised that paid work and domesticity could be considered compatible pursuits. As early as 1850, women's magazines such as *Eliza Cook's Journal* were advising their readerships that the two could be easily combined if women approached their household duties with professional alacrity:

> Two hours a-day would suffice every lady for the discharge of her household concerns, if a little tact and judgment were but brought to bear on the matter: I would point in evidence of my assertion to the fact, that young ladies of attainments and refinement, reduced gentlewomen in fact, who, by living and serving in shops, or working for warehouses; and to whom, in consequence, time stands for money, and work represents wages, despatch their domestic duties with the greatest ease and celerity; and this simply, because they give their minds to the performance of them, and go through with it in a business-like manner. But, it may be urged, house affairs are not like business, that can be transacted and done with: they are continually drawing us off. This is a mistake too.[12]

Beyond assuming the compatibility of household and professional work, this writer urges the introduction of business methods into the domestic sphere. Her call for the professionalisation of domestic duties effectively punctures the sentimentalised picture of the angel perched upon her 'home altar' and introduces the vision of a modern woman as a worker in a modern home run according to industrial principles. Her vision of the modern world thus sweeps aside what, by 1850, had come to be seen as the 'natural' division between public and private. Compatibility was established as a principle in order to protect domestic ideology; however, as this argument reveals, it could also question the separation of spheres that underpinned domestic ideology.

The image of woman's natural role being that of the angel dedicated to her domestic sphere was increasingly challenged both directly and indirectly from many different sources throughout the second half of the nineteenth century. One of the most famous attacks came from John Stuart Mill in his influential treatise, *The Subjection of Women* (1869). Comparing social convention to slavery, Mill wrote, 'So true is it that unnatural generally means only uncustomary, and that everything which is usual appears natural. The subjection of women to men being a universal custom, any departure from it quite naturally appears unnatural'.[13] Similarly, a writer

---

11   The cry for 'something to do' was a common slogan in the mid-Victorian period, appearing as the title for the first chapter of Dinah Craik's lengthy treatise on women's work, *A Woman's Thoughts About Women* (London: Hurst and Blackett, 1858). It also appeared in various other forms, for instance, in an article for *Macmillan's* (Daniel Rose Fearon, 'The Ladies Cry, Nothing To Do!', *Macmillan's* 19 [1869], pp. 451-54).

12   'Advice to the Ladies', *Eliza Cook's Journal* 3 (1850), p. 11.

13   John Stuart Mill, *The Subjection of Women* (Ontario: Broadview Press, 2000), p. 20.

for the *Saturday Review* argued that the division between the spheres only seemed natural because, 'The whole imagination of the race has been fed upon the notion, until the relations between the two sexes have become the one thing on which fancy, sentiment, and hope are taught from childhood to dwell'.[14] Both authors argue that woman as domestic angel was not a role ordained by Nature, but was instead a cultural construction. The writer of 'Facts Versus Ideas' also draws upon this perspective when she comments that what constitutes woman's '"sphere" is so ill defined, so airily constructed, that one never is certain to what extent it may be puffed out, or into how wonderfully small a space it can be contracted'.[15] 'Woman's sphere', this writer suggests, is something that can exist separately from the confined physical space of the home and could therefore be redefined to either incorporate the public into the private or to exclude the domestic altogether.

The disclosure that a number of wives, daughters, and widows were involved in the market economy not only undermined the ideological barrier between paid work and the domestic that formed the basis of the separation of spheres, but also key economic principles such as women's second-class status in the industrial system. No provision was made, for instance, in gendered wage scales for the women who needed to support themselves, yet were forced to subsist on inadequate and unequal pay.[16] The obvious injustice of such gendered standards made these principles easy targets for those who supported the need for change in attitudes towards women's work. When Harriet Martineau reviewed the state of 'Female Industry' in 1859, for example, she attacked the 'supposition ... which has now become false, and ought to be practically admitted to be false; – that every woman is supported (as the law supposes her to be represented) by her father, her brother, or her husband'.[17]

In Martineau's estimation, the returns of the 1851 census, in exposing 'the hard facts' of the changes wrought by industrialisation in women's lives, had also revealed the irrelevance of traditional economic suppositions to modern society. 'So far from our countrywomen being all maintained, as a matter of course, by us "the breadwinners"', she claims, 'three millions out of six of adult Englishwomen work for subsistence; and two out of the three in independence. With this new condition of affairs, new duties and new views must be accepted'.[18] Although Martineau calls for 'new views' on the relationship of women to paid work, her use of a masculine critical voice in order to give her argument more authority signifies the weight of

---

14   'The Goose and the Gander', *Saturday Review*, rpt. in *Englishwoman's Review* 1 (1868), p. 439.

15   ' Facts Versus Ideas', p. 77. See also, 'Employment for Women', *Birmingham Morning News*, rpt. in *Women and Work* no. 37 (13 Feb. 1875), p. 2. For a discussion of the challenge made by women essayists to the idea of a natural sphere for women see Tracy Seeley, 'Victorian Women's Essays and Dinah Mulock's *Thoughts*: Creating an *Ethos* for Argument', *Prose Studies* 19 (1996), pp. 93-109.

16   Harriet Bradley, *Men's Work, Women's Work: A Sociological History of the Sexual Division of Labour in Employment* (Cambridge: Polity Press, 1989), pp. 44-45.

17   Harriet Martineau, 'Female Industry', *Edinburgh Review* 222 (1859), p. 297.

18   Ibid., pp. 294, 336.

the cultural prejudice against female intellectuality. But it also, perhaps, suggests what Deirdre David identifies as Martineau's ambivalent negotiation between her 'uncompromising feminism' and her belief in the 'conventionally feminine qualities of passivity and acquiescence'.[19] Alexis Easley, on the other hand, describes this ambivalence as Martineau's attempt to produce 'objective' cultural criticism.[20] However they choose to describe it, the exploration of this ambivalence has proved enlightening in charting the inherent contradictions of women's interaction with the public sphere.

Recent feminist critics have emphasised the beneficial consequences that a mutable and ambivalent conception of domesticity could hold for middle-class working women. In her important book, *Uneven Developments*, Mary Poovey has repeatedly demonstrated that in key representations of working women the ideology of the domestic sphere could authorise and cultivate women's professional ambitions. Taking the example of the efforts toward the professionalisation of nursing at mid-century, Poovey argues that the way in which the nurse was represented put her in 'the border between the "normal" (domestic) and the "abnormal" (working) woman'.[21] The nurse employed the supposedly intrinsic qualities of supportiveness and care associated with the domestic woman, but brought them into the professional work space. As a result, she was 'able to make the hospital a home and, in so doing, to enhance the reputation of an activity that had been degraded because it was traditionally women's work'.[22] Such 'border cases' as this, Poovey argues, demonstrate that representations of working women not only showed that the supposedly separate spheres were not separate but also enabled women such as nurses to take an active role in the professional public sphere.

Poovey's sophisticated analysis of the social and sexual complexity of the representation of work has been highly influential on criticism since the 1990s concerning the relationship between the domestic ideal and female labour. These critical studies share the broad premise that domesticity could be empowering for women who sought to enter the professional workplace. The professional jobs that were part of the new 'service sector' such as nursing, teaching, and the retail trade, Jane Rendall notes, were deemed suitable for women because, as light and non-industrial 'service' work that required at least some education, they were 'posts which fitted the middle-class Victorian conception of womanhood'.[23] Judy Lown has also

---

19   Deirdre David, *Intellectual Women and Victorian Patriarchy: Harriet Martineau, Elizabeth Barrett Browning, George Eliot* (Ithaca: Cornell University Press, 1987), pp. 31, 32.

20   Alexis Easley, 'Gendered Observations: Harriet Martineau and the Woman Question', *Victorian Women Writers and the Woman Question*, Nicola Diane Thompson, ed. (Cambridge: Cambridge University Press, 1999), p. 83.

21   Mary Poovey, *Uneven Developments: The Ideological Work of Gender in Mid-Victorian Britain* (London: Virago, 1989), p. 14.

22   Ibid.

23   Jane Rendall, *Women in an Industrializing Society: England 1750-1880* (Oxford: Basil Blackwell, 1990), p. 71.

described how women's servicing role in the family was used to justify their entry into the professional fields of nursing, teaching, and the service sector because 'all of these occupations were consistent with an interpretation of "feminine qualities"'.[24] And Monica Cohen has convincingly shown how many nineteenth century authors asserted the respectability of their authorship by depicting their domestic duties as professional work and their writing, therefore, as a household task.[25] In their analyses these critics identify the strategies through which the rhetoric of the domestic ideal was called upon to justify the expansion of woman's sphere to include paid work. They usefully trace the processes through which certain types of work came to be described, according to the nineteenth-century notion of the separation of spheres, as falling 'naturally into women's "sphere"'.[26]

But this construction unnecessarily limits our understanding of the mid-Victorian perception of the middle-class woman's relationship to work. While all of these studies correctly identify the way in which the discourse of domesticity was used to refine the image of work for women, they still adopt a standpoint intrinsic to the ideology of separate spheres, assuming that entering the public sphere was considered to be fundamentally a degrading act for women. Positive representations of women in the workplace thus tend to be read in terms of their resistance to, subversion of, or conflict with, dominant social, cultural, and economic ideology. These representations are seen to be working in what Anne Digby has termed 'gender borderlands'. Digby describes these borderlands as spaces in which middle-class women could safely enter and manipulate the public world without overstepping the bounds of their

---

24 Judy Lown, *Women and Industrialization: Gender at Work in Nineteenth-Century England* (Cambridge: Polity Press, 1990). Lown lists the jobs contained within the 'service sector' as shopwork, clerical work, telegraphy, book-keeping, art and design, watchmaking and piano-tuning. See also Ellen Jordan, *The Women's Movement and Women's Employment in Nineteenth Century Britain* (London: Routledge, 1999); and Mary Jane Corbett, *Representing Femininity: Middle-Class Subjectivity in Victorian and Edwardian Women's Autobiographies* (Oxford: Oxford University Press, 1992).

25 Monica Cohen, *Professional Domesticity in the Victorian Novel: Women, Work, and Home* (Cambridge: Cambridge University Press, 1998).

26 Jane Rendall, *Women in an Industrializing Society*, p. 78. Some other studies that describe the separation of spheres include Patricia Branca, *Silent Sisterhood: Middle-Class Women in the Victorian Home* (London: Croom Helm, 1975); Leonore Davidoff and Catherine Hall, *Family Fortunes: Men and Women of the English Middle Class, 1780-1850* (Chicago: University of Chicago Press, 1987); Lee Holcombe, *Victorian Ladies at Work* (Newton Abbot: David & Charles, 1973); Angela V. John, ed., *Unequal Opportunities: Women's Employment in England 1800-1918* (Oxford: Basil Blackwell, 1986); Elizabeth Langland, *Nobody's Angels: Middle-Class Women and Domestic Ideology in Victorian Culture* (Ithaca: Cornell University Press, 1995); Philippa Levine, *Victorian Feminism, 1850-1900* (London: Hutchinson, 1987); F.M.L. Thompson, *The Rise of Respectable Society: A Social History of Victorian Britain 1830-1900* (Cambridge, MA: Harvard University Press, 1988); and Chris Vanden Bossche, 'The Queen in the Garden/The Woman of the Streets: The Separate Spheres and the Inscription of Gender', *Journal of Pre-Raphaelite Studies* 1 (1992), pp. 1-15.

'domestic territory'.[27] The perspective of gender borderlands, or the 'border cases' as Poovey brands them, has helped to describe women's entry into professions which were seen as partially domestic or 'semi-public'. These professions, such as nursing and teaching, are credited with 'providing middle-class women with respectable work, and making work respectable'.[28]

This book uses the structure of the gender borderland established within these studies to describe women's relationship to work, but also takes it further in order to explore the ways in which these 'borderlands' were transformed by nineteenth century writers into mainstream images of female life. It is one of the central purposes of this book to show how the notion of work for women was not only refined by reference to the domestic ideal, but also came to be seen as an experience with intrinsic refining qualities in itself. I use the term 'refining work' to describe women's complex relations to the public sphere in the nineteenth century. Firstly, according to my account, it describes the process, similar to that identified by Poovey and others, through which certain industrial and public types of employment that were considered inappropriate or undesirable for middle-class women were increasingly refined, that is, represented as suitable occupations. Secondly, it refers to the conventional – and undoubtedly class and gender-inflected – refinement that was seen to be inherent to the 'high culture' discipline of the fine arts. The third, and perhaps, most significant sense of 'refining work', I will argue, relates to the notion that the intrinsic refinement associated with artistic professions could also be afforded to work itself, in all its forms, in a way that could challenge the perception of work as a degrading activity for women. I consider the relationship between female creativity and the marketplace and demonstrate that, to a varying degree, work for women could be represented as suitable if it was characterised according to the principles of art. For this reason, I choose to concentrate on four professions that were consistently associated with the high culture domain of art throughout the second half of the nineteenth century – sewing, painting, writing, and acting.

This association with high culture, however, was complicated by the gendered cultural division that, by the end of the eighteenth century, had come to signify the limits of female creativity.[29] This distinction is succinctly stated by the literary critic J.M. Ludlow when he declares, 'We know, all of us, that if man is the head of humanity, woman is its heart'.[30] In identifying women as the heart of humanity, critics such as Ludlow and R.H. Hutton applied the logic of the ideology of the separation of spheres to female creative production. When reviewing a selection

---

27   Anne Digby, 'Victorian Values and Women in Public and Private', *Proceedings of the British Academy* 78 (1992), p. 210.

28   Laura Morgan Green, *Educating Women: Cultural Conflict and Victorian Literature* (Athens: Ohio University Press, 2001), p. 14.

29   For a good discussion of this gendered division in relation to woman writers of the late eighteenth and early nineteenth century see Gary Kelly, *Women Writing, and Revolution: 1790-1827* (Oxford: Clarendon Press, 1993), esp. chaps. 1 and 5.

30   [J.M. Ludlow], 'Ruth', *North British Review* 19 (1853), p. 168.

of Dinah Craik's novels for the *North British Review* in 1858, for instance, Hutton writes:

> Though women have usually finer spiritual sympathies than men, they have not the same power of concentrating their minds in these alone, and living apart in them for a time, without being disturbed by the intrusive superficialities of actual life and circumstances. Their imagination is not separable, as it were, in anything like the same degree, from the visible surface and form of human existence.[31]

Women's imagination, Hutton argues, is trusting and devoted. Men's, on the other hand, is searching and questioning, and the masculine mind dwells in the realm of the abstract, delving below the 'surface of life' in order to conceptualise ideas rather than events.[32]

This same variation is echoed by Eric Robertson in the introduction to a historical survey of women poets when he claims, 'Faith is woman-like, doubt is man-like. The man digs, but the woman gleans'.[33] Like their imagination, men's spirituality is represented as a transcendent experience that lifts them out of everyday experience and leads them to question and scrutinise the very foundations of belief, probing the religious to reach the divine. Women's, on the other hand, entails an unfailing trust in the commonplace dictates of the established Church, and their morality is signified by the repetition of standard religious platitudes. Although Lydia Becker, in the *Englishwoman's Gazette*, blames this supposedly mundane and earthly bent in women on the 'artificial restraint' of social conditioning and biased education that forced women's minds to be 'pent up in a small corner', her argument, like that of Hutton and Robertson, allows the assumption that women's thinking has been bounded within 'what is considered their legitimate sphere of exertion'.[34] Whether this limitation was thought of as natural or imposed, the division between feminine and masculine forms of creative work in the mid-Victorian period, as in earlier periods, continued to connote a distinction between the earthly and emotional and the abstract and intellectual.

The image of the woman as the moral, sentimental, and emotional centre of art suggested a mainstream form of female creativity that was considered to be domestic, didactic, moral, and charming. Its more negative attributes, however, included its propensity to be shallow, sentimental, pedantic, and mundane. Masculine creativity, on the other hand, was associated with the intellect and the imagination. As Ellen Messer Davidow argues, 'Gender ideology organized a literary economy of public and domestic, contemplative and decorative, vocational and avocational transactions

---

31 [R.H. Hutton], 'Novels by the Authoress of *John Halifax*', *North British Review* 29 (1858), p. 467.

32 Ibid.

33 Eric Robertson, *English Poetesses: A Series of Critical Biographies* (London: Cassell, 1883), p. xiii.

34 Lydia Becker, 'Is There Any Specific Distinction Between Male and Female Intellect?' *Englishwoman's Gazette* 1 (1868), pp. 484, 483.

conducted, respectively, by men and women. In practice, male authors and readers monopolized works of antiquity, traditional genres, intellectual and professional subject, high styles and public import'.[35] Although Davidow is writing here specifically about eighteenth-century literature, this division continued throughout the nineteenth century to characterise dominant thinking about all the fine arts.[36] In poetry, for example, the epic was seen as a masculine genre whose heroic themes and classical narrative were beyond the talents of women.[37] In painting, this distinction surfaced in the ideological restriction of women artists to the lesser genres of landscape and domestic realism and the lesser medium of watercolours.[38] In music, Phyllis Weliver notes, it resulted in the branding of the harp, the piano, and the guitar as the most appropriate instruments for female musicians. It also, she argues, contributed to a general attitude that female musical composition 'should be melodious, graceful music for voice and/or piano. Only men should write powerful, theoretically rigorous music for large-scale, public works like symphonies and operas'.[39]

While these examples describe widespread cultural assumptions about the effect of the essential differences of gender on artistic production, it is also important, as Deborah Cherry points out, to guard 'against over-simplistic comparisons between women's art and men's art' because 'neither women nor men artists in the nineteenth century comprised undifferentiated groups'.[40] Not all women painted watercolour landscapes, nor did all think women's art must exhibit earthly and mundane sensibilities. What these distinctions do illustrate, though, is the range of what feminine artistry and the image of the female artist could signify for mid-Victorian culture. Furthermore, the association with the mundane and the concrete that identified feminine art with everyday life also created a link between the supposedly opposed domains of art and the modern world of capitalist industry. As Kathy Psomiades has shown, femininity worked in the second half of the nineteenth century 'to mediate between the aesthetic and economic realms in which art must

---

35   Ellen Messer-Davidow, '"For Softness She": Gender Ideology and Aesthetics in Eighteenth-Century England', *Eighteenth-Century Women and the Arts*, Frederick M. Keener and Susan E. Lorsch, eds (London: Greenwood Press, 1988), p. 49.

36   For a fuller discussion of the differences between the masculine and feminine writing in relations to the Victorian novel see Nicola Diane Thompson, *Reviewing Sex: Gender and the Reception of Victorian Novels* (London: Macmillan, 1996).

37   For a discussion of the gender distinctions in poetry see Isobel Armstrong, *Victorian Poetry: Poetry, Poetics and Politics* (London: Routledge, 1993), esp. pp. 318-32.

38   Clarissa Campbell Orr, *Women in the Victorian Art World* (Manchester: Manchester University Press, 1995).

39   Phyllis Weliver, *Women Musicians in Victorian Fiction, 1860-1900: Representations of Music, Science and Gender in the Leisured Home* (Aldershot: Ashgate, 2000), pp. 23-24.

40   Deborah Cherry, *Painting Women: Victorian Women Artists* (London: Routledge, 1993), p. 12.

necessarily find itself [and allowed] for the simultaneous figuration of the category of the aesthetic as subject to market conditions and as inviolable by them'.[41]

In addition to its impact on the relationship between the aesthetic and the economic, however, the conjunction of femininity, art, and commerce also opened a new perspective on the working woman's engagement with the industrial marketplace. This perspective is articulated, for instance, by a writer for the *Artist*, who denounced the cultural nostalgia expressed by medieval enthusiasts such as John Ruskin as a short-sighted philosophy because, even though it raised the artistic reputation of woman's needlework, the vogue for skilled handwork that it inspired provided work for only a small number of women. To train women to work in the design and production of textiles in the manufactories, however, he argues, 'puts women's art capacity en rapport with the march of commerce, and tends to the artistic improvement of modern manufactures':

> Instead of banning machinery the England of to-day wants the man – or perhaps the woman – who will recognise it, go amongst it, and consecrate it with a baptism of art; organizing a system by which its capacities may be most artistically utilized, instead of turning his back upon it and railing. It wants, too, a movement like the New York Woman's Technical Institute, by which women's artistic aptitudes may be systematically utilized by Birmingham, Manchester, and Kidderminster. It wants such a movement for the sake of art, and for the sake of women.[42]

England already had such a movement that was supported by the training that some women received in the technical schools like the London Female School of Design (later the Female School of Art) and publicised by exhibitions like the Bristol 'Exhibition of Women's Industry'.[43] This article participates in the surge in support throughout the 1860s to the 1880s for the expansion of women's participation in the 'art-industries'. While attesting, therefore, to the capacity for art to refine even the most industrial work of the textile factories, this writer's argument also demonstrates the increasing possibility as the century progressed for industrial work to be defined as suitable work for women and for conventionally designated women's work to become industrialised. The refining effect this movement would have on the female worker was described by a writer for *Women and Work*, who noted that 'The Nottingham looms will turn out lace so delicate in execution, that only practised eyes could distinguish it from handwork, and though the designers of these elegant and artistic patterns get well paid, they need not be needleworkers at all, but only

---

41   Kathy Alexis Psomiades, *Beauty's Body: Femininity and Representation in British Aestheticism* (Stanford: Stanford University, 1997), p. 3.

42   'Art Work for Women', *Artist* 4 (1883), p. 39.

43   The Bristol exhibition was one of many to feature women's design work. A description of the aims of this exhibition can be found in, 'Women's Industries', *Englishwoman's Review* 15 (1884), pp. 509-12.

artists'.[44] Participation in the art-industries could thus be seen to lift women above the realm of industrial labour and into that of art.

The example of the art industries thus offers a good illustration of the capacity for work itself to be seen as a source of refinement. Borrowing from the principles embodied in Thomas Carlyle's articulation of 'gospel of work' in which he preached that 'all true Work is Religion', many argued that labour itself had the power to purify.[45] The gospel of work developed out of what Alan Gilbert describes as the 'metamorphosis' religious culture underwent in response to the increasing secularisation of Victorian society. By mid-century, Gilbert argues, the conservative religious establishment had adopted the nonconformist tenet that work could be the path to salvation in order to adapt to the 'artificial rationality of an industrialised economy'.[46] Although initially an androcentric concept, this gospel of work was increasingly applied to the issue of women's work in the 1850s, particularly after the publication of Anna Jameson's 'The Communion of Labour' in 1856 in which she stressed women's religious duty to participate in some form of charitable work.[47] While Jameson's traditionalism kept her notions of middle-class women's work within the realm of philanthropy, this principle was brought into the discussion of paid work by, among others, her associate Barbara Leigh Smith (later Bodichon) when, in her treatise on 'Women and Work' in 1857, she maintained, 'Women must, as children of God, be trained to do some work in the world'.[48] Furthering her description of work as a religious duty, Bodichon adds:

> Think of the noble capacities of a human being. Look at your daughters, your sisters, and ask if they are what they might be if their faculties had been drawn forth; if they had liberty to grow, to expand, to become what God means them to be. When you see girls and women dawdling in shops, choosing finery, and talking scandal, do you not think they might have been better with some serious training?[49]

In this essay, Bodichon overturns conventional notions of women's 'natural' existence by placing what she sees as their present restricted life in contrast with her vision of their more noble potential. God, she implies, meant for women to work. And if they were allowed to work, fellow feminist Josephine Butler argued, if 'permission is granted them not only to win bread for themselves, but to use for the good of society,

---

44 *Women and Work* no. 56 (26 June 1875), p. 4.

45 Thomas Carlyle, *Past and Present* (London: Chapman and Hall, 1897), p. 200.

46 Alan D. Gilbert, *Religion and Society in Industrial England: Church, Chapel and Social Change, 1790-1914* (London: Longman, 1976), p. 203.

47 Ellen Jordan, *The Women's Movement and Women's Employment*, p. 153. See also, Judith Johnston, *Anna Jameson: Victorian, Feminist, Woman of Letters* (Aldershot: Scholar Press, 1997).

48 Barbara Leigh Smith, 'Women and Work', rpt. in *The Exploited: Women and Work*, Marie Mulvey Roberts and Tamae Mizuta, eds (London: Routledge, 1995), p. 4.

49 Ibid., p. 10.

every gift bestowed on them by God, we may expect to find, (as certainly we shall find) that they will become the *more* and not the *less* womanly'.[50]

The principle of the gospel of work was sometimes used specifically to suggest a degree of parity between women's moral role in the household and paid work. In doing so, it not only obscured the boundary between public and private, but it also refuted the contention that entering the public sphere was an inherently degrading act for women. Supporting her assertion by quoting a 'great and profound thinker', the author of 'Facts Versus Ideas', for instance, claimed that 'Work is the spell which brings forth the hidden powers of nature: it is the triumph of the spirit over matter, the rendering serviceable, remodelling, or transforming the material substances for the use and embellishment of life'.[51] This rather magnificent peroration expands the horizons of the working day, imbuing the most mundane work with universal significance. Even the lowest forms of drudgery promise to give the worker the god-like ability to bring order to chaos. 'With this conception of the true meaning of work', she concludes, 'can any one imagine it to be a degradation and not a privilege?'.[52] By 1879, Jane Chesney, in recommending commercial horticulture as an appropriate occupation for women, could not imagine it to be so and was able to declare decidedly that 'It is now admitted on all hands, not only that work is no degradation to gentlewomen, but that as it is manifestly needful for a large number of them to earn their own bread, it is desirable to find them as many suitable openings as possible'.[53] Chesney agrees with dominant notions of female labour – that there is such a thing as 'suitable' types of employment for women. Significantly, however, the question of work as a degrading experience seems no longer even worthy of debate and is accordingly dismissed.

Even 20 years earlier when this debate was receiving much attention, particularly in the periodical press, conservative expressions of dominant ideology were often met with scepticism and resistance, but also, occasionally, with positive and constructive reproach. One such argument was played out over a six month period in the *English Woman's Journal* in response to a letter written in 1861 by an 'old-fashioned' 'West-End Housekeeper'. In this letter, the writer comments that 'if a woman is obliged to work, at once, she (although she may be Christian and well bred) loses that peculiar position which the word *lady* conventionally designates; and having once been obliged to step from drawing-room dignity, she need not hesitate as to where she steps down'.[54] The scope of the journal's readership who found this scathing opinion unjust was attested to repeatedly over the next six months by the vehement responses it provoked. The main complaint voiced in these responses refers to what they see as

---

50   Josephine Butler, *The Education and Employment of Women* (Liverpool: T. Brakell, 1868), p. 18 [emphasis in original].

51   A.R.L. 'Facts Versus Ideas', p. 77.

52   Ibid.

53   Jane Chesney, 'A New Vocation for Women', *Macmillan's* 40 (1879), p. 341.

54   'Letter to the editor', *English Woman's Journal* 8 (1861), p. 139.

an antiquated and unenlightened prejudice in the West-End Housekeeper's definition of a 'lady'.

To one respondent, this West-End Housekeeper represents one of 'two worlds of social feeling' – that portion of English society that 'mould[s] all their ideas of social life upon the theory of the middle ages; – the feudal theory'.[55] The other world she describes is that of social democracy in which 'every Englishman [knows] that nothing prevents him from rising, and securing at least to his children or grandchildren the advantages of any and every class above him'.[56] Neither of these social theories, this author concludes, are sufficient for the peculiar difficulties of the working woman's position in which she is placed between the need to work on the one hand and the ideological injunctions against striving and self-promotion on the other. Instead of these conventional theories, she constructively describes a new social system for working women based on the moral power of work, rather than the traditional distinctions of rank:

> Let the workers create their own caste, their own social guild, and don their own strong armour of self-respect; and whether they are nominally admitted to the same rank or not, it is very certain that *ladies* and *gentlewomen* will treat them with no disdain ... Train up yourself and your daughters to higher ideals; and it is ten to one that having done so, having nurtured your children's imagination on the only Example of Life which truly teaches *gentle breeding*, you will find that even in this mortal existence, and in the vigorous, many-sided, illogical England, the chances of their career will secure them that worldly position which it is as ungraceful as it is generally fruitless to struggle to attain.[57]

Although this author relies on conventional notions of womanliness in the construction of this visionary social system, work takes the place of domestic privacy as the true path to feminine grace and gentility. In addition to their attempts to change or undermine the prejudices and constraints of existing gendered social structures, then, some writers who commented on the position of working women in the second half of the century also brought a more dynamic approach to this issue, seeking to leave this debate behind. Those who argued for the desirability of work for women were not condemned merely to tread the narrowly prescribed argumentative space of the 'gender borderlands', but offered a perspective that saw work as an element of responsible citizenship and a means to moral ascendancy. 'We may expect', wrote one author for *Work and Leisure* in 1880, 'that the special gifts and graces developed by this necessity of work as a means of livelihood to women will lift the whole sex higher in the scale of their common humanity, and strengthen and enrich the average of character among all women, whether married or single'.[58] The increasing attention that was focused as early as the end of the 1840s, particularly

---

55   'West-End Housekeepers', *English Woman's Journal* 8 (1861), p. 252.
56   Ibid., pp. 252-53.
57   Ibid., p. 254.
58   'Women and Work', *Work and Leisure* 5 (1880), p. 2.

in representations of working women that appeared in fiction and in the periodical press, on the desirability of paid work for middle-class women thus posed an intriguing challenge not only to the foundation of the separate spheres ideology, but also to the prevailing conceptions about the workings of the capitalist marketplace.[59] In this book, I examine the structure of this challenge and the impact representations of desirable work for women had on the perception of the marketplace.

I have chosen to keep this study to the years 1848-1890 because, as Edward Higgs explains, these years represent a significant change in the reporting and quantifying of women's work. The sizeable change in the number of working women registered in the census from one and a half million in 1841 to two and a half million in 1851 was due in large part not to a great influx of women into paid employment, but instead to a change in the instructions for completing the census. The 1841 census only counted as work the employment for which women receive wages. Helping in a husband's shop, for instance, was not to be recorded. The instructions for the 1851 census, however, requested that women's home work, excluding domestic duties, be 'distinctly recorded'.[60] The effect of this change was that many women who under the 1841 instructions would have merely been listed as 'wife' or 'daughter' were now shown to be making some form of economic contribution. In 1881, these instructions changed again, and once again women's unwaged work was excluded.[61] The years 1848-1890, then, represent a period of specific institutional interest, typified by these changes in the census, in recording the intersection between conventional propriety and women's work. Also, following particularly on the social unrest generated by the various revolutions in Europe and the threat of Chartist revolt in England in 1848, the second half of the nineteenth century was a time when the status of women inside and outside the home took on political, economic, and cultural significance in debates about social stability.[62] By the end of the 1880s, the emergence of the New Woman as a social, cultural, and political icon of the *fin-de-siècle* marked a substantial change in women's relation to aesthetics.[63]

In order to trace the evolution of women's relationship to the marketplace, I examine the representations of working middle-class women in fiction, paintings, and the periodical press from the end of the 1840s to the end of the 1880s that specifically addressed the intersection between issues of domesticity, creativity, remuneration, and refinement. Such representations, I argue, used the image of the working woman

---

59   For a discussion of the increasing coverage in the periodical press of questions concerning work for women see E.M. Palmegiano, 'Mid-Victorian Periodicals and Careers for Women', *Journal of Newspaper and Periodical History* 6:2 (1990), pp. 15-19.

60   Edward Higgs., p. 63.

61   For some of the problems corresponding to the interpretation of nineteenth-century census data see Jane Humphries, 'Women and Paid Work', *Women's History: Britain, 1850-1945*, June Purvis, ed. (London: UCL Press, 1995), pp. 85-107.

62   Karen Chase and Michael Levenson, *The Spectacle of Intimacy: A Public Life for the Victorian Family* (Princeton: Princeton University Press, 2000), esp. pp. 3-6.

63   Rita S. Kranidis, *Subversive Discourse: The Cultural Production of Late Victorian Feminist Novels* (London: Macmillan, 1995).

to figure female respectability and moral value outside dominant social and economic structures. In each chapter, therefore, I have chosen to concentrate on specific forms of feminine artistry in order to trace the impact the representation of the female artist had on the perception of work for the middle-class woman, in particular, and of the marketplace, in general.

The relationship between the figure of the seamstress and the capitalist marketplace is the subject of chapter one. Throughout the nineteenth century, needlework was considered to be one of the most feminine employments. From the lowest slopworker to the Queen herself, from piecework to embroidery, all women sewed in one form or another. As a result, the figure of the seamstress was imbued with far-reaching iconic significance as needlework came to be seen as one of the most powerful metaphors of feminine existence, and the life of the needlewoman preoccupied the Victorian imagination. Generally represented earlier in the century as a woman forced by poverty to labour at this economically unrewarding and physically exhausting work, the seamstress, like her fellow worker, the governess, became the pitiable heroine of shocking melodrama, narrative painting, social problem literature, and poetical pathos. Whereas the governess worked exclusively in the home, though, the seamstress worked in the home, in the workshop, and in the factory. Her association with both the domestic and the commercial sphere thus made her a convenient image of the passive worker victimised by the cruel and inhuman economic system of capitalism. By the end of the 1840s, the figure of the oppressed seamstress had developed into a symbol of working-class vulnerability and social injustice in all its forms. This chapter explores the way in which this early connection of the seamstress with the commercial sphere influenced the changing representation of the needlewoman after 1850 when the realisation of the urgent need to find respectable work for middle-class women surfaced. The seamstress, as I will show, was an important figure in the refinement of the image of paid work as a respectable, and even natural, activity for women.

The relationship between artistry and the industrial economy is also the subject of chapter two. But whereas the seamstress's practical labours were refined by her reference to artistic tradition, in the case of the female artist, industrialisation brought a transformation to artisanal practices. This chapter investigates the means through which representations of the working female artist contributed to the development of the fields of industrial design and factory-based decorative work as suitable occupations for women. Representations of the woman artist in the second half of the century tended to assert the compatibility of art as a paid profession with women's domestic duties. While these representations of independent working women are undermined by the self-sacrificing role associated with woman's place in the domestic sphere, I argue, they also promote female self-sufficiency by developing female creative spaces that exist outside patriarchal control. I describe these spaces metaphorically as screens that protect the woman's privacy while enabling her to work freely. These images find further expression in the development of the idea of art-sisterhoods and in female-led artistic institutions, both of which established models of female-centred artistic education and community. This chapter traces the influence of the wide-ranging application of the adjective 'domestic' on the industrial workplace and contends that, by the end of the 1880s, the image of the working woman could be refined even by reference to the industrial employments contained within the 'art-industries'.

Chapter three picks up on the issues associated with the principle of compatibility in order to explore the difficulties that women writers faced in negotiating between the private world of domesticity and the public world of self-revelation that the profession of writing entailed. As with the issue of compatibility for the female artist, the combination of the public world of authorship with the qualities of domesticity aided in the characterization of writing as a suitable employment for women, but it also engendered what many critics have seen as the woman writer's divided subjectivity. In representing the woman writer, authors negotiated between the degradation of engaging in self-publicity to earn money and the supposedly unassailable virtue contained within the woman's role as the domestic angel in order to develop an image of the woman writer as a respectable, though public, woman. Drawing on metaphors of child-rearing, some authors represented the woman writer's public work as an extension of the mother's functions to teach and nurture her children. Such justifications, however, contributed to the classification described above of woman's creativity as earthly and mundane. These domestic qualities were seen to keep women's writing out of the 'first rank' in comparison with men's, consigning it to the realm of popular culture rather than high art. But, as I will show, this ghettoisation of women's writing opened up for the modern woman writer exclusively feminine spaces based on models of female experience. This chapter investigates those representations that use the figure of the female writer to explore these feminine spaces and suggests that this figure came to represent a form of professional work for women that was inherently refined.

Chapter four concludes the exploration of the relationship between refining work, creativity, and the marketplace in representations of the working middle-class woman by returning to the issue of publicity examined in chapter three. Unlike the more tangible works of the seamstress, the artist or the writer, the product of the actress's performance was her physical presence on the stage. In some senses the very profession of acting seems to typify the publicity that was anathema to the ideal of feminine privacy. However, even acting, arguably the most public and socially degrading occupation, could be represented as respectable work for women. This refinement was achieved through the redefinition of performance, popularly imagined as a form of sexual display, to a lengthy and arduous routine of study, rehearsing, costuming, and acting. Such 'unceasing industry' coupled with an image of domestic morality projected by the microcosmic society of the stage contributed to a general rise in the social status of the actress in the second half of the century. This chapter examines the reasons behind this rise and describes the way in which the actress was shown to be able to manipulate her public image so that the respectability previously contingent upon the woman's domestic role could be accredited to her, regardless of her actual domestic situation.

Although it reached its most sophisticated expression by the turn of the century in the case of the actress, this capacity for manipulating public image had always been affiliated with women working in artistic professions. It is not sufficient, I contend, simply to define this development in terms of women's response to often-repressive cultural and institutional pressures. It is important to see women's relationship with the public sphere as a fundamental interaction with work itself and the world of work. Rather than assigning working women to the margins of patriarchal culture, this book attempts to show how representations of creative women, by both male and female writers, participated in and shaped new forms of mainstream culture. Though this book deals mainly with representations in literature and the periodical press, it also sees self-presentation as a form of representation. Throughout the following chapters, therefore, I also emphasise the active role taken by creative women in developing their professional careers and their public identities. While work was defined as a masculine concept by the dominant ideology of the separation of spheres, what this book reveals is the way in which, in the second half of the century, the creation of female-centred experiences and institutions of work increasingly refined the public perception of work for women.

Chapter 1

Needlework and Creativity in Representations of the Seamstress

> By the way,
> The works of women are symbolical.
> We sew, sew, prick our fingers, dull our sight,
> Producing what? A pair of slippers, sir,
> To put on when you're weary – or a stool
> To stumble over and vex you... 'curse that stool!'
> Or else at best, a cushion, where you lean
> And sleep, and dream of something we are not
> But would be for your sake. Alas, alas!
> This hurts most, this – that, after all, we are paid
> The worth of our work, perhaps.[1]

In *Aurora Leigh* (1857), Elizabeth Barrett Browning identifies the needle as a symbol of the drudgery and worthlessness of a middle-class woman's domestic existence. As a standard accomplishment and ubiquitous activity for the proper middle-class woman, needlework restrains Aurora's independence and literary creativity, tying her physically to the material world of prosaic womanhood. This opposition between the needle and the pen was a familiar device used by women authors throughout the eighteenth and nineteenth centuries, and it contributed to an image of female authorship in which woman's conventional roles and responsibilities were represented as constraints on creativity.[2] Elizabeth Gaskell, for instance, warned an aspiring young writer of the difficulties of pursuing a literary career, noting the ease with which the writer could neglect the 'thousand little bits of work, which no sempstress ever does so well as the wife or mother who knows how the comfort of those she loves depends on little peculiarities'.[3] Charlotte Brontë noted a similar

---

1   Elizabeth Barrett Browning, *Aurora Leigh*, Kerry McSweeney, ed. (Oxford: Oxford University Press, 1993), Book I, lines 456-58. Further references to this edition will be given by book and line numbers in the text.

2   Cecilia Macheski, 'Penelope's Daughters: Images of Needlework in Eighteenth-Century Literature', *Fetter'd or Free? British Women Novelists, 1670-1815*, Mary Anne Schofield and Cecilia Macheski, eds (Athens: Ohio University Press, 1986), pp. 85-100.

3   Elizabeth Gaskell, 'Letter to an unknown correspondent', *The Letters of Mrs. Gaskell*, J.A.V. Chapple and A. Pollard, eds (Manchester: Manchester University Press, 1964), letter 515. For an in depth discussion of Elizabeth Gaskell's exploration of the needle/pen dichotomy

conflict 12 years before *Jane Eyre* was published: 'I have endeavoured not only to observe all the duties a woman ought to fulfil, but to feel deeply interested in them. I don't always succeed, for sometimes when I'm teaching or sewing, I would rather be reading or writing'.[4] Barrett Browning also invokes this tradition in her semi-autobiographical representation of Aurora when her stultifying feminine education and the monotony forced upon her slow down the poem and lead Aurora into the rather clumsy rhetorical digression introduced with the unpoetic 'By the way'. For Aurora, needlework's incompatibility with poetry appears fundamental. Even taking needlework as the subject of poetry proves disruptive as the reader is also forced to slow down over the spondaic repetition in the description of women as they 'sew, sew'. Writing about needlework, then, seems almost as tedious for her as sewing itself. In Aurora's experience, needlework is oppressive and uninspiring. From this perspective, even the little efforts the handy needlewoman makes to add to the comfort of her domestic sphere become markers of her degradation and subordination. The obliging wife, like the cursed stool or serviceable cushion, becomes an object to be despised and disregarded.

The needle, which repeatedly pricks the finger of the woman as she sews, is 'symbolical' for Aurora of the injurious and degrading effect of traditional domesticity. It also signifies woman's complicity in the system that denigrates her and her work. Through Aurora's antipathy to what was considered by many to be the epitome of feminine employment, Barrett Browning questions the value of conventional domestic 'work'. For Aurora, this work is demeaning because it is representative of the traditional role Romney wants her to assume and of the fate she refuses to submit to:

> Once, he stood so near
> He dropped a sudden hand upon my head
> Bent down on woman's work, as soft as rain –
> But then I rose and shook it off as fire,
> The stranger's touch that took my father's place. (*Aurora Leigh*, I.541-45)

In this wordless exchange, sewing helps to confirm the woman's subordinate position within the conventional patriarchal hierarchy. As her cousin and closest living male relative, Romney attempts to claim a proprietorial authority over her. It is an emotional desire that is both encouraged by and reflected in their relative physical positions within the scene. In portraying Aurora with her head bent upon the 'woman's work' of her sewing and her eyes averted away from Romney as he

---

in her fiction see Marie Fitzwilliam, 'The Needle and Not the Pen: Fabric (Auto)biography in *Cranford, Ruth*, and *Wives and Daughters*', *Gaskell Society Journal* 14 (2000), pp. 1-13.

4   Charlotte Brontë, 'To Robert Southey, 16 March 1837', *The Letters of Charlotte Brontë, 1827-1847*, Margaret Smith, ed., 2 vols (Oxford: Clarendon Press, 1995), 1, p. 169. For a discussion of the use of needlework in Charlotte Brontë's fiction see Sally Hesketh, 'Needlework in the Lives and Novels of the Brontë Sisters', *Brontë Society Transactions* 22 (1997), pp. 72-85.

stands over her, Barrett Browning employs a descriptive shorthand symbolising proper feminine modesty and dominant masculine power. The scene is set for the performance of conventional gender roles. In this scene, however, Barrett Browning frustrates the traditional symbolic function of needlework, subverting its place as a marker of proper feminine behaviour. Sewing, here, does not ultimately signal womanly modesty and compliance. In shaking off Romney's hand, Aurora expresses her independence from patriarchal domination and her commitment to her poetry. The oppositional relationship between the needle and the pen established early in the poem is soon complicated as Aurora finds new uses for her sewing. Needlework may fail as a fulfilling activity and aesthetic object, but it provides a practical aid to her aesthetic development as a screen behind which she conceals the 'quickening inner life' of her poetic soul (*Aurora Leigh*, I.1027). Instead of existing in opposition, Aurora's needle acts as a precursor to her pen, aiding her in both her rejection of conventional femininity and in her poetic development.

As both a domestic and an industrial employment, sewing formed one of the most central experiences of work throughout the nineteenth century for all women regardless of class or economic status, and the needle came to embody a powerful metaphor for feminine existence. Whatever their social position, little girls were taught to sew, and whether they applied this skill to the plain sewing of buttonholes and seams or the decorative work of embroidery, most women, at one point or another, sewed. Sewing's unique place as almost exclusively 'women's work', Ellen Jordan notes, identified it as one of the only suitable remunerative occupations for women prior to 1850.[5] The needle thus became a symbol of both the constraining drudgery of domestic femininity and of the possibility of escaping the domestic sphere through work. The needle, Carol Wilson argues, has since the late-eighteenth century 'been the site of intense debates about women's roles and the potential for artistic and political expression'.[6] The complex relationship between Victorian women writers and needlework, typified by *Aurora Leigh*, was played out metaphorically within the needle's power to both stitch together and pierce the artist's fragmented subjectivity.[7] This chapter investigates that relationship and the impact needlework had on ideas of female art and creativity.

Representations of the seamstress in fiction and the periodical press contributed to and reflected a revolution, which began to take place in the 1850s but was not firmly established until the end of the 1880s, in the popular conception of needlework. This

---

5   Ellen Jordan, *The Women's Movement and Women's Employment in Nineteenth Century Britain* (London: Routledge, 1999), pp. 65-66.

6   Carol Shiner Wilson, 'Lost Needles, Tangled Thread: Stitchery, Domesticity, and the Artistic Enterprise in Barbauld, Edgeworth, Taylor, and Lamb', *Revisioning Romanticism: British Women Writers, 1776-1837*, Carol Shiner Wilson, ed. (Philadelphia: University of Pennsylvania Press, 1994), p. 169.

7   Sandra Gilbert and Susan Gubar discuss this dual function of sewing for the female author in relation to Emily Dickinson, for instance, in *The Madwoman in the Attic: The Woman Writer and the Nineteenth-Century Literary Imagination*, 2nd ed. (New Haven: Yale University Press, 2000), pp. 638-42.

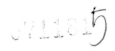

change can be glimpsed in two articles, separated by 20 years, which were written for the *Art Journal*. The first article, written in 1856, remarked that ladies' embroidery, or 'Fancy-work', can 'never aspire to the dignity of a fine art' because it entails mere 'manual dexterity' rather than originality of design.[8] Embroidery, as it is described in this article, is the non-creative and thoroughly private time-consuming activity of the bored housewife. The second article, written in 1877, contradicts this position and details the growing professionalisation and institutionalisation of embroidery as an art-form. Reviewing an exhibition of 'art-needlework', the author comments on the recent establishment of schools of embroidery that sought to teach women the more creative aspects of needlework. Such training in technique and design, the author argues, 'has the two-fold object of giving suitable employment to gentlewomen who need it, and of restoring ornamental needlework to the high place it once held among the decorative arts'.[9] Such extensive training was necessary because, as William Morris noted, 'For such an art nothing patchy or scrappy, or half-starved, should be done: There is no excuse for doing anything which is not strikingly beautiful; and that more especially as the exuberance of the beauty of the work of the East and of medieval Europe, and even of the time of the Renaissance, is at hand to reproach us'.[10]

In remarking upon the 'relatively high position among the arts anciently occupied by textiles', writers for the periodical press expounded, as Morris had, upon the exalted position embroidery historically enjoyed as the pastime of queens and as an aesthetic rival to painting.[11] Needlework was located within a context of dignity and respectability in order to show that it 'has a claim to estimation as an art'.[12] Over the course of the second half of the nineteenth century, and aided greatly by the general popularity of the Arts and Crafts movement, embroidery rebounded from historical obscurity and took its place as a valid, although contested, art. 'Not many years ago it would have been pronounced the height of affectation to talk of needlework as art', a writer for the *London Quarterly Review* noted, 'Now the pendulum has swung the other way … and the faded hangings which had been banished to the attics are brought out and cleaned and touched up'.[13] Unlike the other fine arts, embroidery was traditionally seen to be the province of women. With increasing frequency from the early 1870s onward, needlework was promoted as an art that 'has from the earliest times been sacred to the fair sex: and one in which they have ever been successful'.[14] Proponents of art-needlework as a serious occupation for women sought to establish a matrilineal heritage of sewing women. Ancient examples such as Homer's Penelope and the Greek legend of Arachne provided needlework with a link to high culture

---

8   'A Novelty in Fancy-Work', *Art Journal* 8 (1856), p. 139.

9   Mrs. Bury Palliser, 'The School of Art-Needlework', *Art Journal* 29 (1877), p. 213.

10   William Morris, 'Textiles', *William Morris: Artist, Writer, Socialist*, May Morris, ed. (Oxford: Basil Blackwell, 1936), p. 249.

11   'Lady Marian Alford on Art Needlework', *Edinburgh Review* 164 (1886), p. 146.

12   'Needlework', *Macmillan's Magazine* 28 (1873), p. 429.

13   'Needlework', *London Quarterly Review* 66 (1886), pp. 284-85.

14   'Institute of Art', *Artist* 1 (1880), p. 358.

through its classical ancestry.[15] More modern examples such as Queen Matilda's Bayeux Tapestry and the patient sewing of Mary, Queen of Scots, and even Queen Elizabeth established its home-grown English pedigree.[16] Even folklore and literature were mined for antecedents as medieval and early modern figures such as the Lady of Shalott and Mariana gained currency as images of the creative needlewoman at work.[17] It was a genealogical programme that culminated in what were considered to be serious and scholarly book-length treatises on women sewing throughout the ages.[18] By the end of the 1880s, then, art-needlework was considered by many to be a legitimate and genteel form of female creative production, 'the revival of which', the *Art Journal* argued, 'is one of the most encouraging and best achievements of the age'.[19]

The most popular and widely cited of these scholarly treatises was Lady Marian Alford's *Needlework as Art* (1886). Alford herself, along with the Princess Louise and a number of other aristocratic ladies, supplied a variety of designs for modern needlework and legitimised needlework's modern position within the context of historical patronage. Aesthetic legitimacy was also sought, and the most regularly reproduced patterns came from original designs by established artists such as William Morris and Edward Burne-Jones. And the religious importance of needlework was asserted by the revival in ecclesiastical embroidery.[20] As with all arts, however, imitation suggested mere manual dexterity, and originality was required along with skill in order to cement needlework's artistic reputation. Originality in dress design, for instance, became a prized commodity.[21] And some dress houses wooed customers

---

15   For general contemporary discussions of the ancient history of art needlework see Lady Marian Alford, 'Art Needlework', *Nineteenth Century* 9 (1881), pp. 439-50; and Eugéne Müntz, *A Short History of Tapestry from the Earliest Time to the End of the Eighteenth Century* trans. by Louisa J. Davis (London: Cassell, 1885). See also Cecilia Macheski, 'Penelope's Daughters'. The legend of Arachne tells of a dyer's daughter from Colophon who 'chose for her subjects the various loves of Jupiter ... and grew so proud of her work that, for challenging Minerva to do better, the goddess changed her into a spider' ['A Celebrated Needlewoman', *Melbourne Paper*, rpt. in *Women and Work* no. 86 (22 Jan. 1876), p. 5]. See also [Anne Ritchie], 'Arachne in Sloane Street', *Cornhill Magazine* 29 (1874), pp. 571-76.

16   For a discussion of the nineteenth-century use of the image of Queen Matilda see Rosemary Mitchell, 'A Stitch in Time? Women, Needlework, and the Marking of History in Victorian Britain', *Journal of Victorian Culture* 1 (1996), pp. 185-202. For contemporary representations of the needlework of England's queens see 'Needlework', *Macmillan's Magazine*; Lady Alford, 'Art Needlework'.

17   See, for instance, E. Shannon, 'Poetry as Vision: Sight and Insight in the Lady of Shalott', *Victorian Poetry* 19 (1981), pp. 207-23.

18   For a review of four of these books see 'Lady Marian Alford on Art Needlework', *Edinburgh Review*, p. 140.

19   'Art Publications', *Art Journal* 30 (1878), p. 144.

20   See, for instance, Agnes D. Atkinson, 'Modern Art Needlework', *Portfolio: An Artistic Periodical* 16 (1886), pp. 129-33.

21   See, for instance, 'With Needle and Thread: The Work of Today', *Lady's World* (1887), pp. 32-33.

by the boast of their own in-house designers.[22] As a result, embroidery schools such as the Royal School of Art Needlework encouraged its students to explore the more creative aspects of embroidery and taught the principles of design. Practical lessons in such artistic work, however, were a privilege denied to lower-class women. The rules of the Royal School of Art Needlework, for instance, required that an applicant for admission 'must be a gentlewoman by birth and education'.[23] Established in 1873, the Royal School was placed under the patronage of the Princess Christian, the Princess Mary of Teck, and an assortment of other well-born and well-meaning ladies, including Lady Alford as one of its most vocal supporters. Proponents of the institutionalisation in schools of the instruction of sewing had argued throughout the 1870s that real excellence in needlework could only be achieved through systematic teaching.[24] As the foremost institution established for training in art-needlework, then, the Royal School's exclusive committee and exclusionary admission requirements had the effect of establishing creative embroidery as a respectable remunerative occupation while marking this work the speciality of women of the upper classes.[25]

Yearly exhibitions of students' creations and special exhibitions such as the 'Special Loan Exhibition of Decorative Art Needlework' at the South Kensington Museum in 1873 rounded off the comparisons with the conventionally high art genres of painting and sculpture and contributed to the institutionalisation of embroidery as a serious art form.[26] Every effort was made to rescue embroidery from its debased reputation as mindless fancy-work and to initiate a style of modern art needlework that could express the 'fundamental truths of art'.[27] As an example of 'women's work *par excellence*', needlework constituted a unique outlet for images of female creativity that helped shape the representation of other forms of female artistic production.[28] Jennie June Croly asked in *Women and Work*, for instance, whether a woman should be an author or a dressmaker, concluding that ultimately one is as good as another because, while women 'need not be afraid of a loss of caste ... by becoming dressmakers instead of authors', a 'well-known artist only found out

---

22 'Milliners and Dressmakers', *Women and Work* no. 19 (10 Oct. 1874), p. 2.

23 'Rules of the Royal School of Art Needlework', *Woman's Gazette* 2 (1877), p. 53.

24 See, for instance, Fanny Heath, 'Needlework in the German Schools', *Macmillan's Magazine* 40 (1879), pp. 405-13; and 'Exhibition of School Needlework', *Woman's Gazette* 1 (1876), p. 75.

25 For a discussion of issues of class in relation to embroidery see Rozsika Parker, *The Subversive Stitch: Embroidery and the Making of the Feminine* (London: The Women's Press, 1984).

26 For descriptions of these exhibitions see, for instance, 'Needlework', *Macmillan's Magazine*; 'Ladies' Dressmaking and Embroidery Association', *Woman's Gazette* 4 (1879), p. 184; and 'Notes of an Exhibition of the School of Art Embroidery', *Art Journal*, 28 (1876), pp. 173-74.

27 'Needlework', *Artist* 1 (1880), p. 123.

28 F.R. Conder, 'Women's Work in Austria', *Art Journal* 27 (1875), p. 106.

that she could paint by embroidering for a living'.[29] In Croly's opinion, all forms of female artistry are equally respectable and interchangeable. Rather than acting as a conventional barrier to creative life, embroidery, in the case of the 'well-known artist', stimulates this creativity. Ultimately, Croly argues, the form of expression a woman chooses is less important than the actual 'exercise of faculties':

> You may not be able to put your talent or your acquirements into painting or writing or acting. But what matter? There are hundreds of poor painters and writers and actors who cannot keep the wolf from the door. Put them into what you can – into good healthful cooking; into intelligent laundry or chamber-work; into artistic dressmaking, tasteful millinery, or healthful flower or fruit culture.[30]

Here Croly expands the definition of female creativity beyond the confines of traditional artistic professions in order to suggest that even the most menial domestic tasks, if performed with an originality of thought and an eye to design, can stimulate a woman's creative instincts. The development of artistic skill is taken out of the realm of education and leisure and made more accessible to women. The poetic soul can develop, as it does for Aurora, while a woman sews, cooks, or cleans. In this respect, woman's work in general can be refined, lifted out of its domestic usefulness and transformed into a medium for artistic education.

Croly's emphasis on a domestic genesis for creativity resonated with embroidery's still primary function as a decorative feature of domestic objects. But even these prosaic objects, it was argued, could provide a woman with a firm grounding in basic principles of decorative art.[31] One supporter of art needlework as a profitable employment argued that in the design of patterns for various household embellishments, aesthetic concerns should outweigh those of fashion. Nature and art alone, Miss Scott argued, should influence designers because public taste is capricious. Fashions change, but 'where a thorough knowledge of the principles of art is gained, as one door shuts another opens … If you do not debase your art to a mere article of fashionable furniture, its principles are your own, imperishable, and everlastingly adaptable'.[32] Needlework, then, seemed to offer a basic introduction to aesthetic education and adaptable artistic principles that could be an avenue to creative production for an unlimited number of women. As a way into the professional culture of high art, needlework represented a potentially subversive feminine activity cloaked in an appearance of respectability and traditional domestic experience. In particular, it brought to the foreground a basic contradiction in conservative thinking in which the traditional appreciation for women's domestic work was confronted by the equally traditional disapproval of remunerative female labour. The

---

29   Jennie June Croly, 'An Author or a Dressmaker', *Women and Work* no. 23 (7 Nov. 1874), p. 2.

30   Ibid.

31   See, for instance, Mrs. Merrifield, 'On Design as Applied to Ladies Work', *Art Journal* 7 (1855), pp. 37-39, 73-75, 133-37.

32   Miss Scott, 'Art Embroidery II', *Woman's Gazette* 1 (1876), p. 59.

professionalisation of sewing raised questions about the intrinsic value of women's work in both the domestic sphere and in the marketplace, and the figures of working seamstresses that appeared in fiction and the popular press from the 1850s through the 1880s negotiated these questions in ever more sophisticated ways. As sewing was increasingly institutionalised in the schools of art needlework, dressmaking establishments, and cooperative organisations, the figure of the seamstress provided an emotive image of a working woman more deserving of sympathy and support than chastisement and neglect.

Pity and Patronisation: The Distressed Seamstress in the 1840s

In the early 1840s, the plight of what was estimated to be 15,000 distressed seamstresses in London alone became a cause of general concern for the philanthropic middle classes. The Second Report of the Children's Employment Commission, published in the spring of 1843, had shocked the public with its descriptions of the terrible conditions in the backrooms and garrets in which these seamstresses worked, and many were horrified by the revelation that thousands of vulnerable women were being exploited by the indifferent mechanisms of the commercial world. Almost everyone was united in pity for these 'white slaves of England'. While this term was used to refer in general to all those exploited by the free market system, it held special resonance for seamstresses who were seen to be among the most oppressed and who were stamped with the imagery of subjection by Grainger's judgment that 'no slavery is worse than that of the dress-maker's life in London'.[33] Shortly after this report was presented Thomas Hood published his own version of the pitiable life of the distressed seamstress in his emotive poem 'The Song of the Shirt'. When this poem was published in *Punch* in 1843, the public interest in the life of the needlewoman ensured its favourable reception. But the poem, with its considerable pathos, proved so successful that it allegedly tripled *Punch*'s circulation.

The success of Hood's poem lay in his representation of his seamstress as the solitary figure of a woman working alone in her garret. Fatigued and harassed by her unceasing and unrewarding labour, she longs to escape from her burdensome toil. She is a passive victim of the evils of the industrial world, a slave to economic forces of capitalism, and a martyr to the callous public's demand for cheap clothing, 'sewing at once, with double thread / A shroud as well as a shirt'.[34] In other words, she is a perfect example of a modest and reluctant worker who can be unproblematically pitied. This lonely figure was a popular image for art and literature that, while extremely pathetic and sensibly moving for the general public,

---

33   R.D. Grainger, 'Second Report of the Commissioners Inquiring into the Employment of Children in Trades and Manufactures', *Parliamentary Papers* 14 (1843), F30.

34   Thomas Hood, 'The Song of the Shirt', *Punch* 5 (16 December 1843), p. 260.

had little basis in the reality of the seamstress's life.[35] But her qualities of moral purity and feminine modesty made her a safe and convenient figure throughout the 1840s for charitable appeals to the middle class. The popularity of Hood's poem inspired a host of imitators to create their own version of the lonely seamstress, the first and most influential being Richard Redgrave's 1844 Royal Academy entry, *The Sempstress*. Although this piece is now lost, Redgrave painted a second version in 1846 that reproduced the visual iconography of the first and cemented what was to be the most influential template for representations of the seamstress (Figure 1.1).[36] Redgrave's painting features a single, gaunt figure working alone in an attic room. A clock on the wall behind her reads 2:30, and the darkness outside attests to the lateness of her work. A dying plant on the windowsill and a bottle of medicine on the mantelpiece emphasise the unhealthiness of the work, and a broken basin and scant furniture signify her extreme poverty. With her work on her lap, her eyes look to heaven, marking her only route of escape from her dismal situation. Following the exhibition of Redgrave's painting, a number of artists replicated the spirit of these details, including G.F. Watts, John Everett Millais, Frank Holl, George Hicks, and Edward Radford. The seamstress's desperation and piety was stressed throughout, as in Anna Blunden's *Song of the Shirt* (Figure 1.2), and the single gaunt figure, bare attic room, dying plant, late hour, and window to the outside world appeared over and again as a representation of the crushing burden of the free market.

As a symbol of the exploitation of the vulnerable working class, the seamstress was a central figure not only for melodrama, but also for the social problem novelists of the 1840s.[37] The public interest in this pitiable figure was fed throughout the decade by a succession of remarkably similar narratives that presented the story of the needlewoman's life as a sensational tale of a working-class woman's degradation from respectable poverty into penury, illness, and sometimes even prostitution.[38] Three such narratives were Frances Trollope's *Jessie Phillips* (1844), Charlotte Tonna's *The Wrongs of Woman* (1844), and Elizabeth Gaskell's *Mary Barton* (1848). Each of these texts features seamstresses who are clearly identified as members of the socially and economically vulnerable working class – prime candidates for middle-class protection. These novels all urge reform of the problems that led to

---

35   For a comprehensive explanation of these realities see Wanda F. Neff, *Victorian Working Women* (London: Frank Cass & Co., 1966), and Ivy Pinchbeck, *Women Workers and the Industrial Revolution* (London: Frank Cass & Co., 1969).

36   Susan Casteras, *Images of Victorian Womanhood in English Art* (Rutherford, N.J.: Farleigh Dickinson, 1987).

37   For a discussion of these novels in relation to the social problem genre see Joseph Kestner, *Protest and Reform: The British Social Narrative by Women* (London: Methuen, 1985), pp. 81-107.

38   Among these are H.M. Rathbone, 'The Seamstress', *Working Man's Friend and Family Instructor* 1 (1850), p. 306-308; [Eliza Meteyard], *Lucy Dean: The Noble Needlewoman*, *Eliza Cook's Journal* 3 (Jan. 1850-Jan. 1851); Elizabeth Stone, *The Young Milliner* (London: Cunningham and Mortimer, 1843); Camilla Toulmin, 'The Orphan Milliners: A Story of the West End', *Illuminated Magazine* 2 (1844), pp. 279-85.

such vulnerability for the seamstress as well as the working class as a whole, but they also deal specifically with the difficulties women faced when they worked in the industrial sphere.[39] Their sexual vulnerability as unprotected women in the public domain, in particular, formed a central area of concern and investigation. Dickens's *Nicholas Nickleby* (1837) provides an early example of this vulnerability in the character of Kate Nickleby. As a day worker at Madame Mantilini's dress shop, Kate's walks home from work, often late at night, expose her, like Mary Barton, to the improper advances of a caddish upper-class rogue. Even when she walks home with her mother, Kate still feels the danger of her situation and her powerlessness to protect herself. But Dickens only briefly exposes Kate to such danger, identifying it as a possibility and then removing her from harm's way when she loses her job. In this way, Kate's sexual vulnerability as a working woman is emphasised without injuring her reputation. Although insulted, Kate retains her purity, and her respectability and virtue remain intact.

The consequences are somewhat more severe for Mary Barton, however. In encouraging Harry Carson, Mary shows herself to be both frivolous and foolish. Proud of her beauty and unconcerned for her reputation, Mary engages in an improper and immodest flirtation that, although shown to be obviously wrong, is portrayed more as a sin of thoughtlessness rather than sexuality. While Mary faces external dangers during her walks home at night, her vulnerability is increased by her own vanity and her sexual innocence; she invites Harry Carson's attentions because she believes he wants to marry her. Unlike Kate, she does not understand the motives of upper-class men. Like Dickens, Gaskell introduces the issue of the seamstress's vulnerability through the possibility of the sexual fall, and in this narrative, she also saves her heroine from that fate worse than death. But Mary only just realises in time that, as a result of her flirtation, 'She had hitherto been walking in grope-light towards a precipice'.[40] The obvious sexual imagery of Mary's walk in 'grope-light' is offset by her turn away from the edge. Importantly, Mary's indiscretion does not constitute a fall. She has, however, committed a sexual transgression, and as a result must be redeemed before she can be rewarded with marriage to Jem. Mary's public humiliation and resultant fever thus constitute the penance that mitigates her sin. Through Mary, Gaskell candidly examines the issue of the sexual dangers that plagued the working woman without alienating her readers or sealing the fate of her heroine and suggests, rather boldly, that the problem is social rather than moral. It is Mary's late nights, her motherlessness, and her need to work that are shown to be

---

39   For a full analysis of these novels, see Lynn Alexander, *Women, Work, and Representation: Needlewomen in Victorian Art and Literature* (Athens: Ohio University Press, 2003).

40   Elizabeth Gaskell, *Mary Barton: A Tale of Manchester Life*, Edgar Wright, ed. (Oxford: Oxford University Press, 1998), p. 153.

Figure 1.1   Richard Redgrave, *The Sempstress* (1844)

Figure 1.2   Anna Blunden, 'For Only One Short Hour' *(A Song of the Shirt)*,
1854 (oil on canvas).

primarily at fault.[41] As a result of her class, then, Mary appears more vulnerable than
Kate and, consequently, less responsible for her actions.

An even more daring attempt to locate the sexual difficulties of the seamstress in
a social rather than a moral context was made by Frances Trollope in *Jessie Phillips*.
Taking her heroine over the precipice, Trollope depicts her seamstress as a fallen

---

41   For a discussion of Gaskell's use of *Mary Barton* as an argument for protective
legislation for working women see Kristine Swenson, 'Protection or Restriction? Women's
Labour in *Mary Barton*', *Gaskell Society Journal* 7 (1993), pp. 50-66.

woman. Jessie is seduced and becomes pregnant, but throughout the narrative it becomes apparent that her seamstress is merely a vehicle for Trollope's larger critique of the injustices of the New Poor Law. Even though a fallen woman, Jessie, as a member of the working class, can still be pitied by the reader, just as she is pitied by the most sensible character in the novel, Martha Maxwell. Another representation of the working-class seamstress that defied sexual strictures was Dickens's seamstress in *David Copperfield* (1850), Little Emily. Although Little Emily is redeemed after her fall, in part, by her emigration to Australia, further mitigation is offered in her remorseful and pathetic claim that her seducer Steerforth 'had used all his power to deceive me, and that I believed him, trusted him, loved him!'[42] In this justification, the blame for her fall is subtly shifted from Emily to Steerforth, from any notion of her sexual deviance onto another example of the upper-class exploitation of the working class's vulnerability.[43] As these representations of working-class seamstresses make clear, the distressed seamstress was a convenient figure for complaints against the predatory commercial world. Although sexually susceptible, she could still engage the interest and sympathy of socially-concerned readers.

These images of the distressed seamstress thus provided an eloquent shorthand for a series of cultural anxieties concerning the dangers of an indifferent commercial world which did not discriminate between the class, gender, or vulnerability of its workers. Described as slaves, seamstresses became identified as exchangeable commodities whose health and well-being were an unnecessary and unprofitable consideration in a labour market overrun with willing workers.[44] Cooperative institutions such as the Distressed Needlewoman's Association and the Institution for the Employment of Needlewomen allowed the middle class to soothe their conscience through schemes of philanthropic aid. Some reformers even described the ways in which individuals could make a difference, such as urging middle-class women to be ethical shoppers, advising them to buy either directly from the seamstress or from houses that had good reputations for treating their workers well.[45] Pity and patronisation were thus fused in the public consciousness as an appropriate and adequate response to the seamstress's situation. But the development of an established iconography of this easily pitiable figure contributed to a social inertia that codified the middle-class response to the issues plaguing the seamstress and allowed the middle class to deal with their anxieties about industrial alienation without feeling personally implicated in such scenes of distress. The feeling of sympathy alone, T.J. Edelstein notes, 'would tend partially to satisfy the urge to reform these very problems. Thus, these visual works

---

42   Charles Dickens, *David Copperfield*, Nina Burgis, ed., (Oxford: Clarendon Press, 1981), p. 615.

43   For a discussion of the representation of the seamstress in Dickens' fiction see Lynn M. Alexander, 'Following the Thread: Dickens and the Seamstress', *Victorian Newsletter* no. 80 (1991), pp. 1-7.

44   See, for instance, 'Our Suffocated Sempstresses', *Punch* (4 July 1863), p. 46.

45   See, for instance, 'On the Best Means of Relieving the Needlewomen', *Eliza Cook's Journal* 5 (1851), pp. 189-91; and 'How Can the Young-Ladyhood of England Assist in Improving the Conditions of the Working Classes?', *The Sempstress* 1 (1855), p. 8.

tend to assuage concern while they incite it'.[46] Middle-class audiences could feel sorry for the seamstress or might contribute to a philanthropic organisation such as the Distressed Needlewoman's Association, but in the course of such objectification she was reduced to a symbol of working-class vulnerability that was convenient for reformers who thought women and the working classes unable to help themselves.[47] The middle classes could help if they chose, but the difficulties of the seamstress did not appear in the end to affect them directly.

Regardless of her association to conventional femininity through the common activity of sewing, then, the distressed seamstress throughout the 1840s appeared alien and unconnected to the domestic sphere and the middle-class woman. This point is succinctly made, for instance, in a short feature that appeared in *Eliza Cook's Journal* in 1850. This tale, entitled 'The Seamstress' tells of the healthy country girl Rosie who goes to London in order to make money that will help send her younger brother to school. In just six months, however, the girl, who is at first described as having a 'sunburnt face' with 'dimples showing upon her cheeks and chin, lips rosy and full, eyes sparkling with life and health' and a 'frame radiant with rural beauty and vigour', is transformed into a 'feeble remnant of womanhood – pale, wasted, almost ghastly'.[48] Rosie's story pithily depicts the narrative of degradation that characterised representations of the seamstress, but it also presents a hopeful conclusion as she recovers from her experience when, after a dangerous illness, she is brought home by her parents. Although she is reintegrated into the country idyll, she has lost the innocent enjoyment of life that she had previously known; her step still trips along, 'though not so gaily as before'.[49] This loss of innocence also brands her, leaving, along with her emotional scars, a physical reminder of her experience in her face 'stamped by the deep marks of care'.[50]

The representation of Rosie, like that of Mary Barton, Jessie Phillips, and Little Emily, attests ultimately to middle-class authors' desire throughout the 1840s to employ an image of the working-class seamstress that, while evoking pity for her helpless state, also asserted her distance from the middle-class woman and conventional domesticity. Even when these heroines are re-established within a conventional domestic existence, the distance remains, whether it is the literal space that is embodied in Mary Barton's move to Canada and Little Emily's emigration to Australia, or the physical and emotional breach of Rosie's experience. After 1851, however, this distance began to close. As the public became more aware of the number of middle-class women forced to work, the debates concerning work for women could no longer ignore the more problematic issue of the middle-class

---

46   T.J. Edelstein, 'They Sang "The Song of the Shirt": The Visual Iconography of the Seamstress', *Victorian Studies* 23 (1980), p. 184.

47   Helen Rogers, '"The Good Are Not Always Powerful, Nor The Powerul Always Good": The Politics of Women's Needlework in Mid-Victorian London', *Victorian Studies* 40 (1997), pp. 589-623. See also Lynn Alexander, *Women, Work, and Representation*.

48   'The Seamstress', *Eliza Cook's Journal* 3 (1850), pp. 17, 19.

49   Ibid., p. 19.

50   Ibid.

woman's place in the commercial sphere. The leniency toward sexual transgression granted to the representation of the working-class seamstress could not be replicated in the case of the middle-class working woman. The intertwined problems of sexual and economic vulnerability had now to be substantially addressed and became the foundation for a much broader critique of conventional social morality as an out-moded system. The contradictions of this system were brought into sharp focus in the 1850s by the figure of the middle-class woman reduced to the indignity of a working-class economic status and forced to work to support herself. The reduced gentlewoman as seamstress provided a convenient figure through which this public space could be negotiated because, Helen Rogers argues, she 'linked the plight of all women to their lack of educational and employment opportunities'.[51] The image of the working woman forced by circumstance to go against her upbringing cut an even more sympathetic figure for bourgeois audiences than that of mere economic destitution. As a result, she became a key figure in a more controversial debate concerning the acceptability of work for all women. By the 1850s, the genteel seamstress came to embody what Deborah Logan describes as the 'notion that "goodness" is a transcendent quality that cannot be tainted by corporeal concerns'.[52] Indeed she was used throughout the 1850s as an identifiable symbol of ideal womanhood that was defined by her relation to her work instead of more arbitrary markers such as class.

The Reduced Gentlewoman: Representing the Genteel Seamstress in Elizabeth Gaskell's *Ruth*

The concerns over the exploitation of seamstresses that were repeated throughout the 1840s faded considerably from the public consciousness after the early 1850s.[53] Nevertheless, although less visible, the needlewoman continued to be associated with the issues of social, sexual, and economic vulnerability raised in the social problem novels. As a symbol of working-class and female exploitation, the figure of the seamstress occupied a pivotal role in discussions about the value of individual human life in the capitalist system. The social problem novels that had used the seamstress as the representative of the working class had introduced the rhetoric of the family and domestic ideology into an industrial setting. As Catherine Gallagher notes, the metaphor of family relations had become a useful paternalistic model

---

51   Helen Rogers, 'The Politics of Women's Needlework', p. 611.

52   Deborah Ann Logan, *Fallenness in Victorian Women's Writing: Marry, Stitch, Die, or Do Worse* (Columbia, MO: University of Missouri Press, 1998), p. 31.

53   Occasional incidents re-ignited the public interest in the problems of the seamstress. The death of Mary Anne Walkley in June 1863, for instance, led to a public outcry against the apprenticeship system in which girls were housed in cramped and unhealthy conditions. For a discussion of the publicity surrounding Walkley's death see Christina Walkley, *Ghost in the Looking Glass*, esp. chap. 3.

for the reconciliation between the workers and their masters.[54] At the same time, however, it also contributed to the development in the 1850s of the image of the seamstress as a genteel member of the moral middle class. When Hood created his famous seamstress, he made the point that she was not born to this life. While imagining a peaceful, natural scene, she pines:

> For only one short hour
> To feel as I used to feel,
> Before I knew the woes of want
> And the walk that costs a meal![55]

In the representations that followed Hood, especially in the visual representations where an iconographic shorthand was necessary, this disjunction between the seamstress's origins and situation developed into the difference between gentility and poverty. Respectable but threadbare dresses, nice decorative objects now cracked and chipped, and dead or dying plants all pointed towards the seamstress's faded by inherent refinement. The purity, modesty, and domestic setting that repeatedly appeared in representations that proceeded from Hood asserted that, although forced to work for a living, the genteel seamstress was still imbued with the feminine features of the ideal domestic woman. The difference between the working-class and the genteel seamstress, however, also extended beyond these surface signifiers. Most notably, the iconographic descendents of Hood's seamstress were allowed less sexual freedom than their working-class contemporaries. Even while sharing the same economic deprivations as the lowest slopworker, their actions are judged according to the strict code of middle-class morality. Dickens's Little Dorrit, for instance, maintains her respectability even while living with her family in the unwholesome atmosphere of Marshalsea prison.

Similarly, the orphaned seamstress of George W.M. Reynolds's *The Seamstress, or The White Slave of England* (1853), Virginia Mordaunt, remains virtuous even as those around her try to convince her otherwise.[56] To the housemaid Jane, Virginia's fall into prostitution is inevitable: 'Well, it's a pity – a great pity, such a sweet creature as you are – and quite a lady too: but your fate is fied, as the saying is'.[57] For the seamstress turned prostitute, Miss Barnet, such a fate is the outcome for all seamstresses: '"Hope for the virtuous seamstress!" ejaculated Miss Barnet with a bitter laugh. "No, no Virginia – ten thousand times no!"'.[58] But even among her immoral companions and in her destitute state, Virginia remains strong against

---

54   Catherine Gallagher, *The Industrial Reformation of English Fiction, 1832-1867* (Chicago: University of Chicago Press, 1985).

55   Thomas Hood, 'Song of the Shirt', p. 132.

56   Although only published in novel form in 1853, this story originally appeared in serialised parts in 1850 in Reynolds's journal, *Reynolds's Miscellany*.

57   G.W.M. Reynolds, *The Seamstress, or the White Slave of England* (London: John Dicks, 1853), p. 4.

58   Ibid., p. 44.

the goading of her acquaintances and the advances of the Marquis of Arden who approaches her as she walks through Grosvenor Square on errands for her shop. Even in a fashionable West End neighbourhood, Virginia is not safe from the dangers that accompany the reduced gentlewoman's sexual and social vulnerability, and she must be rescued by the gentlemanly representative of the moral middle class, Mr. Lavenham, in order to escape from the profligate and perverse aristocrat. Caught between the profligacy of upper-class luxury and the sexual vulnerability of the working class, Virginia is cast in the mould of the genteel seamstress, defending her virtuous position alone in her garret and sewing by candlelight.

Reynolds's previous success with *The Mysteries of London* (1844-1864) had secured his place as a popular author of penny dreadfuls, but his Chartist sympathies ensured that much of the horror described in his sensational tales was attributed to the appalling working and living conditions to which working classes were subjected.[59] As an editor and author for Chartist publications such as *Reynolds's Political Instructor* who had on more than one occasion employed the figure of the needlewoman as an example of wider class oppression, Reynolds used the difficulties of Virginia's situation as a seamstress to support the idea of a general populace that was more right-minded and capable than supposedly superior upper classes.[60] He further supports this position by comparing his virtuous, destitute seamstress with her socially respectable mother, the Duchess of Belmont. Although she has had an illegitimate child, the Duchess can occupy a position as a paragon of society because her title and economic status grant her unquestioned respectability. But in the difference between her respectable image and the scandalous secret that she hides, the Duchess represents the superficial nature of social morality. While virtue in the shape of Virginia is vilified and shunned by polite society, transgression in the shape of her mother is embraced and lauded.

In addition to criticising hypocritical social structures, Reynolds also demonstrates through the economic difficulties of the seamstress the corruption in the institutional mechanisms of the market and the evils of the capitalist economy's primary logic of competition:

> It is this accursed system which makes the emporium of Messr. Aaron and Sons flourish for the benefit of its proprietors; while the vapours of demoralization, despair, famine, sickness and death, emanate from its portals and infect the atmosphere that is breathed by a large portion of the community. The towering edifice, so grand without and so superb within … [is] built with the bones of the white slaves of England.[61]

---

59   Peter Haining, *The Penny Dreadful, or, Strange, Horrid, & Sensational Tales!* (London: Victor Gollancz, 1975), pp. 83-85. For a discussion of the popularity of *The Mysteries of London* see Ellen Bayuk Rosenman, 'Spectacular Women: *The Mysteries of London* and the Female Body', *Victorian Studies* 40 (1996), pp. 31-64.

60   See, for instance, G.W.M. Reynolds 'Warning to the Needlewomen and Slopworkers', *Reynolds's Political Instructor* 1 (1850), pp. 66-67, 74-75.

61   Reynolds, *The Seamstress*, p. 88.

Reynolds uses the language of contagion in order to describe the polluting effect of the dressmaker's establishment and the free-market system. The unwholesome atmosphere of the workroom is shown to infect society at large, and the struggle for virtue to survive amidst such widespread infamy is represented as an example of the individual's resistance to a degenerate social system. But the most startling and perhaps most disturbing element of Reynolds's story for his middle-class audience was the comparison that he draws between Virginia and her mother.

The dangers evoked by this type of comparison can be seen most clearly in one of the book's illustrations that juxtaposes the image of Virginia at work with an image of her customers, including her mother, enjoying a society party (Figure 1.3). Virginia's poise and her clean-cut and respectable appearance in lowly surroundings lend her an angelic appearance and signify moral integrity well beyond that of the Duchess. But the society women enjoy a level of social respectability to which the seamstress can only aspire. Besides highlighting the injustice of the discrepancy between the lives of the seamstress and customer, Henry Anelay's woodcut also emphasises certain key similarities between the two. Both Virginia and her mother share a common class origin which circumstances and the obscurity of Virginia's birth do nothing to conceal. The physiognomic similarity between mother and daughter emphasises that the position of each on either side of the needle is a mere matter of circumstance, that the reduced gentlewoman and the feminine ideal are exchangeable in all but means.

The association between a conventional feminine existence and the genteel seamstress was not only used, as it is by Reynolds, to illustrate the degradation in prevailing social systems. It was also used by those more specifically interested in the plight of the seamstress to argue for her innate refinement. When the first, and only, volume of the journal *The Sempstress* was published in October 1855 by the Distressed Needlewoman's Society, the editor stated the aim of the publication to be that of giving publicity to the plight of all seamstresses. But he pays particular attention to the number of reduced gentlewomen forced into the needle trade because their genteel upbringing makes them more pitiable than those who were born to work:

> There is a class of individuals with whose labours neither the rich nor the poor can dispense – a class consisting, in a very large proportion, of persons who have been well educated in early life, who have mixed with the high and the noble; but who, from reverses, are compelled to employ that which they did as a pastime as the means of obtaining their daily bread.[62]

In giving publicity to the plight of the seamstress, the Distressed Needlewoman's Society also publicised the close association between the genteel seamstress and the middle-class domestic woman. As in Anelay's illustration, all that separates

---

62   *The Sempstress* 1 (1855), p. 1.

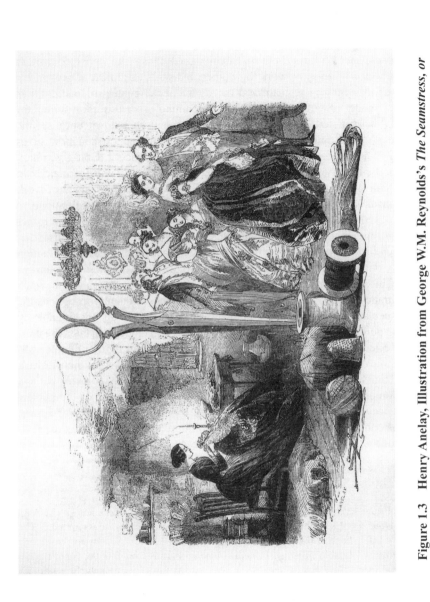

Figure 1.3   Henry Anelay, Illustration from George W.M. Reynolds's *The Seamstress, or The White Slave of England* (1853)

her from the higher classes with whom she previously mixed are the tools of the needle trade, the scissors, thread, needle, and thimble of the seamstress. Through this kind of association, the difficulties encountered by the genteel seamstress could be seen to impinge directly on the security of the domestic ideal. The revelation that a woman of the middle class could be subjected to such degradation threatened the very foundations of domestic ideology.

In order to dispel the fears about such degradation, those who were interested in promoting the acceptability of work for women invested in a project of gentrifying the image of the working woman, and the figure of the genteel seamstress was offered as a model of virtue and modesty. Becoming a seamstress, a writer for *Women and Work* noted, was not necessarily a social step down because, the writer notes, 'social opinion is now undergoing rapid changes, and now gives forth a somewhat uncertain sound. At all events the paramount, God-given duty of honest self-support ought to overrule the conventional decisions of man'.[63] In setting the conventional beliefs of society about the degrading influence of work on women against the idea of work as a 'God-given duty of honest self-support', this writer describes a notion of moral integrity that exists in the individual rather than in their relationship to established social structures. The moral relativism that characterises virtue as a quality of the individual places the emphasis on action rather than environment.[64] Virtue, therefore, can thrive even in the most degrading of situations. This point is made in an article for the *English Woman's Journal* in which the needle trade is described as a place where there was 'frequently to be seen the sublimest spectacle on earth – Virtue in the presence of Infamy uncontaminable by surrounding pollution'.[65] By maintaining her gentility and modesty in even the most difficult of circumstances, the virtuous seamstress could be a figure of comfort to all those who worried about the degrading effects of the workplace on the woman's fragile constitution. While traditional boundaries that separated the working woman from the domestic were being questioned and redrawn, the figure of the genteel seamstress became the focus of debates about the morality of remunerative labour. As a touchstone for the moral probity of which the working woman was capable, the image of the genteel seamstress offered a measure of reassurance to a worried public.

---

63   'Ladies as Dressmakers', *Labour News*, rpt. in *Women and Work* no. 12 (22 Aug. 1874), p. 3. Other articles on the social position of the middle-class seamstress include, 'The Dressmaker's Life', *English Woman's Journal* 1 (1858), pp. 319-25; 'Society for Promoting the Employment of Women', *English Woman's Journal* 5 (1860), pp. 388-96; Ellen Barlee, 'The Needlewomen', *The Times* (8 Dec. 1866), p. 10; and M.E. Phillips, 'On the Necessity for Studying Practical Needlework', *Woman's Gazette* 1 (1876), p. 170.

64   For a discussion of the development of moral relativism in the Victorian period see Christopher Herbert, *Victorian Relativity: Radical Thought and Scientific Discovery* (Chicago: University of Chicago Press, 2001).

65   'Warehouse Seamstresses. By One Who Has Worked With Them', *English Woman's Journal* 3 (1859), p. 168.

Part of this reassurance, however, was challenged by the publication in 1853 of Elizabeth Gaskell's *Ruth*. Although most of the reviews of *Ruth* ranged from favourable to ambivalent, many raised questions about the wisdom of placing a fallen woman at the centre of the narrative. Gaskell herself felt sure that the story of Ruth's fall and redemption would be determined to be an 'unfit subject for fiction', and the early reviews in particular debated this very issue.[66] One reviewer for *Eliza Cook's Journal* asked that the same consideration be given to Ruth as that which was allowed other errant seamstresses. It was this reviewer's position that Ruth's sin was unconscious and deserved charity and understanding rather than condemnation.[67] But the justification of ignorance was one reserved primarily for use with the working-class seamstress. Even without Ruth's early grounding in middle-class morality, a reviewer for the *Spectator* noted, 'the idea of the innocence and ignorance of Ruth ... is hardly consistent with sixteen and some months' experience in a milliner's workroom'.[68] Unlike Jessie Phillips, Little Emily, or even Mary Barton, Ruth is a reduced gentlewoman who should by rights 'know better'. It was this idea of Gaskell's implausible appeal for sympathy for Ruth, based upon her innocence, that prompted the reviewer for *Sharpe's* magazine to claim that Ruth was 'not a veritable type of her class'.[69] But Gaskell goes to great lengths to show that, indeed, Ruth is very much a typical middle-class reduced gentlewoman.[70] Her sensitivity, her beauty, and her love of nature set her apart from the other women in the workroom, with the exception of Jenny whose illness and uncomplaining self-denial bestow on her a sense of virtue and otherworldly wisdom that raises her thoughts above the base concerns of the other seamstresses. Jenny's beatific disposition aligns her naturally with Ruth's sensitive soul, but her 'warning voice and gentle wisdom' suggest that unsentimental resignation is the only way for a seamstress to get through her apprenticeship.[71]

Gaskell depicts Jenny and Ruth as exemplary portraits of the two most popular and influential images of the working seamstress: the respectable and pitiable working-class needlewoman and the reduced gentlewoman. On the one hand, she offers Jenny as a standard portrait of her type, grounded in the economic concerns that characterised representations of the working-class seamstress. All other considerations pale in comparison to the economic, including the monotony and the unhealthiness of her work. Gaskell uses Ruth's position as a reduced gentlewoman, on the other hand, to

---

66   Elizabeth Gaskell, 'Letter to Anne Robson', *The Letters of Mrs. Gaskell*, p. 220.

67   'Ruth', *Eliza Cook's Journal* 8 (1853), pp. 277-80.

68   'unsigned review', *Spectator* 26 (1853), rpt. in *Elizabeth Gaskell: The Critical Heritage*, Angus Easson, ed. (London: Routledge, 1991), p. 213.

69   'unsigned review', *Sharpe's London Magazine* n.s. 2 (1853), rpt. in *Elizabeth Gaskell: The Critical Heritage*, p. 208.

70   For a discussion of how Ruth's middle-class upbringing contributes to her seduction see Suzann Bick, '"Take Her Up Tenderly": Elizabeth Gaskell's Treatment of the Fallen Woman', *Essays in Arts and Sciences* 18 (1989), pp. 17-27.

71   Elizabeth Gaskell, *Ruth*, Angus Easson, ed. (London: Penguin Books, 1997), p. 29. Further references to this edition will appear in the text.

explore the difficulties of reconciling this kind of economic concern with ideas of womanliness and domesticity. In particular, she draws on needlework's middle-class image as a marker of respectable domestic activity in order to establish a context for sewing beyond the remunerative work of Mrs. Mason's house. In the strictly conventional middle-class household of the Bradshaws, needlework rounds off an evening visit with polite activity and reinforces the domineering influence of the patriarch when 'the ladies produced their sewing, while Mr. Bradshaw stood before the fire, and gave the assembled party the benefit of his opinions on many subjects' (*Ruth*, p. 157). Gaskell also calls on needlework's protective function when Jemima Bradshaw uses it as a screen for her modesty. Angered by her father's efforts to establish a match between her and his business partner, Mr. Farquhar, and distressed by what she sees as Farquhar's dislike for her, Jemima meets him with civility, but immediately begins to 'work away at her sewing as if she were to earn her livelihood by it' (*Ruth*, p. 186). Although this industrious sewing protects her feminine delicacy, it also points out the economic implications for female sexuality. The indignation and embarrassment that prompt Jemima's sewing stem from her father's cold-hearted reckoning of the economic advantages of marrying Farquhar. The needlework that had previously denoted her feminine propriety and her value within the domestic sphere becomes linked with the economic value of remunerative sewing. In contrast to the working-class woman, however, Gaskell locates the value of the middle-class woman in her sexuality rather than her work.

Ruth's delicately poised social position between Jenny and Jemima allows Gaskell to negotiate between the economic difficulties of the working-class woman and the sexual and domestic value of the middle-class woman. And, by making her a fallen woman, Gaskell explores the question of redemption through self-sufficiency.[72] As Ruth McDowell Cook argues, Gaskell often uses work to stress women's autonomy and fulfilment outside the domestic role.[73] And in the three jobs that Ruth has in the course of the narrative, Gaskell achieves a substantial analysis of this issue. Ruth's three jobs constitute the three types of remunerative work that were considered to be the most womanly – seamstress, governess, and nurse. Although Ruth's early life as a seamstress ends shortly into her story, it is in this first job that Gaskell sets the tone for Ruth's relationship with all forms of womanly work. However much she is told she must become inured to her situation, she spends her short work breaks at the workroom's window, 'pressed against it as a bird presses against the bars of its cage' (*Ruth*, p. 8). Through Ruth's sense of dissatisfaction with the life to which she has been consigned, Gaskell explores the restrictions popular notions of womanly work put on the reduced gentlewoman. The opposing requirements of necessity and middle-class respectability force Ruth into a job that is both unfulfilling and unsuitable, and the restrictive order of the feminine workplace imprisons her in

---

72   Laura Hapke, 'He Stoops to Conquer: Redeeming the Fallen Woman in the Fiction of Dickens, Gaskell and Their Contemporaries', *Victorian Newsletter* no 69 (1986), pp. 16-22.

73   Ruth McDowell Cook, 'Women's Work as Paradigm for Autonomy in Gaskell's *My Lady Ludlow*', *Gaskell Society Journal* 11 (1997), pp. 68-76.

what is to her an unbearable situation. While the family model upon which Mrs. Mason's house is run is supposed to protect the virtue of the vulnerable seamstress, its moral function is shown to have been corrupted by greed and economic interests, and the inhabitants of the house are subjected to the uncompromising governance of Mrs. Mason's 'motherly' supervision without the love and understanding of the true domestic sphere.

Ruth's subsequent ruin when she turns to Mr. Bellingham for the protection denied to her by this corrupt system thus warns against imposing class and gender-based models of work and respectability on the individual. Forced into an unfulfilling and unremunerative job by an uninterested guardian, Ruth embodies a harsh lesson about the way in which patriarchal notions of female labour served to create and to preserve the vulnerability of the working woman. Needlework, however, is only the first instance of this type of work. When the opportunity arises for Ruth to become a governess for the Bradshaws, her most sympathetic supporter, Mr. Benson, questions whether someone with her history should be placed in such a position of trust. Moreover, when Jemima Bradshaw warns Ruth that her 'taste and refinement' will 'unfit' her for work as a nurse, she openly acknowledges Ruth's stunted potential to enter a different social and economic position when she tells Ruth, '[Y]ou were fitted for something better' (*Ruth*, p. 318). Jemima's judgment is supported by Ruth's basic unfitness for what was conventionally considered acceptable work for women, and each womanly job Ruth undertakes proves disastrous for her, leading, respectively, to her seduction, the publication of her sin, and eventually to her death. This judgment is also supported in the difference Gaskell creates between Ruth and her working-class companions. In her representation of life in the workroom, Gaskell suggests that Ruth's innate gentility, her unsuitablity for such mundane work, and her powerful imagination all signify a refinement in her character that goes beyond that instilled by a middle-class upbringing. Unlike the other girls in the workroom who use their break to eat the meagre supper they are provided, huddle around the fire, or fall asleep at the table, Ruth contemplates the way even the most ugly things can be transformed into beautiful objects by a light covering of snow. Rosemarie Bodenheimer calls this Ruth's 'pastoral drive', which, she argues, leaves Ruth unfit for the claustrophobic life of the seamstress and oblivious to the realities of a social existence.[74] Jenny looks out of the same window as Ruth, but even she 'could not be persuaded into admiring the winter's night' (*Ruth*, p. 9). Instead, she thinks only of how the cold weather makes her illness worse. Where Ruth forgets physical discomfort in her contemplation of the beauty of the scene, Jenny sees only its corporeal impact. Jenny can be sympathetic to Ruth's difficulty in accepting her life as a seamstress, but she cannot really understand why she has such trouble submitting to it.

---

74 Rosemarie Bodenheimer, *The Politics of Story in Victorian Social Fiction* (Ithaca: Cornell University Press, 1988), p. 156.

Ruth's innate gentility is further emphasised in her workroom experience by her relationship to the work she does.[75] Gaskell's choice of needlework as the first job for her heroine, rather than the work of the governess or nurse, allows her to capitalise on the contemporary social investment in the particular vulnerability of the seamstress, and helps her to justify Ruth's fall. In doing so, however, she also draws on needlework's potential to open a private space in which the seamstress can transcend the mundanity of her work. Needlework may prove dangerously confining for Ruth, but it also has a creative potential that is revealed at the hunt-ball when Ruth's poetic nature is awakened to the beauty it desires:

> Ruth did not care to separate the figures that formed a joyous and brilliant whole; it was enough to gaze, and dream of the happy smoothness of the lives in which such music, and such profusion of flowers, of jewels, of elegance of every description, and beauty of all shapes and hues, were every-day things. She did not want to know who the people were; although to hear a catalogue of names seemed to be the great delight of most of her companions. (*Ruth*, p. 16)

In this scene, Gaskell implies the various ways in which needlework has the capacity to influence creativity. Not only does it provide Ruth with a point of comparison through which her experience of drudgery and confinement makes nature and beauty precious to her, but it also introduces her to such brilliance as she encounters at the ball. Unlike the other seamstresses who revel in gossip about the people they are watching, Ruth's admiration of the scene is a subjective reaction to colour, texture, and composition. Where Jenny and the other girls are realistic, Ruth is poetic. Facts and details intrude into her aesthetic enjoyment, and 'to avoid the shock of too rapid a descent in the common-place world of Miss Smiths and Mr. Thomsons, she returned to her post in the ante-room. There she stood thinking, or dreaming' (*Ruth*, p. 16). Through this uncommon form of refuge, Gaskell introduces the possibility for needlework to open up an imaginative space, as it does for Aurora Leigh, for creative production. And the place that is set up for her to work, where all the 'wares' of the milliners are arranged, acts as a haven in which her reverie can be prolonged (*Ruth*, p. 15).

Her retreat from the world of practicality, however, is only temporary and ends when Ruth is 'startled back to actual life' by a petulant dancer with a tear in her gown (*Ruth*, p. 16). The dream that the scene inspires is presumably one of abstract beauty and artistic elegance, but it is a state of poetic inspiration that is short-lived. Her poetic soul is silenced by economic constraints, and she is rapidly returned to the position of a typical seamstress – on her knees at the feet of the upper class. The jarring image of Ruth being pulled down so low from the heights of her artistic reverie emphasises the difference between Ruth's inner world and the social world that surrounds her. The smile she cannot suppress when she catches Mr. Bellingham's eye is understood by him as a coquettish act. For Ruth, however, it is the simple

---

75 Terence Wright, *Elizabeth Gaskell: 'We are Not Angels': Realism, Gender, Values* (London: Macmillan, 1995), pp. 75-76.

result of being 'infected by the feeling' of excitement and amusement attendant upon such an occasion (*Ruth*, p. 17). Although a natural reaction for a woman with a poetic soul, such a personal show of emotion is unacceptable for a proper and demure seamstress. Ruth's experience thus serves to highlight the contradictory function of needlework for the artistic woman. Although it opens up a space for her poetic soul to exist, it also introduces her to the domestic and sexual existence that dominates her life after she loses her job.

This domestic life, first as Mr. Bellingham's mistress and then as Leonard's mother, signals the end of her creative life as her poetic dreamings are replaced by dreams of Mr. Bellingham's love. Even the slight artistic elements in the bright colours and exquisite materials of the ball gowns are replaced by needlework of the 'coarse and common kind' when later she takes up sewing again as a means to earn money (*Ruth*, p. 301-302). The free time in which she had allowed her imagination free reign is captured by the all-consuming domestic ideal, which transforms all forms of female production into domestic duties. As Ruth's imagination is powerfully constrained, she turns with self-sacrificing dedication to the mundane duties of household management, most notably the womanly chore of plain sewing: '[S]he had been devoting every spare hour to the simple tailoring which she performed for her boy (she had always made every article he wore, and felt almost jealous of the employment)' (*Ruth*, p. 261). Her own tailoring for Leonard is dictated by economic necessity, but within this simple task Ruth discovers fulfilment in womanly selflessness. This type of fulfilment, however, proves to be temporary when Leonard asks 'when he might begin to have clothes made by a man' (*Ruth*, p. 261). As Anita Wilson argues, 'Ruth's only flaw as a mother' is her complete 'adoration of her son'.[76] Ruth's devotion is thus both self-sacrificing and self-destructive, leading her naturally to a martyr's death when, having nursed her neighbours and even Mr. Bellingham back to health from a deadly typhus epidemic, she succumbs to it herself.

In *Ruth*, Gaskell does not attempt to resolve the incongruity between domesticity and creativity. Instead, Ruth's poeticism is channelled into her motherly care for her fellow men and ultimately into her devotion to God. In fact, Deborah Deneholz Morse argues, 'Gaskell intends that God be interpreted as Mother ... In her progress toward perfect redemption, Ruth becomes not only a saint but saviour figure to her community.[77] In Ruth's situation, Gaskell illustrates the way in which a woman's creative potential can be used in order to instruct and nurture those around her. As I will show in chapter three, this insight had special resonance for all women writers. Gaskell's work, particularly in *Ruth*, was praised by some critics for the moral lessons of Christian forgiveness and redemption that it taught, but it also contributed to an

---

76   Anita C. Wilson, 'Elizabeth Gaskell's Subversive Icon: Motherhood and Childhood in *Ruth*', *Gaskell Society Journal* 16 (2002), p. 96.

77   Deborah Deneholz Morse, 'Stitching Repentance, Sewing Rebellion: Seamstresses and Fallen Women in Elizabeth Gaskell's Fiction', *Keeping the Victorian House: A Collection of Essays*, Vanessa D. Dickerson, ed. (New York: Garland, 1995), pp. 62-63.

image of the needlewoman in which her innate gentility is described as saintliness. Ruth herself teaches such lessons to the people of Ecclestone through her hard work and womanly devotion, and in return, 'many arose and called her blessed' (*Ruth*, p. 352). Although sainted by the people of Ecclestone, Ruth remains, as Stacey Gottlieb, argues, a product of 'rational, Enlightenment materialism' as opposed to the 'emotional Romantic idealism' of Elizabeth Barrett Browning's fallen seamstress, Marian Erle.[78] But Gaskell's description of needlework's role in Ruth's ultimate sanctification anticipates the more overtly religious image of the needlewoman, epitomised by Marian, that was emerging from the spiritualist fervour of the religious revival that was burgeoning at the end of the 1850s.[79]

Martyrs and Saints: The Value of Needlework in Elizabeth Barrett Browning's *Aurora Leigh*

Carrying on in a logical progression from ideas of sacrifice and martyrdom, the figure of the saintly seamstress emerged from the popular discourse concerning the pious seamstress.[80]Although generally working class, the saintly seamstress exhibited the same qualities of self-denial, sacrifice, and moral integrity as her more secular predecessor, but these qualities were given centre stage as the focus of, and the purpose for, the seamstress's behaviour. As generally a pious and respectable woman, the reduced gentlewoman as seamstress was endowed with an innate and unassailable morality and virtue; in representations of the working-class saintly seamstress, proving this virtuous integrity became the vital concern. One such effort appears in a pamphlet published in 1859 as part of a series called *The Revival: A Weekly Record of Events Connected with the Present Revival of Religion*. This pamphlet, entitled *The Sempstress and the Actress; or, The Power of Prayer*, featured the story of a lonely and destitute seamstress who prays to God for work. Although her prayer seems to be answered when an actress appears with a valuable consignment of work, the seamstress fears that in accepting work from an actress she would be 'serving the devil instead of serving the Lord Jesus'.[81] As a tool of religious

---

78   Stacey Gottlieb, '"And God Will Teach Her": Consciousness and Character in *Ruth* and *Aurora Leigh*', *Victorians Institute Journal* 24 (1996), p. 65.

79   For a history of the mid-century religious revival see L.E. Elliott-Binns, *Religion in the Victorian Era* (London: Lutterworth Press, 1936).

80   Less pointed examples than those which follow can be found in, for instance, 'The Dressmaker's Life'; 'Institution for the Employment of Needlewomen', *English Woman's Journal* 5 (1860), pp. 255-59; and 'The Blackburn Sewing-Schools', *Temple Bar* 7 (1873), pp. 339-48. Although the last article contains no actual saintly seamstress figure, the church's use of unremunerative needlework as a way to maintain moral order and raise the spirits of women and men during the 1863 cotton shortages provides a striking example of the way in which many saw needlework as a saving and redemptive force.

81   *The Sempstress and the Actress, or, The Power of Prayer* (London: J.F. Shaw, 1859), p. 2.

instruction, this pamphlet suggests that God's grace lies primarily in the seamstress's moral protection. The money she could get for such work becomes a conduit for the devil's temptation, and earthly concerns are unimportant as she struggles with the implications of the actress's offer. In this seamstress, the author of the pamphlet offers an ideal example of the way in which the working woman could keep herself above the brutalising influence of the industrial economy. By refusing work when it would contradict Christian principles of right and wrong, this seamstress acts as a model of a working woman who can exist in the marketplace without being governed solely by the ungodly rules of competition.

While the issues of necessity and morality were integral elements of the image of the working-class seamstress, the more extreme example of moral integrity embodied in the figure of the saintly seamstress did not strive so hard to accommodate both. One such example was given in the biography published in 1868 of a French peasant woman who lived at the beginning of the century. Known as the 'sempstress of Saint-Pallais', Marie-Eustelle Harpin is described by her biographer as a poor, devout woman who found her calling in her needlework:

> Having herself no treasures to bestow, she offered her ardent desires in compensation, and laboured to the best of her ability to adorn, and induce others to help in adorning, the humble church which was the nearest object of her solicitude.[82]

Marie-Eustelle's story follows the typical narrative of the life of a saint. The anecdotes the author relates about her emphasise the signs of God's grace that blessed her life; upon finding that she has no money for a new covering for the altar, she prays to the Virgin Mary and receives a donation the next day amounting to the exact sum required. Also, when her friends remonstrate with her that her sacrifice for the church was too great, that 'she gave herself no rest, and that her health was visibly declining', she is reported to have replied, 'It is a need with me rather than a sacrifice'.[83] Miracles, raptures, compelling devotion, and eventual martyrdom, with her early death at the age 28 brought on by her unceasing work, complete the cycle in this story of the life of a modern saint. As an unofficial patron saint of needlewomen, Marie-Eustelle embodied the religious promise that good and hard work brings heavenly rewards. Her earthly concerns, however, are as neglected by her biographer as they reportedly were by Marie-Eustelle herself. In fact, although the author describes her desperate financial need, necessity never appears to influence her at all. The church's failure to supply her with a subsistence wage or even with adequate funds to use in her work is rendered unimportant through the sense of gratitude and unworthiness she feels for the privilege of serving God. In the place of economic concerns, religious sentiment serves as her only motivation and reward. Unlike the representations of the working-class seamstresses of the 1840s,

---

82   *The Life of Marie-Eustelle Harpin, The Sempstress of Saint-Pallais* (London: Burns, Oates, & Co., 1868), p. 219.

83   Ibid., p. 220

the saintly seamstress was held to the same, if not higher, standards as her middle-class counterpart.

The figure of the saintly seamstress appeared to discount a number of anxieties raised by her pitiable forerunner. It shifted responsibility from middle-class pity and patronisation and invoked God as the seamstress's primary protector. Also, it put distance between an activity that occupied a central role in the structure of the domestic ideal and the degradation of public, remunerative work for women. Most importantly, though, the saintly seamstress projected an image of a working-class woman as the moral equal of the reduced gentlewoman. Ideologically, in fact, the work of the saintly seamstress had more in common with the decorative work of the lady embroiderer than the slopwork of the lowest needlewoman. This point was illustrated most overtly in Dante Gabriel Rossetti's depiction of the Virgin Mary herself as a seamstress in his painting, *The Girlhood of Mary Virgin* (1849). This work was derived from a popular medieval narrative sequence about the life of Mary in which Mary's mother, Anna, is shown to be teaching her daughter from a book.[84] In Rossetti's painting, however, the book is reduced to a pedestal for a lily that Mary and her mother use as a model for their embroidery. Rossetti exchanges the image of book-learning for that of Mary's instruction in embroidery in order to assert Mary's ideal femininity in a social world that saw needlework rather than classical education as the apotheosis of womanly activity. In representing needlework as one of the definitive elements of Mary's early life, this exchange also invests needlework itself with an edifying role in the education of the sainted woman. The image of the saintly seamstress attributed to needlework a moral and social function that raised both its profile and that of the woman who sewed.

The association between needlework and the Virgin Mary that Rossetti uses as a shorthand for the ideal domestic woman's virtuousness was also employed in representations of the seamstress toward the end of the 1850s, which often sought to assert the seamstress's ability to embody virtuousness regardless of the situation she was in, or the indignities that were visited upon her. This assertion, for instance, was made in a story for the *English Woman's Journal* in 1859 entitled 'Seamstresses Again'. The author of this tale tells of a self-denying woman named Dorothy who gives up her own small comforts in order to help those around her. Dorothy is shown to leave the comfort of her 'neat, cosy apartment' and 'old-fashioned arm-chair' for the sexual vulnerability, the dulling hopelessness, and the public humiliation of the world of industrial needlework in order to help her ill neighbour.[85] Rather than experiencing any form of degradation when among the other seamstresses, Dorothy is described as a woman 'who, though she had the same sort of bundle as the rest, was clearly not of the sisterhood. She was a neat, elderly, motherly body, and young eyes were fastened on the kindly face just as you stand before some exquisite Madonna, while a spell is being woven about the senses, and every

---

84 Parker, *Subversive Stitch*, p. 38.

85 'Seamstresses Again: A Story of Christmas Eve', *English Woman's Journal* 5 (1859), p. 238.

thought is concentrated to a wondering admiration'.[86] Dorothy is not only a virtuous woman herself, but also provides a beatific example for all who see her.

This image of the saintly seamstress was also used by Barrett Browning in *Aurora Leigh* in order to assert the moral respectability of her own Madonna figure, Marian Erle.[87] As a part of her critique in *Aurora Leigh* of the economic injustices of contemporary society, Barrett Browning portrays the labour of her working-class seamstress Marian Erle as an example of the exploitation of the worker. The death of Marian's fellow seamstress, Lucy Gresham, provides yet another illustration of the evils of the industrial system, and Marian's value to her employer is expressed in simple economic terms:

> She knew, by such an act,
> All place and grace were forfeit in the house,
> Whose mistress would supply the missing hand
> With necessary, not inhuman haste,
> And take no blame. But pity, too, had dues:
> She could not leave a solitary soul
> To founder in the dark, while she sat still
> And lavished stitches on a lady's hem
> As if no other work were paramount.
> 'Why, God', thought Marian, 'has a missing hand
> This moment; Lucy wants a drink, perhaps.
> Let others miss me! never miss me, God!' (*Aurora Leigh,* IV.31-42)

Although Marian suggests that the treatment she receives from her employer is 'necessary, not inhuman', the inhumanity of the market economy is clear. To the mistress of her house, Marian is nothing but the 'hand' that plies the needle, a tool that can easily be replaced if it malfunctions. In leaving her job to nurse Lucy, however, Marian acknowledges a value system contrary to the economic as Barrett Browning separates personal integrity from the pressures of the industrial system. Set against Lucy's suffering, Marian's work as seamstress is represented as frivolous and unimportant. Serving God is offered instead as more valuable work, and a more satisfying reward comes from serving others because ''Tis verily good fortune to be kind' (*Aurora Leigh*, IV.52). The value of needlework as a remunerative profession is surpassed by the demands of duty and compassion as Barrett Browning establishes a moral economy to rival that of the market. Based on a currency of kindness, this moral economy is structured on the principles of exchange, as Marian's kindness is met with kindness in return, and investment, as her compassion brings the promise of a better life with Romney. Individual morality does not just compete with the doctrine of the market, it replaces it as the measure of value and success as Marian is raised up morally, socially, and emotionally through her compassionate work.

---

86   Ibid., p. 236.

87   For a discussion of the Madonna figure in *Aurora Leigh* see Patricia Murphy, 'Reconceiving the Mother: Deconstructing the Madonna in *Aurora Leigh*', *Victorian Newsletter* no 91 (1997), pp. 21-27.

Although Barrett Browning disregards the economic value of needlework, she does not dismiss it outright as worthless. In fact, through Romney's idealistic belief in its beneficial potential for Marian, she provides another perspective on needlework as a vehicle through which moral integrity can be achieved:

> Hope he called belief
> In God – work, worship – therefore let us pray!
> And thus, to snatch her soul from atheism,
> And keep it stainless from her mother's face,
> He sent her to a famous sempstress-house
> Far off in London, there to work and hope.
> With that, they parted. She kept sight of Heaven,
> But not of Romney. He had good to do
> To others: through the days and through the nights
> She sewed and sewed and sewed. (*Aurora Leigh*, III.1227-35)

As her representative of liberal social reform, Romney demonstrates what Barrett Browning reveals to be the fundamental flaw in such trusting idealism. The 'hope he called belief' that he instils in Marian is the expectation of eternal reward without a thought for material comfort. As Marian sews for heaven instead of herself, her sewing is continuous and unspecific. Details are as unimportant as rest when the work is done for God rather than man. It is in the details, however, that subsistence is gained. As an unskilled, untrained, friendless girl, the most Marian could earn are starvation wages, and her continued work as a seamstress would most likely lead to her death as it did for Lucy Gresham. The image of Marian that Barrett Browning lays at the feet of the social reformers, then, is that of the pious but desperate descendant of Hood and Redgrave's pitiable seamstresses. Alone and starving, she looks to God for salvation from her distress. Her piety is expressed in her prayer, and her trust in God emerges in her resignation to her plight. From the perspective of the social reformer, Marian is compelled to take on the role of the compliant, naïve, and unthinking female. The middle-class principle of patriarchal support and protection is invoked as Marian puts her faith in God and Romney, but Barrett Browning eventually shows this trust to be misplaced. Moral integrity alone proves useless against the brutalising forces of modern society as Marian's virtue is wrested from her.

Ironically, Marian proves most vulnerable when she most closely approaches the domestic ideal. In fact, Virginia Steinmetz sees the images of dead, abandoning, and abandoned mothers in the poem and the negative influence of 'mother-want' on the characters as evidence of Barrett Browning's awareness of detrimental effect of the Victorian ideal of the conventional mother.[88] Barrett Browning reverses conventional thinking on woman's vulnerability and names as the most dangerous enemy the very system of patriarchal authority that was allegedly in place to protect her. But

---

88   Virginia V. Steinmetz, 'Images of "Mother-Want" in Elizabeth Barrett Browning's *Aurora Leigh*', *Victorian Poetry* 21 (1983), pp. 35-48.

in her approach to the domestic ideal of the pious, virtuous, and worthy woman, Marian stands as legitimate representative of the potential for social mobility within the moral economy Barrett Browning constructs. As the distressed needlewoman, 'Upon whose finger, exquisitely pricked / By a hundred needles, we're to hang the tie / 'Twixt class and class in England' (*Aurora Leigh*, III. 660-62), Marian personifies a moral order indifferent to class barriers. Here, Barrett Browning offers a vision of society in which a person's social value is determined by the work they do, and it is the dream of such a meritocracy that is embodied in Romney's proposal to Marian: 'My fellow worker, be my wife!' (*Aurora Leigh*, IV.150).

Although Romney's vision, without love to support it, is doomed to collapse under the weight of both middle and working-class defiance, Barrett Browning continues to explore the possibilities of this utopian scheme through the story of Marian. When neither the economic nor the moral uses of needlework are shown to be adequate for the protection and support of the seamstress, Barrett Browning develops instead an alternative vision of needlework based on a system of female co-operation and compassion that fosters both:

> I found a mistress-semptress who was kind
> And let me sew in peace among her girls.
> And what was better than to draw the threads
> All day and half the night for him and him?
> And so I lived for him, and so he lives,
> And so I know, by this time, God lives too. (*Aurora Leigh*, VII.108-13)

The trope of death and salvation that is initiated by Marian's fall removes her entirely from the insignificant concerns of the social world and its detrimental influence on female self-sufficiency. Marian's value is not measured by conventional markers of respectability such as her social class, her upbringing, or her economic situation, but by the work she judges to be most important to her, namely supporting and caring for her child. Throughout *Aurora Leigh*, Barrett Browning contributes a reformist perspective to the cultural and social debate over the value of women's work. Beginning with the scathing review of the worth of the middle-class woman's domestic needlework mentioned at the beginning of this chapter, she challenges various received notions of the forms of work deemed valuable and worthwhile. The domestic woman's efforts to make her home comfortable through the traditional pastime of embroidery are held to be worthy of nothing but ridicule and disdain because they are unnecessary and merely decorative. Marian's remunerative needlework, on the other hand, is represented as noble and useful. The value of needlework, then, is intrinsically tied to what is produced and the ideals of those who produce it.

In contradistinction to prevailing attitudes toward sewing as an indifferent, or overwhelmingly good, activity for women, Barrett Browning demonstrates the moral relativism of needlework. It is not an intrinsically good or bad occupation for women. She offers instead the concepts of valuable and worthless work. She names ladies' fancy work and the exhausting work of the reduced gentlewoman and the saintly seamstress as inferior because it unthinkingly reproduces, with each stitch worked, woman's subordinate and helpless position in an oppressive patriarchal system. The work that Marian finds, on the other hand, subverts received notions of what is economically and morally appropriate when a kind mistress allows a fallen woman to work amongst her girls. In sewing for God and for her son, Marian finds a balance between the necessities of body and soul that is mutually beneficial for her and her son's physical and moral health. Work is her salvation, both religious and economic, but it is work that is mediated by her overwhelming sense of duty to her child and facilitated by a matriarchal system of labour relations. The utopian system in which Barrett Browning places Marian is one in which the mother has complete control over and responsibility for her child, and work is dictated by female forms of experience. Freed from patriarchal and social controls, Marian stands out as an epitome of virtue in contrast to the immoral but respectable upper-class women who 'keep / Their own [virtue] so darned and patched with perfidy, / That, though a rag itself, it looks as well / Across a street, in a balcony or coach, / As any perfect stuff' (*Aurora Leigh*, VII.96-100). The metaphor of shoddy needlework that Barrett Browning uses to expose the apparent hypocrisy of a society that prefers the appearance of respectability over true moral integrity underscores the distance between what she sees as valuable needlework and mainstream female experience. Even though, or, more accurately, because, Marian's character does not conform to conventional standards of womanliness, purity, or respectability, Barrett Browning offers her as an ideal example of a proper and domestically-minded, yet independent, working woman.

In *Aurora Leigh*, Barrett Browning locates the value of needlework in its symbolic function. As an activity common to all types and classes of women, needlework provides a central point of comparison for discussions about the general principles of women's work, whether domestic or remunerative. In showing conventional measures of its value, its market price, its domestic importance, and its moral power, to be inadequate determinants alone, she highlights the absence of real debate, unbiased by patriarchal preconceptions about femininity and domesticity, about the value of women's work. The popular images of needlework and needlewomen, she implies, subordinate and silence the women they represent under the auspices of traditional ideals and social acceptability. But Barrett Browning also finds that they can open up a utopian space within women's work in which the subjection of the worker is transformed into moments of transcendent agency. Paradoxically, then, the value of needlework for the individual worker lay in the very constraints it levelled upon that worker. The restrictive iconography of the saintly seamstress and the reduced gentlewoman appeased cultural preconceptions concerning female labour while also asserting work's genuinely subversive power to facilitate self-determination. Needlework, for instance, provides Aurora with a convenient screen behind which she can develop her unwomanly poetic genius.

The links between needlework and creativity that Gaskell alludes to in *Ruth* surface here in a more pointed exploration of the influence of issues of women's work and self-sufficiency on the development of the artist. Aurora verbalises this association when she calls Marian 'sweetest sister' and 'my saint', and in an ultimately self-reflexive gesture, Barrett Browning acknowledges Marian as a kindred spirit and an admirable model for the woman writer (*Aurora Leigh*, VII.117, 127). Barrett Browning draws on the image of the saintly seamstress in her representation of Marian not only to suggest the value of needlework in the moral economy she constructs, but also to suggest the importance of needlework as a symbol of female creativity when Marian's newfound power of self-determination surfaces ultimately in her most creative act, motherhood.[89] In declaring that her child has no father, Marian invokes the purity of the virgin birth in order to assert her own guiltlessness in her fall, but she also claims for herself alone the power of creation and self-expression. As a sister and saint for the woman writer, Marian thus provides an example of the working woman in which, rather than forming a barrier to creativity, domestic experience can serve as the source of self-sufficient, female-centred creation.

Needlework as Art: Representing the Creative Seamstress in Margaret Oliphant's *Kirsteen*

The representation of needlework as a potential stimulant to creative production had, I have argued, a beneficial influence on the artistic credentials of embroidery, but it also had an impact on the general perception of plain sewing. Even dressmaking, that tedious and oppressive occupation for Ruth, Virginia, Mary, Kate, and many other seamstresses throughout the 1840s and 1850s, could be considered in artistic terms.[90] In *Ruth*, Gaskell hinted at the artistic element of dressmaking, noting, with slight condescension, the way in which some of the seamstresses at Mrs. Mason's would, during their short breaks, hold 'up admiringly the beautiful ball-dress in progress, while others examined the effect, backing from the object to be criticised in the true artistic manner' (*Ruth*, p. 7). Gaskell depicts the seamstresses' artistic interest as affectation; they appear rather silly and superficial in contrast to Ruth's earnest and private poetic musings. By the mid-1860s, though, as the artistic dressmaker was being given more serious consideration, Dickens offered a portrait of a professional dressmaker whose work he 'imaginatively transmuted' from the actualities of working experience.[91] Instead of focussing solely on the economic and physical difficulties of her sewing, he openly refers to her work as art. Although Jenny Wren, his maker of dresses for dolls in *Our Mutual Friend* (1865), describes herself like an ordinary seamstress, Dickens represents her work in artistic terms:

---

89   For a discussion of the sisterly relationship between Aurora and the female artist see Michele Martinez, 'Sister Art and Artists: Elizabeth Barrett Browning's *Aurora Leigh* and the Life of Harriet Hosmer', *Forum for Modern Language Studies* 39 (2002), pp. 214-26.

90   See, for instance, 'Notes of an Exhibition of the School of Art Embroidery'; and 'Ladies' Dressmaking and Embroidery Association', *Woman's Gazette*, 2 (1877), pp. 75-76.

91   Brian Cheadle, 'Work in *Our Mutual Friend*', *Essays in Criticism* 51 (2001), p. 309.

'Perhaps', said Miss Jenny, holding out her doll at arm's length, and critically contemplating the effect of her art with her scissors on her lips and her head thrown back, as if her interest lay there, and not in the conversation; 'perhaps you'll explain your meaning, young man, which is Greek to me. – You must have another touch in your trimming, my dear'. Having addressed the last remark to her fair client, Miss Wren proceeded to snip at some blue fragment that lay before her, among fragments of all colours, and to thread a needle from a skein of blue silk.[92]

Unlike most dressmakers, Jenny does not work from a pattern, nor does she pre-make her skirts because dolls are 'very difficult to fit too, because their figures are so uncertain. You never know where to expect their waists' (*Our Mutual Friend*, p. 332). Each doll's dress is designed, made, and fitted individually, and each constitutes in its own small way a work of art. Although Dickens describes Jenny's work artistically, he avoids making too outrageous a claim for the cultural significance of dressmaking (especially dressmaking for dolls), which was considered by most to be, at the least, a necessity and, at best, a 'decorative art'.[93] To this end, he marginalizes his artistic dressmaker both socially, through her peculiar behaviour and her physical deformities, and professionally, through her diminutive models and the scavenged bits of 'damage and waste' that serve as her millinery materials (*Our Mutual Friend*, p. 333).[94] But Jenny is not merely a typical Dickensian eccentric. Her talent, her idiosyncratic wisdom, and her indeterminate age all contribute to a sense of ethereality about her – she sees everything and understands more than most. Dickens also imbues her with a fanciful imagination, and her melancholic musings, which transform 'something in the face and action for the moment, quite inspired and beautiful', suggest that beneath her odd conversation and childish appearance lie hidden depths of poetic sensibility (*Our Mutual Friend*, p. 290).

Jenny has often been seen by critics as the best representative of the artist in the novel and as the character who enables Dickens to present an 'Aestheticist argument'.[95] However, the conflicting features of Jenny's character suggest a more ambivalent opinion on the merits of artistic needlework, trivialising the idea of needlework as art while supporting the notion of an artistic needlewoman. The result is the image of a working woman who sews out of necessity, but uses her work as an outlet for her artistic inclination. Seemingly undecided about whether it constitutes

---

92 Charles Dickens, *Our Mutual Friend*, Stephen Gill, ed. (London: Penguin Books, 1985), p. 785. Further references to this edition will be given in the text.

93 Monoure Conway, 'Women as Decorative Artists', *Women and Work* no. 22 (31 Oct. 1874), p. 3.

94 For a discussion of the potential created by Jenny's deformity see Helena Michie, '"Who is this in Pain?" Scarring, Disfigurement, and Female Identity in *Bleak House* and *Our Mutual Friend*', *Novel: A Forum on Fiction* 22 (1989), pp. 199-212.

95 Peter Smith, 'The Aestheticist Argument of *Our Mutual Friend*', *The Cambridge Quarterly* 18 (1989), pp. 362-82. See also Lothar Cerný, '"Life in Death": Art in Dickens's *Our Mutual Friend*', *Dickens Quarterly* 17 (2000), pp. 22-36, and Nancy Aycock Metz, 'The Artistic Reclamation of Waste in *Our Mutual Friend*', *Nineteenth Century Fiction* 34 (1978-80), pp. 59-72.

an art or a trifle, Dickens depicts her work with a seriocomic flourish that belies her consummate professionalism. Whatever her personal and physical difficulties, Jenny is a savvy businesswoman who, in contrast to his earlier vulnerable and helpless seamstresses, professes her self-sufficiency and declares herself, in her constant refrain of, '*I* know their tricks and their manners', to be a shrewd judge of character (*Our Mutual Friend*, p. 274). Dickens makes it clear that the pity with which the other characters patronise her is wasted upon this independent, intelligent, capable, and professional seamstress. In particular, in showing how utterly irrelevant this socially mandated emotion is to Jenny, Dickens emphasises what little effect such responses had on alleviating the seamstress's distress. In Jenny's self-sufficiency, Dickens reflects the distance that had been travelled in the conception of the seamstress since Hood had sung his dolorous song. The rather straight-forward image of the seamstress as vulnerable and distressed that was established by Hood and Redgrave in the 1840s had undergone a slow revolution over the course of the following decades as arguments promoting female autonomy and self-sufficiency gained a strong foothold in public consciousness. Jenny may not have been a typical portrait of a respectable and feminine needlewoman, but even for this poor, working-class girl, issues of art and artistry outweigh those of necessity.

One telling illustration of the diminishing importance of economic concerns in representations of sewing can be found in Christina Rossetti's short story *Speaking Likenesses* (1874). This story is presented as a series of three fairy-tales joined together in the framework that depicts an aunt entertaining her nieces as they sit at their sewing. Although the children complain about the tedium of their work, the aunt remonstrates, 'no help no story … However, as I see thimbles coming out, I conclude you choose story and labour'.[96] The relationship Rossetti develops between the creative work of story-telling and the manual work of sewing suggests a moral lesson to be learned from the revelation that creative production is itself a form of work. The aunt's pronouncement that 'Now I start my knitting and my story together' reinforces the manual labour involved in the construction of narrative and acknowledges the story's debt to the sewing, as if the weaving of the tale proceeds from the stitching of the thread.[97] The completion of the labour both of story-telling and sewing, however, depends on the continued help of the community of girls gathered around their needles. The tales proceed as an exchange of services, the aunt's story for the nieces' help, when the aunt realises that 'I have too many poor friends ever to get through *my* work'.[98] By making it *their* work instead, an impossible task becomes manageable within the confines of Rossetti's story. Working as a community, the women of the story complete both the creative and manual aspects of their work when the fairy-tales and sewing end together.

---

96   Christina Rossetti, 'Speaking Likenesses', *Poems and Prose*, Jan Marsh, ed. (London: J.M. Dent, 1994), p. 339.

97   Ibid., p. 325.

98   Ibid., p. 339. Emphasis in original.

In indicating the didactic potential of creative production, Rossetti acknowledges story-telling, like sewing, as fittingly feminine work.

While Rossetti's story offers a powerful image of the domestic genesis of female creativity, she circumvents any economic implications in such female-centred work by distancing their sewing from financial considerations; her middle-class women ply their needles philanthropically, spinning a series of educative stories instead of earning money. The scene she sets is a familiar picture of domestic activity, moral education, and social duty that played against progressive images of female productivity in the economic sphere. Rossetti, however, admits an implicit connection between the domestic and economic spheres when she draws on the ideology of the Victorian work ethic in order to teach a lesson in domestic duty. Through the process of sewing and listening, the nieces learn an important lesson in methodical production, and by the third story, their aunt no longer needs to cajole them into beginning their work, nor remind them, as she does during the first story, to keep at it. The morals of the individual fairy-tales that teach proper feminine virtues such as obedience, humility, and courteousness are augmented by the overarching lesson that hard work brings ample reward. Although on the surface a thoroughly conventional tale, Rossetti's story reveals the pervasive influence economics had on issues of female creativity, production, and even domesticity.

Throughout the 1870s and 1880s, as needlework was increasingly linked with creative production, discussions over the economic value of the seamstress's work gave way, in terms of the number of column inches devoted to it in the periodical press, to debates over the artistic merits of the middle-class lady's supposedly amateur sewing. Issues of monetary import did not, however, disappear altogether. Even the most vocal supporters of the art of embroidery recognised the economic potential of needlework for all classes of women. Lady Alford's article on 'Art Needlework' for the *Nineteenth Century*, for instance, was written in reply to a letter to the editor asking for information about remunerative employment for women.[99] For working-class women, the rural crafts revival provided employment in spinning, lace-making, and various other handicrafts according to the artistic principles of the Art and Crafts movement.[100] And in institutions such as the Ladies' Dressmaking and Embroidery Association, reduced gentlewomen were taught both artistic and practical sewing so that women 'may obtain a practical knowledge of a business which will be useful to them, either in their own homes or as a means of livelihood'.[101] Not everyone saw economic benefits in needlework, though. A writer for the *Artist* warned that its supporters were 'ignoring the changed conditions of modern life which have killed hand work of this kind for ever, except as an unremunerative though laudable amusement'.[102] Whether a supporter or detractor,

---

99   Alford, 'Art Needlework', pp. 439-49.

100   Anthea Callen, *Angel in the Studio: Women in the Arts and Crafts Movement, 1870-1914* (London: Astragal Books, 1979).

101   'Ladies' Dressmaking and Embroidery Association', *Woman's Gazette*, p. 76.

102   'Art Work for Women', *Artist* 4 (1883), pp. 38-39.

most people writing on art needlework discussed its value in both artistic and economic terms.

The associations that were made between artistry and economics contributed to the refinement of needlework from a domestic activity or mere remunerative occupation to a professional opportunity. Indeed, whereas 20 years earlier, moral strength and virtuousness had signified respectability in the image of the seamstress, creativity was now called upon as a marker of professional and social legitimacy in the representation of the artistic needlewoman. Margaret Oliphant's *Kirsteen* (1889), for instance, traces the career of its eponymous heroine as a seamstress whose artistic flair is a marker of her gentility:

> She was not, perhaps, very intellectual, but she was independent and original, little trained in other people's ideals and full of fancies of her own, which to my thinking, is the most delightful of characteristics … Kirsteen tried her active young powers upon everything, being impatient of sameness and monotony, and bent upon securing a difference, an individual touch in every different variety of costume. She was delighted with the beautiful materials, which were thrown about in the work-room, the ordinary mantua-maker having little feeling for them except in a view of their cost at so much a yard.[103]

Oliphant uses Kirsteen's artistic inclination to separate her, as Gaskell separates Ruth, from the rabble of 'ordinary' dressmakers, but it also marks her out as an independent and self-sufficient 'girl of the period'. Written on the cusp of the New Woman phenomenon, *Kirsteen* portrays a middle-class girl who defies a number of social conventions when she leaves home to avoid a loveless marriage and becomes a successful businesswoman. As a woman and a dressmaker, Kirsteen is firmly located in the 1880s. The story, however, is set in the 1820s, and through this temporal discrepancy, Oliphant demonstrates the change over the Victorian era in ideas of proper womanly behaviour and in the propriety of work for the middle-class woman. In Kirsteen's move from her obsessively traditional home in the highlands of Scotland to the modern, industrial culture of London, Oliphant dramatises the standard clash between the old and the new. Her family despises her decision to enter into such degrading work, and even though Kirsteen uses the money she earns to buy back the ancestral home, her eldest brother, raised by his success in the army to 'Sir' Alexander, states with exaggerated familial pride that rather than her becoming a dressmaker, 'any sort of a man, if he had been a chimney-sweep, would have been better' (*Kirsteen*, p. 341). As the representative of the traditional patriarchal order, Sir Alexander articulates conventional notions of domestic propriety and female support. To owe his home to his sister's work is a lamentable situation, and in order to maintain what he sees as the proper domestic state, 'Kirsteen was a rare and not very welcome visitor in the house she had redeemed' (*Kirsteen*, p. 341). From Sir Alexander's perspective, Kirsteen, having degraded herself and the family name by working, is little better than a fallen woman.

---

103 Margaret Oliphant, *Kirsteen*, Merryn Williams, ed. (London: J.M. Dent, 1984), pp. 164-65. Further references to this edition will be given in the text.

The intense and unjust aversion of Kirsteen's family to her dressmaking career appears overly melodramatic, and the social disgrace engendered by her public work is at odds with the description of her actual life as a seamstress. By no means a scandalous experience, Kirsteen's work is depicted as very ladylike and the shop as a genteel establishment. As dressmakers to the Queen, Miss Jean Brown's serves only the best clientele, and even their all-night work sessions are very civilised experiences:

> They had tea drinking at midnight, when the fine-flavoured tea was served to the work-women all round with dainty cakes, and the highest solace of all, Miss Jean herself sat up and finished *Waverly*, at the risk of making a few needles rust by the dropping here and there of furtive tears. (*Kirsteen*, p. 223)

Oliphant's depiction of this all-night work session is a highly idealised scene that is more reminiscent of a middle-class social visit than the harsh and wearying conditions of the busy seasons that were consistently reported throughout the century. As progressive as her characterisation of Kirsteen is, Oliphant relies on images of domesticity and feminine propriety to balance Kirsteen's work with conventional markers of social respectability.[104] Kirsteen may disobey her father, but Oliphant mitigates her rebelliousness by attributing it to a very womanly cause. She leaves home to escape being forced, at her father's insistence, to marry a local lord, Glendochart, not because he, or marriage itself, is particularly distasteful to her, but because she has promised Ronald Drummond, who is with the army in India, that she would wait for him. In Kirsteen's decision to leave, Oliphant demonstrates the power of romantic love over filial duty. Kirsteen's actions may be ungrateful and unwise, but they are not unwomanly.

The opinion of Kirsteen's family, notwithstanding, Oliphant portrays her as a proper, womanly worker. Unwilling to bring her family name into ill repute, Kirsteen does not use her surname Douglas in her professional dealings, going instead by Miss Kirsteen. Furthermore, when her romantic story becomes known among the customers of the shop, Kirsteen is angered and embarrassed by the impertinence with which they discuss her private life publicly and remark that her life is 'So dramatic! It might go on the stage' (*Kirsteen*, p. 178). In Kirsteen's fears and instances of public exposure, Oliphant recalls the social vulnerability that plagued the reduced gentlewoman. The moral difficulties of the seamstress are also evoked when Kirsteen is subjected to the sexual advances of the caddish Lord John who is her equal socially but her superior economically. After all, the narrator notes, 'these were the days when … milliners were supposed very fair game' (*Kirsteen*, p. 167). As a conventionally womanly worker, Kirsteen is exposed to the dangers that were supposed to afflict all seamstresses. Also, with her virtual ostracism from her family,

---

104 For a discussion of Oliphant's complex relationship with the Woman Question see Merryn Williams, 'Feminist or Antifeminist? Oliphant and the Woman Question', *Margaret Oliphant: Critical Essays on a Gentle Subversive*, D.J. Trela, ed. (Selingsgrove: Susquehanna University Press, 1995), pp. 165-80.

she has no one to protect her. Having taken on this life in order to remain faithful to Ronald, Kirsteen is left desolate and alone when she hears of his death. All she has left is her work, and she realises that her business 'was her established place, and that her life had taken the form and colour it must now bear to the end' (*Kirsteen*, p. 240). In Kirsteen's isolated situation, Oliphant describes the dangers of work for women in Kirsteen's social position. All Kirsteen's plans end, Arlene Young argues, in Kirsteen's, and Oliphant's, 'sad recognition' that 'work and independence would inevitably bear the aspect of just another form of bondage'.[105] But Oliphant also finds that such personal isolation can open up a space for professional success. With Ronald's death, the narrator comments, 'life was over for Kirsteen; and life began' (*Kirsteen*, p. 241). This change in Kirsteen's life is described by Linda Peterson as a movement from the '"old" feminine plot of romance to the "new" masculine plot of public achievement'.[106] Her dreams of a conventional womanly life die, but her professional life thrives. She approaches her work with new vigour, reorganising the operation of the workroom and, in general, taking over the running of the business from Miss Jean.

The death of Kirsteen's domestic dream is depicted as a tragedy for which professional success is the consolation. While Kirsteen accepts what her life must be, she sees this change as the 'worst … that could happen' to her (*Kirsteen*, p. 241). But Oliphant also acknowledges the creative, social, and sexual autonomy such a professional life brings with it. Freed from all forms of male domination, Kirsteen sees the way marriage turns love into 'bondage' (*Kirsteen*, p. 254). Men cease to have any influence over her, and she feels 'remote' from the 'agitations' of young love and sexual energy (*Kirsteen*, p. 243). Also, denied the biological creativity of motherhood, she excels even more at the creative work of dressmaking: 'She had never been so inventive, so full of new combinations' (*Kirsteen*, p. 233). *Kirsteen* raises the spectre of the independent career woman so dreaded by conservative thinking throughout the century and offers this figure a positive identity and a confident voice. Her procreativity is channelled exclusively into her work, where it unapologetically dismisses patriarchal presuppositions. As Kabi Hartman has shown, Kirsteen's artistic dressmaking is used by Oliphant as a metaphor for writing.[107] And Oliphant is less concerned with the negotiation between domestic and remunerative female work that had occupied earlier writers than with the simple assertion of a separate space in the marketplace for female creativity, her own included.

By the 1880s the seamstress no longer represented the figure of pitiable vulnerability that had proved so useful to the social problem novelists. In fact,

---

105 Arlene Young, *Culture, Class and Gender in the Victorian Novel* (London: Macmillan, 1999), p. 136.

106 Linda Peterson, 'The Female *Bildungsroman*: Tradition and Revision in Oliphant's Fiction', *Margaret Oliphant: Critical Essays on a Gentle Subversive*, p. 85.

107 Kabi Hartman, '"An Artist in her Way": Representations of the Woman Artist in Margaret Oliphant's *Kirsteen*', *Schuykill: A Creative and Critical Review from Temple University* 2 (1999), pp. 74-84.

the participation of such figures within the patriarchal world-view was now being consigned to an earlier configuration of labour relations. Oliphant does this explicitly, projecting her definitively contemporary critique of the 1880s labour market on traditional ideas of female propriety in the 1820s. She creates a narrative of female empowerment in which the value of needlework develops from the obscurity of its dutiful domestic function into the public world of the modern career. The successful seamstress announces her creative success and in the same gesture enters the modern world of personal opportunity and entrepreneurship that would also be embraced by New Women.[108] Needlework was no longer a symbol of degradation and vulnerability, but was imagined instead as a path to creative expression.

Artistic needlework could signify, as it does for Kirsteen and Jenny Wren, independence and self-sufficiency for the female worker. As the most apposite marker of both proper domestic womanhood and acceptable female employment, the occupation of needlework embodied the promise of remunerative and meaningful employment for middle-class women. Needlework came to symbolise the wealth of opportunity that work opened for women in conditions of economic independence, social mobility, and creative freedom, while the dangers and difficulties traditionally applied to women's ventures into the public sphere were identified as the result of the specific exploitative conditions of the capitalist economy and patriarchal system. In other words, the concept of women's work in general was increasingly refined through its association with female creative production. In defiance of those who were dismissive of needlework's artistic merits, such as the *Art Journal*'s 'grand distinction' between 'the fine Arts and those of industry', supporters of art embroidery married the supposed feminine quality of 'mechanical dexterity' with the masculine and artistic genius for '*originality* of design'.[109] Raising the standard of creative needlework, therefore, meant raising the profile of female creativity. In describing a domestic genesis for this creativity, representations of the seamstress throughout the second half of the century had managed not only to assert the respectability of women working in the public sphere, but had also succeeded in raising a specifically female activity to the level of an art.

Whether or not sewing itself was seen as a creative act, it could be used by writers throughout the second half of the nineteenth century as a means of exploring the social and economic conditions of female creativity and of locating those conditions within a specifically female frame of experience. The description of the compatibility between women's work and the domestic sphere that was central in the representation of the seamstress would also appear in the representations of other creative women throughout the second half of the nineteenth century as economic, educative, and domestic reasons were cited as justifications for woman's entry into the public world of work. But, as the next two chapters will show, the quality of

---

108 For a discussion of the relationship between *Kirsteen* and New Woman fiction see Ann Heilmann, 'Mrs. Grundy's Rebellion: Margaret Oliphant Between Orthodoxy and the New Woman', *Women's Writing* 6 (1999), pp. 215-34.

109 'A Novelty in Fancy-Work', p. 139 [italics in original].

self-sacrificing devotion that characterised the respectable seamstress's existence had a contradictory impact on the image of women working in the more public artistic spaces of painting and writing. Self-sacrifice, after all, was not consistent with the inevitable elements of self-publicity intrinsic to the work and identity of the artist.

Chapter 2

'A Suitable Employment for Women': The Woman Artist and the Principle of Compatibility

In her well-known and influential treatise on 'Female Industry' that appeared in the *Edinburgh Review* in 1859, Harriet Martineau called for an end to what she saw as the 'artificial depreciation' that was levelled at women's work. Although generally thought of as secondary in the factories, women's work, she argued, was crucial to the continuing success of England as an industrial nation:

> We look to cultivated women ... for the improvement of our national character as tasteful manufacturers. It is only the inferiority of our designs which prevents our taking the lead of the world in our silks, ribbons, artificial flowers, paper-hangings, carpets and furniture generally ... The greater part of the work remains to be done; and it is properly women's work. [1]

The manufacture of artistically designed merchandise, such as silks, ribbons, and paper hangings, was termed in the second half of the nineteenth century the 'art-industries'. This term related not only to the design of such items, but also to the production of a wide variety of related crafts from etching and engraving to pottery painting and photograph tinting. Often grouped with art-needlework, these crafts were demarcated as one of the branches of 'low art' that were mainly inhabited by women. [2]

In characterising the art-industries as being 'properly woman's work', then, Martineau is reproducing the sexual divisions between art and craft. [3] But in linking women's work in the art-industries to the 'improvement' of the 'national character', Martineau also demonstrates that public industry could be seen to be compatible with private femininity. Social responsibility and commercial prosperity are shown to mitigate women's presence in the public and degrading industrial sphere. They also take the place of domestic respectability and feminine accomplishment in the identification of the 'cultivated' woman. The association Martineau makes between female artistry and the industrial economy evokes a refined image of women's

---

1   Harriet Martineau, 'Female Industry', *Edinburgh Review* 109 (1859), pp. 294, 334.

2   A.C.M, 'Industrial Art Work – No. 1', *Woman's Gazette* 1 (1875), p. 11.

3   Anthea Callen, 'Sexual Division of Labour in the Arts and Crafts Movement', *Oxford Art Journal* 3 (1980), pp. 22-27.

industrial work that was repeated throughout the second half of the nineteenth century. This chapter investigates the development of that image and the impact it had on representations of women in the industrial sphere. In order to trace the influence of these issues on the perceptions of the working woman, it is important first to understand the contribution made by women's perceived relation to 'high art' to the discourse of compatibility.

The Principle of Compatibility: Domesticating the Professional Artist

The argument for the compatibility of women's work with the domestic sphere that was so effectively asserted in representations of the seamstress occupied many mid-Victorian discussions and representations of female artists as well. As Rozsika Parker and Griselda Pollock have shown, 'Victorian writers found a way of recognizing women's art compatible with their bourgeois patriarchal ideology [by] imposing their own limiting definitions and notions of a separate sphere'.[4] Unlike the perception of men as true artists with a genius and a vocation for art, they argue, women artists, since the nineteenth century, have been presumed to have an 'innate lack of talent and a "natural" predisposition for "feminine" subjects'.[5] The mid-Victorian bias against women's art was outlined by the *Art Journal* in 1857 when it noted, 'It has been too much the custom with a certain class of connoisseurs, real or pretending, to speak disparagingly of the productions of female artists – to regard them as works of the *hand* rather than of the *mind* – pretty and graceful pictures, but little else'.[6] Prevailing cultural attitudes toward what constituted 'feminine' art recommended watercolours over oils as a more manageable and pliant medium for the weaker sex, and studies in life drawing from the nude were frowned upon severely. Also, women were discouraged from attempting history paintings because, as the most highly regarded artistic genre, history painting was considered beyond the scope of the female artist's power and imagination. Natural or domestic scenes were offered as genres much more suited to a woman's experience, and landscapes and portraits were consequently deemed suitably feminine subjects.[7] Such methodological prejudices reflected the social bias described by the *Art Journal*, which presumed that the female imagination was inferior to the male; feminine art was compared with the 'pretty and graceful' decorative and ornamental work that formed part of the list of standard female accomplishments.

Parker and Pollock's analysis in 1981 of the detrimental effect this Victorian perception of a feminine style had on the female artist's place in histories of art led

---

4   Rozsika Parker and Griselda Pollock, *Old Mistresses: Women, Art and Ideology* (London: Rivers Oram Press, 1981), p. 12.

5   Ibid., p. 13.

6   'The Society of Female Artists', *Art Journal* 9 (1857), p. 215.

7   For a full discussion of the limits placed on both amateur and professional woman artists, see, for instance, Clarissa Campbell Orr, *Women in the Victorian Art World* (Manchester: Manchester University Press, 1995).

to a reassessment by feminist art historians of the lives of Victorian women artists. Pamela Gerrish Nunn, for instance, used her history, *Victorian Women Artists*, to answer questions such as, 'What were creative women doing while Edwin Landseer was immortalising dogs, stags and the British Royal Family?'[8] Histories such as this have been invaluable in detailing the heterogeneity of nineteenth century women artists' education, experience, and aesthetics and have consistently shown that, despite the overwhelming effort of many Victorian cultural critics to define a form of feminine art, 'there is no single women's perspective or women's culture'.[9] Though critical studies of the literary representations of the female artist have been scarcer than these historical investigations, they too have usefully examined the individual creative woman's interaction with the cultural assumptions that defined the feminine artist.[10] However, although female artists were themselves a heterogeneous group, the principles of feminine art repeatedly surfaced throughout discussions and representations of women artists in the second half of the nineteenth century as the standard by which the talent and the respectability of the female artist could be measured.

When the prominent artist Rosa Bonheur's popular large oil painting, *The Horse Fair* (1855), was reviewed by the *Art Journal*, for instance, the reviewer's appreciation for the work was increased by the fact that it came from the brush of a woman: 'Her large picture would be a wonderful work for any painter; but as the production of a female it is marvellous in conception and execution'.[11] The admiration and the wonder excited by Bonheur's *The Horse Fair* granted the painting and Bonheur herself a 'place among the very first painters of any age'.[12] But a second reaction to this work, also articulated by a writer for the *Art Journal*, demonstrated

---

8   Pamela Gerrish Nunn, *Victorian Women Artists* (London: The Woman's Press, 1981), p. 1.

9   Deborah Cherry, *Painting Women: Victorian Women Artists* (London: Routledge, 1993), p. 16. Some of the studies in recent years include, Whitney Chadwick, *Women, Art, and Society* (London: Thames and Hudson, 1990); Paula Gillett, *Worlds of Art: Painters in Victorian Society* (New Brunswick, NJ: Rutgers University Press, 1990); Jan Marsh and Pamela Gerrish Nunn, *Pre-Raphaelite Women Artists* (Manchester: Manchester City Art Galleries, 1997); Linda Nochlin, *Women, Art, and Power* (London: Thames and Hudson, 1991); Griselda Pollock, *Vision and Difference: Femininity, Feminism and the Histories of Art* (London: Routledge, 1988); Clarissa Campbell Orr, ed., *Women in the Victorian Art World*; and Charlotte Yeldham, *Women Artists in Nineteenth Century France and England*, 2 vols (London: Garland Publishing, 1984).

10   Some of the most notable are, Susan Casteras, '"The Necessity of a Name": Portrayals and Betrayals of Victorian Women Artists', *Gender and Discourse in Victorian Literature and Art*, Anthony H. Harrison and Barbara Taylor, eds (DeKalb: Northern Illinois University Press, 1992), pp. 207-32; and Dennis Denisoff, 'Lady in Green with Novel: The Gendered Economics of the Visual Arts and Mid-Victorian Women's Writing', *Victorian Women Writers and the Woman Question*, Nicola Diane Thompson, ed. (Cambridge: Cambridge University Press, 1999), pp. 151-69.

11   'Mademoiselle Rosa Bonheur', *Art Journal* 7 (1855), p. 243.

12   Ibid.

the pitfalls of such female genius: 'When a Rosa Bonheur, for example, astonishes the world with a "Horse Fair", or a herd of half-wild oxen, then we hear from the same lips some such exclamation as this: – "Clever – very clever, but *decidedly unfeminine!*"'[13] The ironic gaze that the *Art Journal* levels at the condescension of such judgments highlights the influence of the principles of feminine art exerted on the mid-century perception of the female artist's work. The critical approval and disapproval visited on Bonheur's work as reported by the journal are responses to her gender rather than her talent, and as much as her artistic reputation benefits from the impression that she exceeds the expected capability of most female artists, it is also limited by the critics who see her as a woman first and an artist second. Even a periodical like the *English Woman's Journal* could not entirely escape the influence of ideals of femininity when reviewing the work of the unconventional female artist. '[D]etermined not to marry, but to devote herself exclusively to her favourite art', the journal noted, 'Rosa Bonheur may be confidently expected to produce a long line of noble works that will worthily maintain, if they may not heighten, the reputation she has already acquired; while the virtues and excellencies of her private character, will assuredly win for their possessor an ever-widening circle of admiration and respect'.[14] Although Bonheur's dedication to her work is described by the journal in the terms of masculine vocation as the 'path that nature had marked out for her', and her respectability is presumed rather than questioned, the work of the artist is still seen to be bound up with the position of the woman.[15] While work can enhance reputation, femininity is shown to be the key to true success.

Although it fostered such critical condescension, the argument for the compatibility of art with the domestic sphere was instrumental in helping to define the high culture and public occupation of art as suitable paid work for women. As an amateur interest, art could easily be seen as a leisure activity, but a woman who devoted herself to art as her chosen profession, or relied on her skill in order to earn money, offered a worrying challenge to the feminine ideal. To reassure a general public of readers who might worry that the household would be neglected, or that children would be left motherless by the divided attention of the working woman, journals such as the *Art Journal* asserted the principle of compatibility with increasing frequency. Edited since its debut in 1839 by Samuel Carter Hall, the *Art-Union Monthly Journal* (shortened to the *Art Journal* in 1849) quickly rose to prominence as the leading journal on the fine arts and the arts of manufacturing so that, by 1851, the *Art Circular* was able to claim with confidence that 'This journal has now obtained so wide a celebrity that it is almost superfluous to sing its praises'.[16] The *Art Journal* maintained a very vocal support for female artists throughout the century, and frequently argued for the promotion of the economic interests of women. The *Journal* repeatedly asserted the necessity for the recognition

---

13   'The Society of Female Artists, *Art Journal*, p. 215.
14   'Rosa Bonheur', *English Woman's Journal* 1 (1858), p. 241.
15   Ibid.
16   *Art Circular* no. 2 (23 Jan. 1851), p. 10.

and support of female-run and centred organizations such as the Female School of Art and the Society of Female Artists, and it urged manufacturers to employ women as pattern designers for the decorative industries.

Such assertions, however, raised anxieties about the effect the increasingly public and professionalised role of the woman artist could have on her femininity. 'In conformity with the common remark', the respected art critic F.T. Palgrave noted, 'Very high genius for any art is apt ... to be engrossing; occasionally, to be undomestic in its tendencies'.[17] In order to counter this 'common remark', sympathetic journals like the *Art Journal* tried repeatedly to assure their readers of the propriety and domestic virtues of the 'lady painter' (itself a term of condescension). While arguing for continued education for woman artists, for instance, a writer for the *Journal* insisted that 'Of a surety, Art will never take her out of her natural sphere, tempt her to slight or abandon the enjoyments of home, or interfere with the household duties which are, as they ought to be, woman's privilege, pride, and reward'.[18] This particular assurance accompanied the *Journal*'s report on the national prizes won by the Female School of Art in 1871, and located in such a context, it reassures its readers that neither the expanding public role of the woman artist nor the public use or exhibition of her work would endanger her private respectability. With unflappable confidence, the writer expresses his certainty that the professional female artist could remain primarily a domestic woman.

This theoretical proposition was reinforced by more practical advice concerning the combination of artistic and domestic work. Such 'Advice to the Ladies' is offered by *Eliza Cook's Journal* when the author, in an effort to persuade its generally middle-class female readership of the importance of finding something useful to do with their time, insisted that a woman's daily household duties could be completed in two hours and argued that the efficiency with which these domestic duties could be dispatched, as evidenced by the skill of the reduced gentlewoman and those women who had to work, could easily be adopted by all women. Her time would then be free for nobler pursuits, which the optimistic advisor describes as, 'the duty of achieving distinction in some branch of study ... the necessity for *excelling* as an artist ... to open your mind, to enlarge your ideas and understanding'.[19] Here, the woman's duty as the moral guardian of the domestic sphere is broadened and intensified through exposure to the study of art, and art and domestic life are offered as mutual expressions of the responsibilities inherent in the concept of womanly duty. Art, this author contends, would certainly not interfere with a woman's household work; instead, it could enhance the femininity that such work represents. In efficiently dedicating her time to improving herself in order to improve her moral and educative function in her own household, the woman artist could become the linchpin for a rationally ordered

17 F.T. Palgrave, 'Women and the Fine Arts', *Macmillan's Magazine* 12 (1865), p. 127.

18 'The Female School of Art', *Art Journal* 23 (1871), p. 138.

19 'Advice to the Ladies', *Eliza Cook's Journal* 3 (1850), p. 11 [italics in original]. Published from 1849-1854, *Eliza Cook's Journal* was aimed primarily at women readers and dealt with issues that affected and interested middle-class women.

and morally enlightened society. A woman, this writer argues, should not simply study art or pursue an artistic interest. She should, instead, combine her art with her domestic role in order to become a model of artistic, and womanly, perfection.

The issue of compatibility opened a doorway through which the middle-class woman could escape the circumscribed routine of the domestic sphere by enabling her to extend that sphere and fulfil moral duties outside the home. For those, for instance, who saw conventional domesticity as the reason many ladies' lives were 'frittered away in a round of purposeless occupations', painting could allow women to participate in a purposeful scheme of moral philanthropy without leaving the home.[20] This 'suggestion' for women artists proposed that 'They should give their works for the adornment of rooms where working-men meet . . . Would not a faithful representation of mountain wilds, of shady forest, or of some happy domestic scene, do something to elevate the tone of working-men?'[21] This suggestion, which allows the woman artist to exert her moral influence on society from the safety of the domestic sphere, seeks to apply the doctrine of 'feminine influence',[22] a doctrine most famously espoused by John Ruskin in his lecture 'Of Queens' Gardens' (1865). Although Ruskin took this doctrine to an extreme by laying the responsibility for the morality of the state entirely within the woman's sphere, his lecture signalled the ideological power attributed to woman's role as 'the centre of order, the balm of distress, and the mirror of beauty'.[23] For Ruskin, the woman's influence on society and the State was a necessary and natural expansion of her role and duties within her own domain, and her domestic duties were given a public function. Extending this tenet to painting, the author of 'A Suggestion' justifies the public exhibition of a woman's art through its moral purpose. This doctrine could also help allay the fears of exhibition that plagued women artists, fears such as those described by Jan Marsh when she writes, 'Even when it was their work which was on display rather than their bodies, the sense of exposure to insult was similar and acted as a powerful deterrent'.[24] As moral and elevating work, a woman's paintings could be displayed in a very public and common space such as a working-men's room without exposing the artist to public scrutiny or compromising her domestic role. Through the doctrine of womanly influence, then, a domestic quality could be superimposed upon the female artist's work, securing her 'femininity' even while she participated, through the display of her paintings, in her own public exhibition as a working woman.

If venturing beyond the prescribed subjects and mediums, or refusing to maintain the appearance of conventional domesticity, could endanger the perception of a woman's femininity and respectability, then appearing to adhere to the conventions

20   'A Suggestion', *Macmillan's Magazine* 20 (1869), p. 365.

21   Ibid.

22   This was, as the *Saturday Review* argued, religious and social influence, not intellectual ['Feminine Influence', *Saturday Review* 22 (1866), pp. 784-86].

23   John Ruskin, 'Of Queens' Gardens', *Sesame and Lilies* (London: Blackie & Son, n.d.), p. 105.

24   Jan Marsh, 'Art, Ambition and Sisterhood in the 1850s', *Women in the Victorian Art World*, Clarissa Campbell Orr, ed., p. 34.

Figure 2.1   **Henrietta Ward, *God Save the Queen* [engraving in *The Art Journal*] (1857)**

for 'feminine' art could presumably secure a woman's domestic respectability. The artist Henrietta Ward, for instance, used her 1857 Royal Academy contribution, *God Save the Queen* (Figure 2.1), to portray herself as a 'normal', domestic middle-

Figure 2.2 Emily Mary Osborn, *Nameless and Friendless*, 1857 (oil on canvas).

class woman. The painting depicts a woman who is teaching her children to sing the national anthem. The picture the artist creates, however, is not a fictionalised scene of domestic realism but a comprehensible 'family portraiture' of the artist and her children engaged in a patriotic activity.[25] That Ward and her children are recognizable as the subject of her painting is demonstrated by the noted art critic James Dafforne, who off-handedly remarks that 'the lady presiding at the instrument is Mrs. Ward herself, and the youthful choristers are her children'.[26] As one of only 91 paintings by female artists in an exhibition of 1,372 works, *God Save the Queen* publicly advertised Ward's professional ambitions while making them appear comparatively uncommon for women.[27] Her decision to place herself at the centre of this picture could thus seem a strange choice for the domestically-minded woman in light of the 'unfeminine' publicity and the personal display that the self-portrait would entail. But in presenting herself to the public as an artist who gave precedence to her domestic duties, Ward established a self-image that mitigated her real position as a professional artist and a woman exhibiting the spectacle of her privacy at the Royal Academy in order to earn money.

The power this kind of image of domestic womanliness could have in obscuring a woman's professional ambitions can be seen in the way Ward's construction of her identity was unquestioningly reproduced by the mainstream critic Dafforne. In his biographical sketch of Ward for the *Art Journal*, Dafforne portrays Ward's artistry as the almost accidental result of her commitment to fulfil her womanly role as a disciple to her husband. As a prominent artist himself, Edward Ward is cited by Dafforne as the primary influence on his wife's career: 'Mrs. Ward is a skillful performer on the pianoforte, and from a child has been an enthusiastic lover of music; we believe her choice of a husband alone decided her in making painting a more prominent study than music'.[28] Rather than describing the painting as an indication of her professional artistry, Dafforne reads it as a testimony to her feminine propriety and contributes to Ward's efforts to generate a public image of her life as one of conventional domesticity. The discourse of compatibility was thus used by artists and commentators as a bulwark for middle-class respectability. But while the central representation of Ward as the conventional mother works toward establishing a picture of ideal domesticity, Ward also introduces other elements into the painting that destabilise the homogeneity of the woman's role in the domestic sphere.

Opposed to the image of Ward as the domestic angel is a triumvirate of working women who symbolically represent the ambiguity between public and private that women encountered in everyday life. The first image is the just visible figure of the

---

25 'Royal Academy Exhibition', *Art Journal* 9 (1857), p. 167.

26 James Dafforne, 'British Artists: Their Style and Character, no. LXXVII – Henrietta Ward', *Art Journal* 16 (1864), p. 358.

27 These figures come from William Sandby, *The History of the Royal Academy of Arts from its Foundation in 1768 to the Present Time*, 2 vols (London: Longman, Green, Longman, Roberts & Green, 1862), 2, p. 251.

28 Dafforne, 'British Artists', p. 358.

governess who minds the smallest child on the stairs. This figure, only barely in view, reinforces the distinction between the working woman and the domesticated Mrs. Ward and contributes to the delineation of Mrs. Ward as the typical middle-class woman. By embodying the presence of a working woman in the household who was paid to take the place of the mother, the figure of the governess undermined the naturalness of the ideology of separate spheres.[29] The second image is that of Queen Victoria, who is introduced into the painting through the song being taught to the children. Although Queen Victoria was 'furious' over the 'mad, wicked folly of "Women's Rights"',[30] she herself proved the most public example of the 'modern' woman who found it necessary to combine her domestic life with work. By naming the painting *God Save the Queen*, Ward associates herself with the public understanding of a woman whose duty it was to work, but whose image, as Susan Casteras notes, 'was steeped in dedication to country and family, respect for hard work, and respectability'.[31] Ward may also have been recalling the frontispiece to the 1842 *Illustrated Book of British Song* in which the Queen appears as a private woman, without her crown and with her family gathered around her. The words 'God Save the Queen' and the crown appear below the prominently placed domestic scene, and Victoria is shown to be engrossed solely in her children. This scene, Margaret Homans argues, 'is the apotheosis of the royal family as middle-class folks, with the queen imaged as governing, paradoxically, by removing herself absolutely from the sphere of government'.[32] In the spirit of womanly influence, then, this illustration implies that the Queen uses her domestic position to rule the country.

The references to both the governess and the Queen in this painting provide iconographically powerful images of compatibility in action. They also remind the viewer of a third working woman, the artist Ward, who, though outside the frame, is nonetheless present by implication. While the image of Ward as the domestic woman occupies the centre of the painting, Ward the artist is shown to exist in the margins of this domestic identity. Compatibility thus allowed female artists a way to maintain their respectability without denying the public and remunerative aspects of their work. It offered them a solution to the difficulties associated with the issues of work and publicity for women, and it helped shape a domestic image of female artistry that defined the requirements of professional life, such as education, production, and exhibition, as domestic and ultimately private activities. It could be employed to obscure the economic realities of the life of the professional female artist, and the practicalities of an artist looking, or needing, to sell her painting could be concealed,

29   Mary Poovey, *Uneven Developments: The Ideological Work of Gender in Mid-Victorian England* (London: Virago, 1989), p. 127.

30   Quoted in Margaret Cole, *Women of To-day* (London: Thomas Nelson, 1946), p. 150.

31   Susan P. Casteras, 'Her Majesty the Queen', *Images of Victorian Womanhood in English Art* (Rutherford, NJ: Fairleigh Dickinson University Press, 1987), p. 20.

32   Margaret Homans, 'Victoria's Sovereign Obedience: Portraits of the Queen as Wife and Mother', *Victorian Literature and the Victorian Visual Imagination*, Carol T. Christ and John O. Jordan, eds (Berkeley: University of California Press, 1995), p. 176.

as Ward's painting shows, within the domestic qualities attributed to the artist. But the principle of compatibility was also used by artists such as Ward and others to question the very structures it relied upon and maintained. The inclusion of images of public work within Ward's picture of happy domesticity undermines the feminine ideal and subverts the separation of spheres. Throughout the middle of the century, the issue of compatibility and principles of feminine writing were used paradoxically to expand woman's sphere and to define professional work, like their domestic duties, as a 'natural' activity for women.

The Screen and the Margin: Redefining Domesticity

Although Ward chose to depict herself directly as a domestic woman instead of as an artist in *God Save the Queen*, her choice belies what Charlotte Yeldham describes as a general increase around this time in the number of representations of female artists. Between 1850-1869, Yeldham notes, women artists painted a total of three self-portraits, 12 portraits of contemporary female artists, and seven representations of unspecified female artists.[33] Although these figures are not overwhelmingly large, they do point to the women artists' growing desire to move away from the stereotypical female subjects of flowers and landscapes in order to represent the various aspects of their professional life. Florence Claxton's *Scenes from the Life of a Female Artist* (1858), for instance, depicts a woman artist sitting disconsolately in her studio, hovering over a canvas that has just been rejected from the Royal Academy exhibition.[34] But among these various art-related subjects and among the 91 works by female exhibitors displayed at the Royal Academy or the 149 women whose works were exhibited at the newly formed Society of Female Artists exhibition in 1857, only one directly represented the woman artist engaged in an economic transaction.[35] Emily Mary Osborn's *Nameless and Friendless* (Figure 2.2) depicts a young woman's attempt to sell a painting in an art dealer's shop. Although the young woman and the dealer occupy the foreground, the eye is continually drawn to other elements which place this central image in relief: a bourgeois woman and boy leave the store having made a purchase, and two gentlemen in top hats grasp a picture of a ballerina whose costume leaves her arms and legs uncovered. By entering into an economic exchange with the dealer, the girl has placed herself in a very public position that threatens her respectability. Positioned in contrast to the representative of bourgeois maternal respectability and an example of female immodesty, the young woman occupies a space that negotiates between these two social extremes.

---

33   Charlotte Yeldham, *Women Artists in Nineteenth Century France and England*, I, pp. 167-68.

34   The description of this work is recorded in the review of the second exhibition of the Society of Female Artists in the *English Woman's Journal* 1 (1858), p. 209.

35   The figures on the SFA come from Pamela Gerrish Nunn, *Victorian Women Artists*, p. 113.

The three female figures that Osborn portrays in this painting show, like Ward's triumvirate, the woman artist's reliance on alternative images of womanhood in the construction of her public identity. But unlike Ward's picture, which positions the woman artist as a domestic woman, Osborn's alternative images highlight her artist's isolation from respectable femininity and her need for male patronage and protection. To construct this marginal position, Osborn draws on the iconographic properties that characterised the reduced gentlewoman – a proper black mourning dress, a modest, downcast look, and an expression of patient suffering – as the defining physical features of her heroine. It is a move calculated to elicit pity for her artist, and its success is evident in James Dafforne's eloquent interpretation in the *Art Journal* of the 'pathetic story' told by the painting:

> A young orphan girl, an artist, offers to a dealer a picture she has painted. The man examines it critically, and somewhat contemptuously; and one can fancy the result of the inspection will be of this kind – "Afraid I can't find room for it, I'm already overstocked with things of this sort; there's no sale for them". How many heavy hearts of both young and old which have turned from a shop-door with such words ringing in the ears are known only to those who have mingled with the Art-world in its various phases. And this poor girl, whose good looks have drawn towards her the eyes of some loungers in the shop, and whose young brother has accompanied her thither, will doubtless have to retrace her steps through the pitiless rain to try her fortune elsewhere, and, not improbably, be compelled at last to leave her work in the hands of some pawnbroker for advance of a small sum of money to support herself and brother. It is a sad, true story, told without exaggeration.[36]

If, as the author suggests, Osborn tells the story without exaggeration, there is certainly exaggeration in this description. Like Redgrave's *The Sempstress, Nameless and Friendless* provided the male art world and society with an image of the disadvantaged female worker that they could pity, patronise, and rescue. Crucially, the woman's creations, both those of her portfolio and the painting she is trying to sell, are depicted in the hands of two male figures, the boy and the dealer. Seen in this light, the narrative of the distressed gentlewoman may be most clearly understood as an issue of control wherein the image of a woman at the centre of the professional, remunerative transaction was transformed into a cry for help to those who should 'rescue' her from this indignity. Dafforne's suggestion that this 'sad', 'pathetic story' is a common experience for women artists broadens the import of Osborn's picture from the specific context depicted, and the nameless and friendless artist becomes an allegorical representation of the working woman's vulnerability.

The broader social context suggested by Dafforne is also supported by the epigraph Osborn affixed to the painting for its exhibition at the Royal Academy: 'The rich man's wealth is his strong city: the destruction of the poor is their poverty'.[37] While

---

36 James Dafforne, 'British Artists: Their Style and Character, no. LXXV-Emily Mary Osborn', *Art Journal* 16 (1864), p. 261.

37 Quoted in Charlotte Yeldham, *Women Artists in Nineteenth Century France and England*, I, p. 167.

not overtly gender-based, the epigraph's division between rich and poor locates the poor woman in a perilous opposition to the male economic world of the city. As a bringer of destruction, her poverty signifies not only her economic destitution, but also the social and moral difficulties that plagued the anonymous and unprotected girl in a man's world. The presence of a London city street and the dome of St. Paul's, which is visible in the background, inform the viewer that this woman is trying to survive in a city of commerce and economic exchange that is indifferent to the individual's plight. In this way, the allegorical content of the painting refers as much to the expansive city scene viewed through the window as to the intimate narrative portrayed in the foreground. Her modest appearance indicates that she still maintains her innocence and respectability, but her exposure to the male city of commerce highlights her vulnerability and precarious social and economic status. Being both nameless and friendless, she is bereft of an identifiable social position and natural protectors. Without a more specific reference to the domestic character of the woman represented, either through the title or epigraph, or some more direct visual clue, Osborn advertises the woman's marginal position. By failing to provide her subject with a recognisable domestic identity, Osborn leaves the woman morally and socially stranded in the position in which necessity has placed her.

In this picture, Osborn implies that, regardless of her desire or need to sell her painting, the woman artist is dependent on a market that is controlled by male dealers and critics, and which, in any case, was traditionally defined as a masculine arena. The difficulties encountered by the professional female artist in the masculine art world were investigated in more detail in a story entitled 'The Portrait' which was published in the *English Woman's Journal* in 1861. This story features as its heroine an amateur artist, Emily Lindores, who tries to pursue her vocation to study art. The central episode of this story deals with Emily's efforts to paint a portrait of her patroness, Mrs. Bethune, as the medieval Italian sculptress, Properzia Rossi. Emily hopes that this portrait will earn her the approbation of their acquaintance, Mr. Cleveland, who is a professional painter himself, and win her the encouragement to pursue a professional career. Her encounters with the masculine art world through her acquaintance with Cleveland, however, are shown to place her repeatedly at a disadvantage and to undermine her professional identity. The woman's power to control the circumstances of the exhibition of her work is the first issue to be explored when Emily's plans for an elaborate unveiling are dashed. Entering her studio uninvited, Cleveland sees her work before it is finished and properly hung. Although Cleveland praises her painting and validates her talent, the professional imbalance of power between himself and Emily is further emphasised through the engrained condescension apparent in his comment, 'Your picture has a great fault in my eyes ... you cannot amend it ... but I will paint a Properzia and *show* you the amendment'.[38]

---

38 A.R.L., 'The Portrait', *English Woman's Journal* 7 (1861), p. 115. This story was published in five parts from April 1861- August 1861.

Cleveland's amendment replaces Mrs Bethune with Emily herself as his 'ideal Properzia'.[39] Through this alteration, Cleveland usurps Emily's project, displacing her from the easel and projecting her onto the canvas. In his portrait, Emily is transferred from subject to object, from decorator to decoration – from the position of the imaginative female artist to a much more feminine role as the model and inspiration for the male artist. Furthermore, the artistic community corroborates this displacement of female authority. While Emily's Properzia languishes in obscurity, Cleveland's is accepted for exhibition at the Royal Academy. Rather than receiving artistic fame herself, Emily becomes a mere prop to Cleveland's ambitions, inspiring only sexual admiration from viewers of his work. 'I observed' Emily complains, 'that the promoter and encourager of the fine arts seated at the foot of the table stared at me in a manner beyond that which the law of etiquette could justify. I felt the blood mount to my face, for I at once concluded he was thinking of the portrait'.[40]

Emily's encounter with Cleveland removes her, both literally and figuratively, from the heights of artistic excellence. When exiled back to her poor aunt by the jealous Mrs. Bethune, Emily is literally forced to give up her dreams of going to Rome and devoting herself to art. Indeed, in contrast to such lofty ambitions, the fashioning of Emily in the role of Properzia figuratively roots her established artistic identity in a domestic frame, 'for the beautiful Properzia was a notable housewife, as well as a sculptress and a musician'.[41] Cleveland's painting domesticates Emily's identity as a professional artist and ultimately strips her of her expressive power. Recast in public as the proper and domestic sculptress Properzia, Emily is appreciated for her femininity rather than recognized for her artistry. In exploring the result of this recasting, then, 'The Portrait' explores the fate of a woman with talent and vocation whose opportunities are constrained by the dictates of domesticity and the condescension of the masculine art world.

The place of female artistic production in relation to conventional social and economic milieux was an issue that also surfaced explicitly in the two most notable representations of the female artist in the mid-Victorian period – Anne Brontë's *The Tenant of Wildfell Hall* (1848) and Dinah Craik's *Olive* (1850). In her preface to the second edition of *The Tenant of Wildfell Hall*, Brontë highlights this issue as one of the concerns of the novel. In this preface, she attempts to counter the disapproval critics had expressed of the 'vulgar, rough, brusque-mannered personages' and the 'bold coarseness, [and] reckless freedom of language' that many saw as the 'defect which injures the real usefulness and real worth of the book'.[42] The preface exhibits the tension that results when the female artist's desire for freedom of expression

---

39   Ibid.

40   Ibid., p. 255.

41   Ibid., p. 116.

42   'Mr. Bell's New Novel', *Rambler: A Catholic Journal and Review* 3 (1848), p. 65. 'unsigned review', *Sharpe's London Magazine* 7 (1848), rpt. in *The Brontës: The Critical Heritage,* Miriam Allott, ed. (London: Routledge & Kegan Paul, 1974), p. 265. [Charles Kingsley], 'Recent Novels', *Fraser's Magazine* 39 (1849), p. 424.

comes into conflict with the male critic's prejudices about what constitutes proper feminine art. Many readers objected, in particular, to its unusual treatment of the story of marriage and domestic life, which was considered to be the particular forte of the woman writer, when the home, which was supposed to be a refuge and a safe haven, is shown to be a place of danger and violence. In response to such criticism, Brontë claims the right to represent such coarseness for the female writer as well as the male by arguing that vulgarity in representation can be excused if it fulfils a didactic purpose. The correct use for her talents, she concludes, is to speak the truth and teach a lesson through the 'warnings of experience'.[43] Referring to Brontë's exposure to Methodist doctrines of the transformative power of narrative, Melody Kemp notes that this is a 'novel with a purpose ... demonstrat[ing] how a reader should employ his or her time in order to save, or at least improve himself'.[44] Deborah Morse describes Brontë's moral programme in this novel as 'witnessing', the process through which a first-hand account of the experience of evil is given in order to teach a civilising lesson. She notes that 'Books – especially the Bible – are the vehicle of this civilizing process, which is enacted in Anne Brontë's book itself, the work of an artist who insistently incorporates the Word within her own words in order to provide a story that morally educates us through Art while creating her own feminist testament'.[45] Rachel Carnell, on the other hand, sees Brontë's Preface as indicative of her desire to enact, through Helen, an eighteenth century model of improving the public good through rational discourse.[46] Whatever the specific motivation behind the telling of her controversial tale, Brontë frames her story in religious and educative terms. The result of this is that she effects a compromise between female creativity and propriety through the moral function of art, and the daring elements of the book can be justified as examples of the public expression of womanly influence and the extension of domestic duties.

While Brontë attempts to justify her decision to depict an unconventional story, she also reveals the way in which the principles of feminine writing could be manipulated to grant the creative woman greater freedom to express herself. But, as Brontë shows throughout the novel, such compromise comes at a price. The location of art as a domestic activity ostensibly placed art ultimately under the control of the male head of the household in which it was produced, and in *The Tenant of Wildfell Hall* Brontë repeatedly investigates the conflict between a woman's desire to assert her ownership over her own creative work and man's desire to control this

---

43   Anne Brontë, *The Tenant of Wildfell Hall*, Stevie Davies, ed. (London: Penguin Books, 1996), p. 130. Further references to this edition will be given in the text.

44   Melody J. Kemp, 'Helen's Diary and the Method(ism) of Character Formation', in *The Tenant of Wildfell Hall, New Approaches to the Literary Art of Anne Brontë*, Julie Nash and Barbara A Suess, eds (Aldershot: Ashgate, 2001), p. 198.

45   Deborah Denenholz Morse, '"I speak of those I do know": Witnessing as Radical Gesture in *The Tenant of Wildfell Hall*', *New Approaches to the Literary Art of Anne Brontë*, Julie Nash and Barbara A Suess, eds, p. 111.

46   Rachel K. Carnell, 'Feminism and the Public Sphere in Anne Brontë's *The Tenant of Wildfell Hall*', *Nineteenth-Century Literature* 53 (1998), pp. 1-24.

production. Written in the early years of agitation for reform of the laws concerning a married woman's property, this novel explores the helplessness of a woman who has no control over her own property and no legal rights to her child.[47] In fact, this conflict underpins the relationship between Brontë's heroine, Helen Huntingdon, and her husband, Arthur, from the earliest days of their courtship. When Arthur discovers a picture of himself sketched on the back of one of Helen's drawings, he not only takes the picture against her will, but also refuses to return it when she insists upon him doing so. Although the sketch is hers, Helen is unable to assert her control over it, or over him, because Arthur is empowered to claim ownership over her, and her work, by what he sees as a public demonstration of her affection for him. The picture outwardly represents the struggle for sexual dominance in their relationship, but it also signifies the conflict of creative ownership between the woman artist and her masculine critic. Upon seeing the portrait, Arthur assumes that it represents an open admission of Helen's preference for him, and he 'placed it against his waistcoat, and buttoned his coat upon it with a delighted chuckle', effectively pressing it against his heart and defining it as a mere token of her love (*Tenant*, p. 155). Through Arthur's reductive and egotistical assumption, Brontë recalls the socially established rules that sought to confine women's art to the representation of the emotional, the natural, and the mundane. Arthur judges Helen's art to be the sentimental production of the feminine eye rather than the imagination, a mere copy of that which exists before her and an expression of her emotional and sexual desires.

Brontë uses Arthur's perspective on Helen's work to illustrate the compatibility between Helen's domestic desires and her artistic pursuits, which is implied by her choice of Arthur as her subject. However, the beneficial aspects of compatibility are undermined by the hostile struggle for control that is waged over these paintings. While Arthur is not entirely incorrect in his assumption, Brontë shows that the assumption remains unwelcome and, in fact, plays painfully against the artistic ideals that Helen also cherishes. Arthur capitalises on the emotional revelation the picture signifies in order to steal a kiss from Helen, but her indignant reaction to this liberty is not directed at him, but at the painting which has exposed her: 'He would not have done so but for that hateful picture! And there he had it still in his possession, an eternal monument to his pride and my humiliation!' (*Tenant*, p. 157). Helen views this sketch in traditional domestic terms as a symbol of her personal relationship with Arthur, and Brontë uses this incident to explore the interaction of female artistic autonomy with a conventional sexual economy. The alliance between art and domestic feeling that characterises the sketch defines Helen as an amateur artist and signifies her confinement within the role of the traditional domestic woman. As a result, it is

---

47 The first Married Woman's Property Bill was not passed until 1857. For a discussion of the passage of this bill see Lee Holcombe, 'Victorian Wives and Property: Reform of the Married Woman's Property Law, 1857-1882', *A Widening Sphere: Changing Roles of Victorian Women*, Martha Vicinus, ed. (Bloomington: Indiana University Press, 1977), pp. 3-28. Also, Mary Poovey, *Uneven Developments: The Ideological Work of Gender in Mid-Victorian Britain* (London: Virago, 1989), esp. chap 3.

not simply the existence of the sketch that makes her vulnerable to the appearance of impropriety and to Arthur's sexual advances. Helen has brought her sketches to the attention of those in the drawing room because she wants to compete with Miss Wilmot, whose singing is winning Arthur's attention and admiration, and 'Helen's art serves as a method of courtship ... [and] an expression of the young woman's desire'.[48] It is thus this exhibition of her womanly accomplishment and sentiment that exposes her to feminine vulnerability. Brontë reinforces this point by contrasting this incident with a later scene in which Arthur enters Helen's studio uninvited and attempts to appropriate another picture of himself that she has painted. Unlike the previous incident, this time, Helen forcefully retrieves the painting because, in this instance, he has violated her privacy by looking at paintings she had no intention of exhibiting: 'I never let anyone see them ... I *insist* on having that back! It is mine, and you have no *right* to take it' (*Tenant*, p. 160-61). The emphasis Brontë places on Arthur's proprietary arrogance and Helen's adamant possessiveness reveals Arthur's invasion of Helen's private creative space as a further attempt to broaden his control over her by appropriating her most personal productions.

In fact, once she is married, it is not just her money that becomes Arthur's property. Helen also has no power to assert her ownership over her paintings or her painting materials. It is marriage, Brontë suggests, that is most detrimental to creativity and female production. This is a point that Brontë makes repeatedly through both of Helen's marriages. Although Helen has given up her painting by the time she marries Gilbert Markham, Brontë illustrates another instance of presumptive male authority when Gilbert asserts an editorial control over Helen's quasi-literary production, her journal. Many critics see the exchange of the diary between Helen and Gilbert as an instance of Helen's power over Gilbert, expressing such relations as her moral instruction of him or his role as the diffident suitor.[49] But, as Elizabeth Signorotti argues, 'One cannot ignore the evidence within the text that points to an opposite conclusion: Markham's appropriation and edition of Helen's history reflects an attempt to contain and control her'.[50] Gilbert has not stolen Helen's journal nor read it without her permission as Arthur had done, but once he has it, he assumes the right to reproduce it for his friend's amusement. Also when he proposes to relate Helen's history to his acknowledged reader Halford, his friend and the recipient of

---

48   Karen Shaw, '*Wildfell Hall* and the Artist as a Young Woman', *West Virginia University Philosophical Papers* 48 (2001-2002), p. 13.

49   See, for instance, Jan B. Gordon, 'Gossip, Diary, Letter, Text: Anne Brontë's Narrative *Tenant* and the Problematic of the Goth Sequel', *ELH* 51 (1984), pp. 719-45; N.M. Jacobs, 'Gender and Layered Narrative in *Wuthering Heights* and *The Tenant of Wildfell Hall*', *Journal of Narrative Technique* 16 (1986), pp. 204-19; Elizabeth Langland, 'The Voicing of Feminine Desire in Anne Brontë's *The Tenant of Wildfell Hall*', *Gender and Discourse in Victorian Literature and Art*, Anthony H. Harrison and Barbara Taylor, eds (DeKalb: Northern Illinois University Press, 1992), pp. 111-23; and Lori A. Paige, 'Helen's Diary Freshly Considered', *Brontë Society Transactions* 20 (1991), pp. 225-27.

50   Elizabeth Signorotti, '"A Frame Perfect and Glorious": Narrative Structure in Anne Brontë's *The Tenant of Wildfell Hall*', *Victorian Newsletter* no. 87 (1995), p. 21.

his epistolary narrative, he claims that he will provide him with a 'full and faithful' account of the story (*Tenant*, p. 10). The journal, however, is presented 'whole, save, perhaps, a few passages here and there of merely temporal interest to the writer, or such as would serve to encumber the story rather than elucidate it' (*Tenant*, p. 129). The reader, then, is left with a narrative that, despite Gilbert's assurances, is far from full or faithful.

Unlike both her marriages, the seemingly autonomous life Helen builds for herself at Wildfell Hall is one of sexual independence, creative freedom, and professional activity. Escaping Arthur enables her to make an ideal home outside conventional domestic existence. Where marriage only brought fear and despair, work is shown to bring peace and security when, at Wildfell Hall, she can practice her art unmolested and use her womanly accomplishment to support herself and her son. But even here her artistic production is mediated through a male protector – her paintings are delivered to the dealer and sold through her brother. Whatever Helen's domestic or professional situation, Brontë portrays her heroine essentially as an amateur woman artist, attributing the money Helen earns to her moral and domestic duty to her son. While Helen admits that in removing her son from what she sees as the profligate and 'injurious' influence of his father she is brooking the 'world's opinion and the feelings of my friends', her protection of her son is presented as her greatest duty and her most solemn responsibility (*Tenant*, p. 352). To the society that Helen encounters in the novel, however, her motives and justifications are irrelevant. Beyond the moral debate concerning duty and domesticity, Brontë reveals that Helen's position as a respectable woman within the neighbourhood relies more upon societal gossip than informed judgment. With no real complaint against Helen, the censure of the small society that surrounds Wildfell Hall is summed up by Mrs. Markham when she exclaims, 'You see what it is for a woman to affect to be different to other people' (*Tenant*, p. 89). Helen's only real offence is that she does not live strictly according to what this small village society considers to be proper for a lady. Her silence about her husband and family, her social reticence, and, most importantly, her professional career as an artist set her apart from other women in the village and expose her to their unfounded censure. But by placing the world's opinion in conflict with Helen's duty as a mother, Brontë demonstrates the shallowness and the inaccuracy of conventional measures of respectability such as appearance and situation. She offers instead an alternative image of domesticity in which insubstantial and modish conventions of ideal femininity are replaced by the individual's responsibility to fulfil fundamental moral duties. In this light, Brontë celebrates the concept of domesticity as the fulfilment of basic maternal and Christian obligations rather than as the strict adherence to certain physical parameters, and Helen is represented as a domestic woman regardless of her home life and seemingly 'unwifely' behaviour.

Brontë's characterisation of Helen constructs an image of the woman artist in which art comes to be defined as an integral feature of her domestic duty. The heroine of Dinah Craik's *Olive*, Olive Rothesay, is represented with similar domestic tendencies. But, although she insists that as a dutiful daughter and honourable woman she must pursue an art career in order to repay her father's debts and support herself and her mother, her art is also presented as a vocation of the 'dawning artist soul' that drives her to achieve more than a fair talent for copying lady-like watercolours and genteel landscapes.[51] Artistic vocation, however, as it is defined by Michael Vanbrugh, Olive's drawing master and Craik's conventional representative of the creative genius, is a 'dominion [in which] man has the advantage' (*Olive*, p. 126). In the relationship between Olive and Vanbrugh, Craik explores in her own way the mechanisms of power that characterise the female artist's association with a male adviser. To this end, she depicts Vanbrugh's efforts to instruct Olive according to his own conventional image of female artistry. He even desires to control her personal life, issuing directives on how she should wear her hair and offering a marriage proposal that would require her to abandon her own thoughts of a professional career in order to promote his. From a typically restrictive social perspective, Vanbrugh speaks derisively of women artists as worldly and sentimental and defines the great artist as a model of Romantic individuality:

> He, strong in his might of intellect, can make it his all in all, his life's sole aim and guerdon ... But there scarce ever lived the woman who would not rather sit meekly by her own hearth, with her husband at her side, and her children at her knee, than be the crowned Corinne of the Capitol. (*Olive*, p. 126)

Craik, however, suggests that this description of the female artist does not apply to Olive because Olive is not like most women. The slight curve of the spine with which Olive is born seemingly excludes her from 'woman's natural destiny', and her artistic vocation is offered as a consolation and a substitute for the human love denied her by her deformity (*Olive*, p. 127):

> Sometimes chance or circumstance or wrong, sealing up her woman's nature, converts her into a self-dependent human soul. Instead of life's sweetnesses, she has before her life's greatnesses. The struggle passed, her genius may lift itself upward, expand and grow mighty ... Then, even while she walks with scarce-healed feet over the world's rough pathway, heaven's glory may rest upon her upturned brow, and she may become a light unto her generation. (*Olive*, p. 126)

The curve of her spine, her refusal of Vanbrugh's marriage offer, and his definition of creative genius, all signify her exclusion from traditional domesticity. But in this passage, Craik suggests that Olive's self-dependence, artistic vocation, and intellectual power can all be redefined as domestic qualities through the extended function of the doctrine of feminine influence. On this occasion, though, the bearing of feminine influence is seen as the privilege of the desexualised woman. Unlike Ruskin's domestic Queen, whose influence emanated from a fundamental commitment to duties within her private household domain, Craik's heroine only bears influence insofar as she stands beyond the mundane concerns of domestic life.

---

51 Dinah Craik, *Olive: A Young Girl's Triumph Over Prejudice,* Cora Kaplan, ed. (Oxford: Oxford University Press, 1996), p. 65. Further references to this edition will be given in the text.

The various impulses that direct Olive's work create a fundamental conflict in her character between her 'masculine power of mind' and 'woman's natural destiny', but they also compel her to resolve this conflict from the perspective of the professional artist. Craik's representation of Olive offers a reorientation of perceived domesticity and suggests that, like marriage or motherhood, professional artistry can constitute the centre of domestic experience.

In the characterisations of both Helen and Olive, both traditional domesticity and Romantic individualism are rejected as inadequate for the development of a professional artistic identity. What Brontë and Craik construct instead is an uneasy alliance for their heroines between art and domesticity that exists in marginal spaces free from patriarchal control. For both, this marginal space is literally the space of a studio that doubles as a drawing room. While living under the patriarchal control of her husband at Grassdale Manor, Helen transformed the library into her studio. This is a conventionally masculine space in which, as Deobrah Morse notes, she is surrounded by 'books written by men'.[52] Arthur's ultimate exertion of control over Helen's creative production through the destruction of all her paintings and painting materials is foregrounded by her position in this masculine place. Unlike the library, though, the drawing room is a feminine space. Helen is able to receive visitors while she paints, and Olive can pursue her artistic career as she watches over her aged and blind mother. In the drawing room, female creativity can co-exist with domestic propriety. The difficulty of maintaining the balance between these two, however, is depicted in both novels. When Helen is visited by Gilbert Markham and his sister, she not only has to clear the chairs of paintings in order for her guests to sit down, but she also appears distracted and occasionally touches her painting with her brush 'as if she found it impossible to wean her attention entirely from her occupation to fix it on her guests' (*Tenant*, p. 46). But when Gilbert remarks on her obvious eagerness to be painting, she realises her inattention and throws down her brush 'as if startled into politeness' (*Tenant*, p. 47). In trying to perform both roles at once, Helen is successful at neither, but quickly gives priority to the social space of the drawing room.

In *Olive*, however, Craik presents a character who defies all attempts to confine her professional identity within established boundaries or conventional domestic parameters. Even the very public exhibition of her work at the Royal Academy does not encroach upon Olive's impeccable character and stable social status. By embracing the marginal status of the professional female artist, Olive is never subjected to the implicit compromise of drawing-room artistic production that characterized many mid-Victorian representations. Indeed, her marginality is startlingly celebrated by Craik in the spatial metaphor of the 'crimson screen' that separates the drawing room and transforms half of it into a painting studio. This screen promotes Olive's successful combination of the drawing room with the studio because it allows her to work uninterruptedly while painting and to easily and gracefully receive visitors when free. As such, it is the legitimate physical margin that brightens the 'once

---

52   Morse, 'Witnessing as Radical Gesture', p. 108.

gloomy barrenness' of the drawing room as it usurps its domestic function (*Olive*, p. 140). This metaphor of the screen embodies an alternative form of the domestic life that Olive experiences through her professional work, one in which the woman's artistic identity subsumes the domestic.

Although Craik constructs this life around Olive's relationship with her art, what is most interesting is the way she uses the rhetoric of conventional domesticity to describe it. It is a relationship, the narrator comments, that begins with the logical first step: 'She gathered up all her passionate love-impulses into her virgin soul, and married herself unto her Art' (*Olive*, p. 148). In this formulation, the relationship between the woman and her art is described as an ideal marriage that surpasses the 'meanness' of a conventional domestic life. While Olive sees the 'general standard of perfection' in marriage as 'ineffably beneath her own ideal', art offers her alternative means to experience the fulfilment that women were supposed to find in their husbands (*Olive*, p. 148).

The potential for art to provide this kind of experience was a possibility that Craik further developed in her prose exploration of 'The Woman Question' in *A Woman's Thoughts about Women* (1858). Written eight years later, this book provides an interesting perspective on the relationship between Olive and her art. When discussing the creative woman's personal involvement with her work, Craik writes:

> We may paint scores of pictures, write shelvesful of books – the errant children of our brain may be familiar half over the known world, and yet we ourselves sit as quiet by our chimney-corner, live a life as simple and peaceful as any happy "common woman" of them all.[53]

By characterising the woman writer and artist as the 'mother' of the 'errant children' of books and paintings, Craik suggests that work is the 'natural' offspring of the professional woman. Through this suggestion, she delineates an image of the woman's role within the domestic sphere that draws on what Lynda Nead defines as that 'most valuable and natural component' of middle-class femininity, woman as mother.[54] The discourse of domesticity employed to construct Craik's picture of the 'simple and peaceful' life of the woman artist suggests the quiet, traditional domestic life. However, the image she describes posits an alternative experience of motherhood and the domestic sphere. The 'children' of professional women are 'errant children' because Craik's picture of alternative domesticity deviates from the norm by leaving out one crucial element – the man. In this alternative domestic sphere, the mother and child relationship is entirely self-sufficient; there is no reliance on the husband or father as there is in the traditional domestic sphere.[55] Instead, the power of creation,

---

53　Dinah Craik, *A Woman's Thoughts About Women* (London: Hurst and Blackett, 1858), p. 58.

54　Lynda Nead, *Myths of Sexuality: Representations of Women in Victorian Britain* (Oxford: Basil Blackwell, 1988), p. 26.

55　For a discussion of the woman's dependence on the man as a cultural norm, see Lynda Nead, *Myths of Sexuality*, esp. chapter 1.

as well as the peace of a contented household, is granted to the woman alone.[56] Furthermore, by outlining this alternative for the female artist in domestic terms, Craik defines the professional woman as a 'common woman'.

This same notion of alternative domesticity is implicit in Olive's 'marriage' to her art. For Olive, the domestic paradigm is complete when, 'Half-smiling, she began to call her pictures her children, and to think of the time when they, a goodly race, would live, and tell no tale of their creator's woe' (*Olive*, p. 263). The difficulty, however, of fully imagining such a life for a woman in 1850 is made clear by the introduction of the conventional love interest in the form of Harold Gwynne and the resulting change in her relationship to her art. When Olive realises that she loves Harold, the fulfilment her art had given her collapses, and when one of her paintings wins for her great public and professional success, it is no longer enough for Olive: 'When the news came – tidings which a year ago would have thrilled her with pleasure – Olive only smiled faintly, and a few minutes after went into her chamber, hid her face, and wept' (*Olive*, p. 234). Even her artistic inspiration is retrospectively assigned to this conventional love story as the narrator notes that this widely admired painting was 'unconsciously created from the inspiration of that sweet love-dream' (*Olive*, p. 234). Olive's professional vocation gives way to a conventional marriage because, the narrator notes in typically feminine terms, 'it was a natural and womanly thing that in her husband's fame Olive should almost forget her own' (325). Like Helen, Olive is re-established within a traditional domestic sphere in which a drawing room is only a drawing room. But as the qualifying statement that Olive 'almost' forgets her own fame implies, art is not entirely abandoned, nor is the professional ever completely excised from Olive's domestic identity.

While her prose allowed Craik to propose the image of an alternative domesticity without exploring its ramifications or attempting to dramatise it, the detail and the mainstream interests of the fictional portrait perhaps made it too difficult an ideal to be sustained. But in *Olive* Craik, at least briefly, portrays the possibility for the marginal to become the mainstream. And rather than completely subverting the picture of alternative domesticity that she constructs, she depicts Olive's marriage as one in which she and her husband 'both work together for their dearest ones', while their home is one whose comforts will be those 'which she with her slender means could win' (322). Although Craik depicts Olive's ideological self-negation in marriage, the actuality of their married life is one in which husband and wife are at least economic equals. While both these early representations of the professional female artist eventually capitulate to the principles of feminine art and conventions of domestic life, both *The Tenant of Wildfell Hall* and *Olive* imagine a form of professional female creativity that can exist outside the realm of masculine influence and control.

---

56   Tracy Seeley describes Craik's assertion of female-centred experience in this essay as a rhetorical strategy aimed at creating a public authority for women. Tracy Seeley, 'Victorian Women's Essays and Dinah Mulock's *Thoughts*: Creating an *Ethos* for Argument', *Prose Studies* 19 (1996), pp. 93-109.

The difficulty for female creativity to flourish under the conventional, patriarchal domestic setting is also explored by the Pre-Raphaelite artist and writer Amelia Blanford Edwards in her novel *Barbara's History* (1864). As with Olive, Barbara finds that she must devote to her work all of her domestic and sexual resources if she is to succeed as an artist. Before they are engaged, Barbara's lover Hugh Farquhar, who is himself an amateur painter, warns her that in order to be a true artist one must give complete devotion and surrendering self-sacrifice to art. 'Beware of such empty words as home, or love, or friendship', he tells her, 'Devote yourself to your art. Make it your home, your country, your friend. Wed it; live in it; die for it'.[57] Drawn on melodramatically by the overpowering desires of her 'womanly' heart, though, art is never enough for Barbara. 'The humanity that is in me', she laments, 'demands something more than paint and canvas' (*Barbara's History*, p. 164). Through this aspect of Barbara's 'humanity', Edwards depicts the problems of reconciling the woman with the artist, illustrating how Barbara's feminine yearning for love comes between her and her art. Disappointed, for instance, by her family's indifference to her, Barbara explains, 'Profoundly dejected, I painted on, effacing each touch as soon as made, pausing every now and then for very lassitude' (*Barbara's History*, p. 174). Similarly, when her patient love for Hugh is finally rewarded in their marriage, she exclaims, 'Can you not guess, Hugh, why I have been so very, very idle? ... because I am too happy to sketch. Too happy for even Art to make me happier' (*Barbara's History*, p. 258).

While Edwards fulfils conventional expectations by subordinating the artist to the woman once Barbara is married, she subsequently undermines these expectations by disrupting the domestic idyll she creates through a sensational twist in the tale. Barbara's happiness is quickly foreshortened when, shortly after coming to live at Hugh's country estate, she comes to believe he has another wife who he keeps hidden in a secluded part of the house. Appalled and devastated by her discovery, Barbara looks for solace in the company of a like-minded artist-friend, Ida, when she secretly leaves Hugh and goes to live in Rome, the 'artist's Paradise' (*Barbara's History*, p. 136). Barbara and Ida fulfil their schoolgirl dreams of living in the geographical centre of classical artistry where they 'hire a studio; paint together; study together; wander together in the ruins of the Forum' (*Barbara's History*, p. 136). While their practical and sisterly approach to living in Rome might have appeared transgressive under less sensational circumstances, the sensational plot device of the novel offers Barbara a strong justification for her actions. Painting to support herself and her newborn son, Barbara lives a life in Rome that appears respectably domestic and certainly preferable to a bigamous and scandalous marriage.

Although Edwards ultimately re-establishes a more familiar Victorian narrative – showing Barbara's assumptions to have been mistaken, redeeming the disgraced Hugh, and reuniting the estranged couple – Barbara's Roman interlude remains a positive expression of professional female work and mutual support. Thus the

---

57 Amelia Blanford Edwards, *Barbara's History* (London: Rubicon, 2000), pp. 163-64. Further references to this edition will be given in the text.

sensationalist plot device is used to excuse a utopian, if brief, vision of artistic sisterhood. Like *Olive* and *The Tenant of Wildfell Hall*, *Barbara's History* typifies a gathering trend in the 1850s and 1860s to establish and define female-centred spaces for work. Such narratives implicitly opened an alternative to models of female artistic labour commensurable with the patriarchal home. In the case of *Barbara's History*, this alternative is fully realised in the relationship between Barbara and Ida and the sisterly, though limited, community they develop in Rome. The idea of such a community spirit between artistic women also had a significant impact on the perception of artistic production as a remunerative profession for women.

'Art-sisters': Female Communities in the Victorian Art World

Recollecting, in *An Art Student in Munich* (1853), her own experience, Anna Mary Howitt describes how female communities, both actual and notional, could provide a woman artist with the support and inspiration necessary to pursue a career in art. Her participation in a female community begins with a visit she and her fellow student Clare (her pseudonym for Jane Benham Hay) received from Justina (Barbara Bodichon). This visit evokes Justina's enthusiastic desire to establish a female utopia:

> A large scheme of what she calls the Outer and Inner Sisterhood. The Inner, to consist of the Art-sisters bound together by their one object ... the Outer Sisterhood to consist of women, all workers, and all striving after a pure moral life, but belonging to any profession, any pursuit.[58]

Justina sees places in the Sisterhood for not only the artist, but also, among others, the needlewoman and the cook, where each woman works according to her taste and pleasure, serving the general good of the community and allowing the community to be self-sufficient. This vision of a supportive, nonexclusive, female community was derived by Bodichon, in part, from the work she was already involved in for the feminist movements that were emerging at mid-century. Daughter of a Radical MP and a first cousin of Florence Nightingale, Bodichon, along with Bessie Rayner Parkes, became a leader of the women's movements centred around their offices in Langham Place, the birth place of both the *English Woman's Journal* and the Society for Promoting the Employment of Women.[59] This vision later came to fruition in various schemes in which Bodichon was involved such as the establishment of the Portfolio

---

58   Anna Mary Howitt, *An Art Student in Munich* (1853), rpt. in *Canvassing: Recollections by Six Victorian Women Artists,* Pamela Gerrish Nunn, ed. (London: Camden Press, 1986) p. 36. Further references to this edition will be given in the text.

59   Pam Hirsch, *Barbara Leigh Smith Bodichon, 1827–1891: Feminist, Artist and Rebel* (London: Pimlico, 1999).

Club at the Leigh Smith house and the founding of the Society of Female Artists (SFA) in 1857.[60]

While discussing their dreams, the women of Howitt's story experience a moment of 'the sublimest intellectual emotion' in which the three 'art-sisters' transcend the mundane, if only briefly, as they sit in the studio 'and dr[i]nk in the whole spirit of the place' (*Art Student*, p. 33). Howitt expresses the relationship between female artists as a spiritual connection that fosters cooperation rather than competition – a sisterhood 'by which association we might be enabled to do noble things' (*Art Student*, p. 36). The bases for this sisterhood are notions not only of support, but also of mutual stimulus and inspiration. Howitt describes this second feature when she notes that, as Howitt and Clare show Justina around their studio, Justina finds the scene inspirational, and 'having seen what [they] were beginning', she takes 'into her memory all the features of the beloved little room, so that she could picture our lives when she should have again vanished' (*Art Student*, p. 32). Although these women are just students, working under the tutelage of a male painting master, the master is not present in the scene Justina memorises for her future picture. By representing the scene as she has seen it, Justina has the power to reimagine and redefine the women's position from that of students to that of the Art-Sisters they desire to be. Justina can construct her picture so as to promote the aims of her subjects, portraying them as artists, but the scene has also given her the inspiration for her own artistic creation, an image she can take home with her and represent not only for the furtherance of her own career, but also for the inspiration of other female artists. Howitt and Clare have set up their own limited version of artistic sisterhood in Munich where they live and work together for their mutual support and benefit. Along with their painting careers, this community is what they 'have been beginning', and Justina can bring this notion home with her as an example for fellow female artists.

These notions of mutual support and stimulus that characterise this vision of a sisterhood of artists were the model for female associations throughout the second half of the century.[61] They also became an important tool in defending

---

60   Pam Hirsch, 'Barbara Leigh Smith Bodichon: Artist and Activist', *Women in the Victorian Art World*, Clarissa Campbell Orr, ed., pp. 167-86.

61   Jan Marsh, 'Art, Ambition and Sisterhood in the 1850s', pp. 33-48.

female art communities, such as the Female School of Art (FSA)[62] and the SFA,[63] from the criticisms of their detractors. As Martha Vicinus notes, 'Attacks upon single women and their communities generally focused on the threatened loss of a woman's mothering and her denial of family duties'.[64] But, by highlighting the nurturing and protective function of the professional artist to her art 'sisters', arguments in support of such societies countered the censure that such communities could be anathema to a woman's domestic duties. Furthermore, the notion of women helping women also extended beyond the formation of actual communities and the emotional and economic support these communities afforded.[65] Whitney Chadwick explains that a number of women artists 'turned to the writing of women and to history's heroic women for subjects that would enable them to enter the field of history painting'.[66] For many women artists for whom history painting was a male-dominated and unapproachable genre, the use of the female figure as their subject made this genre more accessible. Lucy Madox Brown, for instance, found success with the historical

---

62 The Female School of Art was founded in 1842 by a grant distributed by the government for the establishment of schools for design. For 17 years this school received £500 out of the annual £1500 grant until 1859 when the government decided to discontinue its funding. In 1851 the school was moved, because of its rapidly growing number of students, from its initial home with other schools of design in Somerset House, to cramped and unhealthy premises above a soap manufacturers in the Strand, but the public outcry against such unsuitable premises which were 'in the close vicinity of several gin-shops, pawn shops, and old-rag shops, and some of the worst courts and alleys of London' led to the removal of the school to a better location in Gower Street [(anon.), 'Female School of Design', *Art Journal* 3 (1851), p. 121]. After the withdrawal of public funds, a private subscription allowed the school to continue and permanent premises were bought for it in Queen's Square. For contemporary discussions of the Female School of Art see 'Right Hon. A.J. Mundella, MP.', *Artist* 4 (1883), pp. 100-101; J. Cordy Jeaffreson, 'Female Artists and Art Schools of England', *Art Pictorial and Industrial* 1 (1870), pp. 25-30, 50-52, 70-73; F.D. Maurice, 'Female School of Art; Mrs. Jameson', *Macmillan's Magazine* 2 (1860), pp. 227-35; Louisa Gann, 'The Gower Street (Female) School of Art', *Art Journal* 12 (1860), p. 61. A complete history of the school is contained within, F. Graeme Chalmers, *Women in the Nineteenth-Century Art World: Schools of Art and Design for Women in London and Philadelphia* (London: Greenwood Press, 1998).

63 The Society of Female Artists was founded in 1857 in order to provide women artists with the opportunity to control their own exhibition circumstances. The history of the society is described in detail by Charlotte Yeldham in *Women Artists in Nineteenth-Century France and England*, esp. chap 2, part 3. Pamela Gerrish Nunn also provides an extensive investigation of the importance of the society as a forum for exhibition in *Victorian Women Artists*.

64 Martha Vicinus, *Independent Women: Work and Community for Single Women, 1850-1920* (London: Virago Press, 1985), p. 31.

65 For a fuller discussion of the sisterly relationship between female artists and their fellow artists, subjects, and 'matrons' see Susan P. Casteras and Linda H. Peterson, *A Struggle for Fame: Victorian Women Artists and Authors* (New Haven: Yale Center for British Art, 1994).

66 Whitney Chadwick, *Women, Art, and Society*, p. 189.

figure of Margaret Roper in her large oil painting, *Margaret Roper Rescuing the Head of her Father Sir Thomas More* (1873), and Henrietta Ward was highly praised for her depiction of *Queen Mary Quitting Stirling Castle* (1863). The notion of a sisterhood for all women, therefore, offered the woman artist the means to claim for herself the imaginative freedom and technical superiority generally reserved for the male artist. A history painting would not be considered unfeminine if it depicted, as Madox Brown's did, a shining example of filial duty. Margaret Roper risking her own life in order to give her father a proper burial, or Queen Mary hovering over her child in a final goodbye, offered images of 'proper' feminine behaviour even amidst unusual circumstances and very undomestic events.

The idea of mutually supporting sisterhoods among artists infiltrated every aspect of women's art. In his article on 'Female Artists and Art-Schools of England' for *Art Pictorial and Industrial* in 1870, for instance, John Cordy Jeaffreson focuses on the idea of sisterhood and its domestic associations to describe the form of artistic instruction that most women received. In this article, Jeaffreson chronicles the history of the Female School of Art, beginning with its establishment in 1842 'partly to enable young women of the middle class to obtain honourable and profitable employment and partly to improve ornamental design in manufactures, by cultivating the taste of the designer'.[67] From this economic and manufacturing-based beginning, the Female School of *Design* was transformed into the Female School of *Art* in which 'the majority of the students are the daughters of prosperous and gentle homes', and not more than half the pupils 'have a definite purpose of earning their livelihood by artistic labour'.[68] As art replaced design in the name of the school, the domestic woman replaced the working woman as the pupil of choice in the school prospectus. Accompanying, or perhaps instigating, this conversion was what Jeaffreson claimed to be a transformation in the method of female art instruction. Before the nineteenth century, he writes, female painters were educated in 'the home in which they ministered to the daily needs and promoted the domestic happiness of the men who were at the same time their near relations and their instructors in art'.[69] Against this domestic education, Jeaffreson offers the FSA as a desirable alternative because, 'it is a school maintained exclusively for womankind, that its teachers are all women, and that every care is taken for the preservation of womanly tone amongst the pupils, are facts that commend the establishment to the favour of parents who desire for their girls the benefits of sound artistic culture'.[70] Through the FSA, women's artistic education was no longer the responsibility of men, and particularly their male relations; it became instead the province of a female teacher in a female-run school.

---

67   J. Cordy Jeaffreson, 'Female Artists and Art-Schools of England', p. 52. This article was published in three consecutive issues in the first volume of the journal.

68   Ibid.

69   Ibid., p. 28.

70   Ibid., p. 52.

The role of the male art teacher and male institutions such as the Royal Academy did not, however, disappear in discussions of women's artistic education and exhibition. Even while awarding the annual prizes at the FSA in 1866, the new president of the Royal Academy, Sir Francis Grant, declared his position as a 'warm advocate of the admission of lady students to the Royal Academy'.[71] Although there were no regulations against admitting a woman to the Royal Academy, there were no women students at the Academy until 1860. The first female student, Anna Laura Hereford, was eventually only grudgingly granted entrance, her admittance was allowed after much debate and resistance when it was discovered that the 'L. Hereford' who had applied and been accepted was a woman.[72] Also, despite Grant's assurances, no female students were admitted to the Royal Academy between 1864 and 1868.[73] This exclusion from the Royal Academy was generally seen as a disadvantage to the woman artist.[74] And the formation of alternative institutions, such as FSA and the SFA, offered women a way to combat the monopoly on the marketplace enjoyed by the male-dominated exhibition societies.[75] In reviewing the second exhibition of the SFA the *English Woman's Journal* noted the advantages of such an institution:

> This society affords a new industrial opening to women. It brings a class together, gives them *espirit de corps*, and forcibly draws the attention of the public to the number of those who follow art as a profession, and will stimulate many a young painter who would have despaired of the Royal Academy.[76]

This set of exclusively female-centred art institutions were put in place to deny patriarchal control over women's artistic production and exhibition, and they called for a form of solidarity among female artists. But while the rhetoric of sisterhood flourished, the reality proved somewhat different. The first few years of the annual exhibition of the SFA was, according to the *English Woman's Journal*, marked by the 'absence of notabilities in the world of art'.[77]

The difficulties of this notion of sisterhood are concisely described by Tamar Garb when she writes that 'Bonds of affection, conspiratorial and collusive allegiances,

---

71   'Sir F. Grant at the Female School of Art', *Englishwoman's Review* 1 (1868), p. 396.

72   'Miss Louisa Hereford', *Art Journal* 23 (1871), p. 80.

73   H.C. Morgan, 'The Lost Opportunity of the Royal Academy: An Assessment of its Position in the Nineteenth Century', *Journal of the Warburg and Courtauld Institutes* 32 (1969), p. 415.

74   See, for instance, 'The Royal Academy and Female Artists', *English Woman's Journal* 7 (1861), pp. 71-72; A.R., 'The Royal Academy', *Athenaeum* no. 1637 (12 March 1859), pp. 361-62; C.E.B., *Athenaeum* no. 1638 (March 19 1859), p. 394; 'Female Students at the Royal Academy', *Art Journal* 18 (1866), p. 94.

75   See, for instance, 'Society of Female Artists', *Englishwoman's Review* ns 1 (1871), pp. 149-50.

76   'The Society of Female Artists', *English Woman's Journal* 1 (1858), p. 205.

77   'The Fifth Annual Exhibition of the Society of Female Artists', *English Woman's Journal* 7 (1861), p. 60.

and shared experiences, were offset by envy and competitiveness, rivalry and personal ambition'.[78] Although Garb is writing about the Union of Women Painters and Sculptors in Paris at the end of the century, the lesson is the same. 'Like sisters', she notes, 'the members of the *Union des Femmes Peintres et Sculpteurs* were bonded together against the hostility of an exclusionary outside world, but like sisters they had to deal with the negative emotions which characterise all classic family dramas'.[79] The restrictions of societies like the Paris Union and the SFA were created by the very exclusionary practices they adopted. A woman could only achieve limited success by choosing to exhibit her best work at the SFA rather than the Royal Academy, and throughout the 1850s and 1860s, the *Art Journal* repeatedly pleaded with successful women artists to save at least something for the SFA:

> We do not ask them to forego the advantages attending an appearance in the Royal Academy and elsewhere, but we do ask them to reserve a portion of their strength to further the object of their sisters in Art. A combination of the female 'Art-power' of the country could not possibly fail to make itself felt and respected to an extent which would operate beneficially upon all who might contribute to it.[80]

Those successful women artists who did participate in these seemingly less advantageous exhibitions were highly praised by the *Journal*. For instance, on the occasion of the 15th annual exhibition of the society, the *Art Journal* commented, 'It is highly to the credit of Mrs. Ward and Madame Jerichau (artists of the very highest and best established renown) that they exhibit here, and help a society that works under many disadvantages. They set a high standard, and a high standard is just what woman's work requires in every department of work'.[81] The *Journal* implies that by mere example these renowned artists could help ameliorate the many disadvantages the society worked under, such as limited funding, cramped studios, and inadequate teaching, and that they could in this way raise the standard of women's artwork.

The reaction to the fifth exhibition by the *English Woman's Journal* provides an interesting example of the limits of sisterhood. Itself a female undertaking begun by, among others, Barbara Bodichon, the *Journal* praises the contributions of 'notabilities' from the British art world and French artists like Rosa Bonheur. All paintings, however, are not so equally welcomed. 'There are some few', the *Journal* sneers, 'so irredeemably bad that we can only wonder how they gained admittance; neither the would-be artist nor the art is served by the feeling, kindly though it be, which secures such pictures a place on the walls'.[82] The *Journal*'s comments, while completely consistent with critical practice, disparage the 'kindly' feelings that the ideals of sisterhood demand. In practical experience, the utopian notions

---

78 Tamar Garb, *Sisters of the Brush: Women's Artistic Culture in Late Nineteenth-Century Paris* (New Haven: Yale University Press, 1994), p. 3.

79 Ibid.

80 'The Society of Female Artists', *Art Journal* 9 (1857), p. 216.

81 'The Society of Female Artists', *Art Journal* 24 (1872), p. 90.

82 'The Fifth Annual Exhibition of the Society of Female Artists', p. 60.

of sisterhood bend under the pressures of taste and aesthetics. The very existence of the Society thus helped to establish the kind of hierarchy between the various levels of female artists that it purported to work against. Those successful female artists who forewent the Royal Academy exhibition or saved their lesser pieces for the SFA occupied a similarly condescending position as those male artists and critics who admired and supported the pretty drawings of the 'lady painter'. And the call for them to instruct and protect their fellow artists defined them more as a mother rather than a sister to the ordinary female artist. The principles of sisterhood were thus transformed from an ideal of equality to a practical system of mutual benefit. While the lesser artist could get greater public exposition and the possible sale of her work, the better known artist, through the educative and nurturing qualities of her matriarchal role, could enhance her professional success and her domestic reputation at the same time.

By the 1860s the principle of compatibility was being used to indicate a form of female creativity that could exist independently from conventional domesticity. Whether it was located in institutionalised organisations like the FSA and the SFA or in visions of the transformed drawing room, the principle of compatibility helped shape the image of domesticity as a mutable concept. The very principle that was initially employed to validate female artistry by stressing its connection with the domestic sphere was therefore being used to justify the contention, made by a writer for the *English Woman's Journal* and discussed in the introduction, 'that a woman may be employed in other work than household, and yet be domestic in the simple meaning of the word'.[83] Thus, the process of redefining the woman artist's marginal experience as a form of female-centred artistry proved to be a successful method for constructing an image of domesticity that could exist outside the physical space of the home.

Art and Industry: The Economics of Compatibility

The representations of female artists that asserted the principle of compatibility helped transform the working woman's marginal identity into a mainstream image of respectable femininity, but they also opened the door for respectable employment for middle-class women in the industrial sphere, employment that was determined to be elevating as well as domestic in character. This type of employment is described in an article for *Eliza Cook's Journal* in 1851 in which the author notes:

> In the arts of design connected with our various branches of manufacture, women might be usefully employed. Why should not they be as competent, by proper training, to execute a pattern for a dress, for a chandelier, or for a grate, as to choose one?[84]

---

83 A.R.L., 'Facts *Versus* Ideas', *English Woman's Journal* 7 (1861), p. 74.
84 'The Ladies' Guild', *Eliza Cook's Journal* 5 (1851), p. 277.

In this article, the writer suggests that the primary consumers of domestic goods ought, perhaps, to be the best equipped to design them. Who better to design an attractive and effective grate than someone who personally knows what the customer wants? Bringing the fundamental capitalist principle of supply and demand to bear on the problem of women's work in this way suggested that consumers, producers, and the marketplace in general would benefit if domestic products matched domestic need. In this light, the provision of 'proper training' for women as well as men was a sensible measure dedicated to ensuring that the economy, as well as the home, could be effectively managed. Furthermore, there was no reason to think that such training and labour would in any way diminish women's femininity or the quality of their work. 'Occupations such as these are perfectly elegant', confirms the author, adding, 'they are also highly remunerative'.[85] Such work would remain 'domestic in the simple meaning of the word', but would enable women to enter the public, commercial, and professional sphere of industrial work.

Although the writer acknowledges the connections between the art-industries and the manufacturing sector, the brief description of items that women could be called upon to design emphasises the domestic character of the work. The design of a dress, a chandelier, or a grate could be used to enhance the beauty of the home, and the woman, in providing the designs for these items, could be considered to be contributing to the ornamentation of her own domestic sphere. The woman's domestic qualifications for providing for the ornamentation of her domestic sphere are noted by a writer for *Harper's Magazine* who argues that 'a wife being gayly adorned, her whole house is embellished; but if she be destitute of ornaments, all will be deprived of decoration'.[86] The link between the woman's traditional function as a decorative feature of the household with her work in art-industries suggests an easy progression from her role as ornament, to ornamentor of the home, and ultimately to a position as designer of these ornaments. The woman's ornamental function could therefore be expanded, step by step, to include her work in a public industry that would otherwise seem at odds with her domestic identity.

This strategy, which gained in strength and scope from the 1860s onward, used association with the domestic sphere in order to define the industrial employment involved in the production of the art-industries as 'suitable employment for women'.[87] In the *Art Journal* in 1860, for instance, John Stewart named 'art-

---

85 Ibid.

86 Monoure Conway, *Harper's Magazine,* rpt. in *Women and Work* no. 22 (31 October 1874), p. 3.

87   J. Stewart, 'Art-Decoration: A Suitable Employment for Women', *Art Journal* 12 (1860), p. 70. Such arguments were repeatedly made in the periodical press, as a very brief survey will show. See 'Photography as an Employment for Women', *Englishwoman's Review* 1 (1867), pp. 219-23; *Women and Work* no. 56 (26 June 1875), p. 4; M.G., 'Industrial Art-Work', *Woman's Gazette* 1 (1875), pp. 11, 27-29, 73-74 ['Industrial Art-Work' was a semi-regular column in *Woman's Gazette* which reported the latest developments and achievement in the art-industries]; 'Art Work for Women', *Artist* 4 (1883), pp. 38-39; B.C. Saward, 'Artistic Occupations for Ladies', *Lady's World* (1887), pp. 29-31, 138-39.

decoration' and other 'kindred branches of Art industries', such as pattern designing for a wide range of domestic items, as suited to women for three reasons: it was not strenuous; it yielded a fair profit that supplied a 'respectable maintenance', and it was a new industry that would not 'interfere with the present employment of men'.[88] Stewart's explanation situates art-decoration as a much more genteel occupation than other industrial employments available to women and implicitly suggests that art-decoration differed significantly from the types of labour carried out by women of the working class. It is not strenuous like the physically demanding work required from the women workers on farms and in coalmines; it realises a fair profit unlike the more common piecework professions such as needlework and homework; and the women workers would not be filling positions that had previously belonged to men as they did in the potteries and cotton mills.[89] In spite of this important distinction, the 'art-industries' were directly dependent on the manufacturing sector. Many factories employed pattern designers full-time, exposing the designers to the evils of factory life. While some (though not all) designers worked directly in the factories for which they designed patterns, the associations that were made between such design work and the domestic sphere discursively 'de-industrialised' their work and reimagined it as a domestic activity. In characterising the art-industries as a genteel occupation suitable for women, Stewart considered the female designer as an 'artisan' rather than a factory worker.[90]

The domestic character that permeated the art-industries was chronicled by a regular column that appeared in the monthly journal the *Artist*. This column, titled 'Art in the House', included recent innovations and issues within the art industries such as designs for tapestries, jewellery, furnishings, and wall papers. As the journal explains, 'It is intended to be, in a measure, the Ladies' Column of the paper'.[91] Although the column dealt principally with these industrially produced commodities, it assigned them to the province of 'art and taste'. It tended to de-industrialise these art-industries by associating them with the work of women in the domestic sphere and with the elevated status of artistic work. In fact, many new areas of employment for women were justified by emphasising their artistic credentials. The 'art of mosaic working', the tinting of photographs, or the cutting of shell-cameos were all promoted as both artistic and remunerative employment.[92] Etching, for example,

---

88   Stewart, 'Art Decoration', p. 70.

89   For a discussion of occupations of working-class women, see, for instance, Duncan Blythell, 'Women in the Workforce', *The Industrial Revolution and British Society,* Patrick K. O'Brien and Roland Quinault, eds (Cambridge: Cambridge University Press, 1993), pp. 31-53.

90   Harriet Martineau, 'Female Industry', p. 334.

91   'Art in the House', *Artist* 1 (1880), p. 85.

92   'Mosaic Working as an Employment for Women', *Women and Work* no. 8 (25 July 1874), p. 3; 'Photographic Colouring', *Women and Work* no. 13 (29 Aug. 1874), p. 2; 'Cameo-Cutting by Lady Artists', *Builder*, rpt. in *Women and Work* no. 27 (5 Dec. 1874), p. 4. Many of these new 'artistic' employments were promoted by Emily Faithfull's weekly newspaper *Women and Work*, which was published between 1874-76.

was described as an occupation that required 'patience and perseverance, and great care in keeping every thing used clean and free from dust', and this suggested to some observers an employment perfectly suited to the temperament and skills of the domestic woman.[93] Henry Blackburn further outlined the advantages of etching when he argued, 'There is opportunity here for practicing a new field of art (for it is an art), proficiency in which will produce employment'.[94] As with most descriptions of the increasing variety of 'artistic employments' open to women, Blackburn's insistence that etching was an art implicitly assumed the suitability of art as an occupation for women. Such arguments linked women, art, and remunerative work with the domestic sphere, regardless of the actual location in which this work was performed. The art-industries could be conceived of not only in terms of manufacturing work destined for the domestic sphere, but also as extensions of the domestic sphere in which women could unproblematically play their part.

The elevation brought to women working in the decorative industries through their connection with the 'high culture' qualities of art was explored by Margaret Oliphant in her representation of the 'little gentlewoman' and 'young Preraphaelite' Rose Lake in *Miss Marjoribanks* (1866).[95] Daughter of the town's drawing master, Rose is in charge of the female pupils at the local School of Design and spends her spare time creating her own designs. Her sister Barbara also possesses artistic talent, but her talent takes the form of an outstanding singing voice. Although their family is not considered to be socially desirable by the Carlingford gentry, the artistry of Rose's interesting designs and her sister Barbara's striking contralto earn them invitations to Lucilla Marjoribanks's weekly parties. But even though their artistic talents have gained them entry to genteel society, their status as professional women places them on the margins of this society. Elisabeth Jay argues that the artistic professionalism that Barbara and Rose show is mocked within the novel as an endeavour that 'must deprive a woman of all claims to be a "lady"'.[96] But in Rose and Barbara's respective reactions to their marginality, Oliphant offers a perspective on the social power a woman could exert by embracing such marginal status. While Rose only goes to Lucilla's evenings a few times and remains proud and inconspicuous, Barbara's temerity in putting herself forward merely confirms her as 'an intruder into those regions of the blest' (*Miss Marjoribanks*, p. 85). Even the supposed romantic rivalry between Barbara and Lucilla over Mr. Cavendish is depicted, from Barbara's point-of-view, as as much a contest between the two women, as it is about desire for Mr. Cavendish's affection. When Lucilla fails to show jealousy over Barbara's relationship with Mr. Cavendish, 'Barbara could have

---

93   'Etching As an Employment for Women', *Women and Work* no. 9 (1 Aug. 1874), p. 2.

94   Henry Blackburn, 'Artistic Employment for Women', *Women and Work* no. 5 (4 June 1874), p. 2.

95   Margaret Oliphant, *Miss Marjoribanks*, Elisabeth Jay, ed. (London: Penguin Books, 1998), p. 145. Further references to this edition will be given in the text.

96   Elisabeth Jay, 'Introduction', *Miss Marjoribanks*, p. xxx.

eaten her fingers instead of the gloves which she kept biting in her vexation. For to tell the truth, if Miss Marjoribanks was not jealous, the victory was but half a victory after all' (*Miss Marjoribanks*, p. 112). Barbara assumes her equality with the polite society she encounters, and in consequence is frustrated in her ambitions and denigrated by this society until she leaves Carlingford in order to become a governess.

Although only a designer, Rose, on the other hand, assumes a professional identity that places her in a social position that is marginal to both the genteel and the working classes. She tries to convince Barbara that 'The true strength of our position is that we are a family of artists. We are everybody's equal, and we are nobody's equal. We have a rank of our own' (*Miss Marjoribanks*, p. 96). In rejecting traditional distinctions of class and embracing her individual rank as artist, Rose earns the respect of the society she shuns while her sister is rejected by the society she seeks. While Barbara, jilted by Mr. Cavendish, stands alone at one of Lucilla's Thursday evenings, 'all wan and crumpled', Rose 'electrified all the people who were fond of art' (*Miss Marjoribanks*, p. 155). The little attention that is given to Rose by literary critics tends to define her, as artist, as the representative of the author.[97] By setting Rose off against Lucilla, the queen-like figure who rules over her subjects in Carlingford, and Barbara, the poor but beautiful woman who has ambitions to rise above her station through marriage, Oliphant depicts the artist as someone who exists outside the issues that rule conventional women's lives.

Oliphant, however, shows some ambivalence about Rose. This is evident, as Elizabeth Winston has shown, in the diminished role granted to Rose between the serial and the three-volume publication of the novel. Winston argues that in excising a portion of Rose's story, Oliphant moves Rose's story to the margins of the text and 'reduced [her] focus on the professional female artist'.[98] This ambivalence about Rose ensures that her marginal respectability extends primarily to her professional identity. When Lucilla's acquaintance, General Travers, is struck by Rose's beauty, he is 'crestfallen' to learn that she is 'not a lady to speak of, but only a drawing-master's daughter' (*Miss Marjoribanks*, p. 244). Even Rose herself acknowledges that any attention she receives from gentlemen is the result of her artistic ability and tries to define her sister's relationship with Mr. Cavendish in a similar way: '"One of the gentlemen from Marlborough House once took off his hat to me', said Rose, with a certain solemnity. 'Of course I was pleased; but then I knew it was my design he was thinking of – my Honiton flounce, you know. I suppose this other one must have thought you had a pretty voice'" (*Miss Marjoribanks*, p. 95). The gentility Rose possesses is not a product of her birth or her character; it is a direct result of her work as a designer for the art-industries. Rose is, as Linda Peterson notes, is the only female character who looks to something other than marriage in order to

---

97   See, for instance, Gail Turley Houston, *Royalties: The Queen and Victorian Writers* (Charlottesville: University of Virginia Press, 1999), p. 156.

98   Elizabeth Winston, 'Revising Miss Marjoribanks', *Nineteenth-Century Studies* 9 (1995), p. 89.

define her identity.[99] But straying from the accepted pattern of female development is ultimately unsustainable for Rose, who must give up her artistic career in order to look after her family. Yet even after the loss of this career, Rose, unlike her sister, remains 'unspeakably respectable' (*Miss Marjoribanks*, p. 449). In this way, Rose's experience inverts the principle of compatibility, and the domestic is made respectable, and even attractive, by the professional.

The influence of the art-industries on the domestic identity of a woman who worked outside the home also served as the focus of one of Charlotte Yonge's lesser well-known works, *Beechcroft at Rockstone* (1888). In this novel, Yonge deals with the difficulty encountered by a reduced gentlewoman who is forced by economic necessity to take a job as a designer for a marble works. In this job, Kalliope White is frustrated in her desire to create beautiful designs by the manufacturer's demand for items that will sell. But even amidst the atmosphere of the works, which 'was full of ugly slated or iron-roofed sheds, rough workmen, and gratings and screeches of machinery', she maintains her office as a domestic sanctuary.[100] This office, with its 'terra-cotta vase of flowers' and windows 'blocked with transparencies delicately cut and tinted in cardboard', is filled with a 'perfect neatness and simplicity ... which rendered it by no means an unfit setting for the grave beauty of Kalliope's countenance and figure'.[101] Like Brontë and Craik, Yonge offers an image of a woman artist who combines her working with her domestic space, but it is the factory not the drawing room in which Kalliope works. Hers is a marginal space that inverts the artistic colonisation of the domestic sphere by bringing domesticity into the workplace. Domesticity here is shown to be a mutable concept that can be transported outside the sphere of the home.

It is mainly Kalliope's own gentility, along with her decorating and decorative function, which imbues the industrial setting of her workroom with its domestic character. But the quality of her artistic designs also contributes to the domestication of the space. Her beautiful designs hang about the room and form an idiosyncratic wallpaper for her office. Again, domesticity and art work together to define the art-industries as suitable and respectable employment, but the influence of her artistic spirit instils Kalliope with an air of refinement beyond that of mere domesticity. Art elevates Kalliope's domestic identity even while it appeals to the domestic for respectability. Furthermore, it also elevates the workplace and the work conducted within it. Kalliope's office is a microcosm of domestic orderliness and decoration, and it brings a profoundly civilising influence to bear on her colleagues and the rough environment that surrounds it. As such it reflects on the ideologically loaded nineteenth-century conception of the civilising influence the middle classes could

---

99   Linda Peterson, 'The Female *Bildungsroman*: Tradition and Revision in Oliphant's Fiction', *Margaret Oliphant: Critical Essays on a Gentle Subversive*, D.J. Trela, ed. (Selingsgrove, PA: Susquehanna University Press, 1995).

100   Charlotte M. Yonge, *Beechcroft at Rockstone* (London: Macmillan and Co., 1893), p. 55.

101   Ibid., pp. 81-82.

exert on their working-class inferiors. If such civilising influences could ultimately be identified with principles of domestic management and decoration, then the most significant enlightenment projects of the age could also be described as feminine in disposition.

Art-industry, whether realised in the form of house decoration, etching, or pattern design, came to represent employment for women that was simultaneously respectable, remunerative, and domestic, but it also influenced the perception of domesticity itself. Domesticity and remunerative work were no longer irreconcilable alternatives. Indeed, as Martineau implied in 'Female Industry', the currency and status of domesticity might be considerably advanced by its participation in the modern industrial marketplace, whose effective functions were at the heart of Britain's cherished economic dominance. Entering the industrial workplace in order to introduce a civilising influence could also, then, be described as 'properly woman's work'.

Chapter 3

'The Difference is Great in Being Known to Write and Setting up for an Authoress': Representing the Writing Woman

The discourse of compatibility between art and the domestic sphere that was so influential in representations of the artist was also employed by Victorian authors in order to legitimate their characters', and their own, creative ambitions. In *Aurora Leigh*, for instance, Elizabeth Barrett Browning, as I have shown, characterises Aurora's conventional domestic activity of sewing as a screen behind which she can conceal her poetic musings. As Aurora describes her early domestic life, she explains:

> Then I sat and teased
> The patient needle till it split the thread,
> Which oozed off from it in meandering lace
> From hour to hour. I was not, therefore, sad;
> My soul was singing at a work apart
> Behind the wall of sense, as safe from harm
> As sings the lark when sucked up out of sight
> In vortices of glory and blue air.
> And so, through forced work and spontaneous work,
> The inner life informed the outer life,
> Reduced the irregular blood to a settled rhythm,
> Made cool the forehead with fresh-sprinkling dreams.[1]

Whether or not Aurora's sewing actually helps in her development as a poet, or provides a creative stimulus, as Jennie Croly had argued it could, sewing and poetry are at least shown to be compatible. Not only can Aurora soar on the heights of aesthetic sensibility while she sews, but also such a rich 'inner life' helps her meet the drudgery of her womanly duty with equanimity. However, unlike the bright crimson screen that contains Olive Rothesay's artistry while boldly announcing its place in her domestic identity, Aurora's screen of needlework completely obscures her

---

1   Elizabeth Barrett Browning, *Aurora Leigh*, Kerry McSweeney, ed. (Oxford: Oxford University Press, 1993), Book I, lines 1049-60. Further references to this edition will be given by book and line numbers in the text.

inner poetic life from the outside world. In concealing Aurora's artistry in this way, Barrett Browning participates in what Mary Jean Corbett describes as the middle-class woman writer's 'tactful silences'. Such schemes, she argues, were a denial of the public and professional nature of her work: '[K]nowing themselves to be divided between the privacy of the domestic and the publicity of the market, they may yet minimize the effects of their rupture with conventional femininity by not calling attention to it'.[2] Similarly, Valerie Sanders demonstrates that the autobiographies of female writers seemed to attend only rarely to the actual practice of writing.[3] While Corbett and Sanders are speaking specifically about how women writers represent themselves in autobiographical works, I would suggest that this deliberate silence could also account for the relative paucity of representations of women writers in women's fiction of the mid-Victorian period. Although there was a proliferation of fictional female writers in New Woman novels, there are only a few narratives from the mid-Victorian period that feature an authoress as their heroine.[4] Even the number of periodical articles written about women writers does not approach those about seamstresses, artists, or actresses. Where such discussions do appear, they often tend to be in the form of reviews or biographical pieces where the issue of woman as author cannot be so easily ignored. Silence was both a personal choice and a cultural mechanism for diffusing the tensions created by the introduction of the private woman's voice to the public sphere.

While silence may have appeared the preferable option, authors in the nineteenth century faced an increasingly voyeuristic public. Seeking to break this silence, readers sought to uncover the personality of the author behind the work. Some, as Linda Shires points out, looked to the author's life for this information and appropriated the author as a public figure to be gazed at and their private life as a commodity to be consumed.[5] Others looked to the work the author produced as the key that could penetrate the reality behind the name. This view of literature as a key to personality is defined by M.H. Abrams as a 'strange innovation' of the Romantic aesthetic that defines art as the creation of the individual subjectivity of the artist. In his classic work on the Romantic tradition, *The Mirror and the Lamp*, Abrams writes, 'For good or ill, the widespread use of literature as an index – as the most reliable index

---

2   Mary Jean Corbett, *Representing Femininity: Middle-Class Subjectivity in Victorian and Edwardian Women's Autobiographies* (Oxford: Oxford University Press, 1992), pp. 72, 58-59.

3   Valerie Sanders, *The Private Lives of Victorian Women: Autobiography in Nineteenth-Century England* (London: Harvester Wheatsheaf, 1989), pp. 75-101.

4   For a discussion of the woman writer in New Woman fiction, see Lyn Pykett, 'Portraits of the Artist as a Young Woman: Representations of the Female Artist in New Woman Fiction of the 1890s', *Victorian Women Writers and the Woman Question*, Nicola Diane Thompson, ed. (Cambridge: Cambridge University Press, 1999), pp. 135-50.

5   Linda M. Shires, 'The Author as Spectacle and Commodity: Elizabeth Barrett Browning and Thomas Hardy', *Victorian Literature and the Victorian Imagination*, Carol T. Christ and John O. Jordan, eds (Berkeley: University of California Press, 1995), pp. 198-212.

– to personality was a product of the characteristic aesthetic orientation of the early nineteenth century'.[6]

Abrams introduces this idea with an epigraph from Thomas Carlyle's 1840 lecture, 'The Hero as Poet', in which Carlyle, writing about Shakespeare, had claimed, 'His works are so many windows, through which we see a glimpse of the world that was in him'. What this epigraph and Abrams make clear is not only the place of the literary work in advancing the popular interest in personality, but also the critical investment in looking to the work as a marker of the individual author's moral code. 'We hear', Carlyle argues, 'of a man's "intellectual nature" and of his "moral nature", as if these again were divisible, and existed apart … Morality itself, what we call the moral quality of a man, what is this but another *side* of the one vital Force whereby he is and works?'[7] In this lecture, Carlyle expressly ties the issue of social responsibility to the author's cultural production. If the author's personality is believed to be reflected in his work, then the morality of each individual author becomes decidedly significant. Knowing the personality of the author, therefore, becomes not only a matter of public interest, but also one of social importance. Keeping silent or remaining hidden, then, was an ever-decreasing possibility for the woman writer, so much so that by 1883, in his introduction to *English Poetesses: A Series of Critical Biographies*, Eric Robertson felt justified in setting aside a discussion of the women's poetry itself in favour of the 'most lovely qualities of personal character' that the poetry reveals. 'It is the business of subsequent pages', he writes, 'to show how beautiful this poetry is. But there is another beauty which it may be hoped that these pages will also reveal – the beauty of noble lives led by pure and able women'.[8] For Robertson, personality and poetry are qualitatively linked, and beautiful poetry signifies a virtuous woman.

In the light of notions of privacy that were at the heart of the image of feminine respectability, the personal investment associated with such work could also be seen to attract unwanted and unwomanly publicity. 'We have learnt much lately about woman', the poet Dora Greenwell noted in 1861:

> It is surely singular that woman, bound, as she is, no less by the laws of society than by the immutable instincts of her nature, to a certain suppression in all that relates to personal feeling, should attain, in print, to the fearless, uncompromising sincerity she misses in real life; so that in the poem, – above all, in the novel – that epic, as it has been truly called, of our modern day, – a living soul, a living voice, should seem to greet us; a voice so sad, so truthful, so earnest, that we have felt as if some intimate secret were at once

---

6   M.H. Abrams, *The Mirror and the Lamp: Romantic Theory and the Critical Tradition* (London: Oxford University Press, 1953), p. 227.

7   Thomas Carlyle, 'The Hero as Poet', *Lectures on Heroes* (London: Chapman & Hall, n.d.), p. 264 [italics in original].

8   Eric Robertson, *English Poetesses: A Series of Critical Biographies* (London: Cassell, 1883), p. xvi.

communicated and withheld, – an Open Secret, free to all who could find its key – the secret of a woman's heart, with all its needs, its struggle, and its aspirations.[9]

In the spirit of Greenwell's 'Open Secret', many nineteenth-century female authors, as the other chapters in this book show, often explored the contradictions of the creative woman's life through the difficulties experienced by heroines working in other artistic genres. George Eliot, for instance, uses the figure of the actress in her fiction in order to write about the implications of her own performance in the role of 'Great Author'.[10] Greenwell, however, openly describes in this passage the sense of divided subjectivity that is often used to define the image of the woman writer in the mid-Victorian period.[11] Greenwell creates an image of the woman writer as one who is more modern, more sensitive, better educated, and nobler than her frivolous predecessors. But, torn between competing expectations, Greenwell's modern woman writer is forced to confront the ambivalence inherent in the 'Open Secret'. The 'instincts of her nature' demanded that she remain private, but the 'living voice' of authorship dictated that she must reveal the 'secrets of a woman's heart'. In her discourse on the modern woman writer, Greenwell publicly negotiates the taboo on self-publicity and exposes the contradiction inherent to this position.

Having described the difference for the woman writer between real life and the voice surfacing in print, Greenwell argues that society and biology lead women to suppress their true feelings – their soul – while writing allows them to speak with a sincerity that conventional domesticity denies them. Similarly, Barrett Browning's portrayal of Aurora as an apparently 'proper' middle-class woman whose soul privately thrives only in her imaginative work develops a detailed dialogue between the woman writer's outer and inner life. Noting that, for Aurora, 'The inner life informed the outer life, / Reduced the irregular blood to a settled rhythm, / Made cool the forehead with fresh-sprinkling dreams', Barrett Browning identifies Aurora's personal imaginative freedom as the source of her attention to her domestic duty. In doing so, she exposes the performance of conventional femininity as a process of negotiation that enables Aurora to maintain her artistic identity.

This chapter investigates those representations of women writers that explicitly address this process of negotiation between an outer and inner life, between domestic and artistic tendencies.[12] It also explores the impact this dialogue had on popular images of female authorship and argues that in these images we can detect the

---

9   Dora Greenwell, 'Our Single Women', *North British Review* 36 (1862), p. 63.

10   Nina Auerbach, 'Secret Performances: George Eliot and the Art of Acting', *Romantic Imprisonment: Women and Other Glorified Outcasts* (New York: Columbia University Press, 1986), pp. 253-67.

11   For a discussion of the influence of a fragmented subjectivity of the woman writer see, for instance, Elsie Michie, *Outside the Pale: Cultural Exclusion, Gender Difference, and the Victorian Woman Writer* (Ithaca: Cornell University Press, 1993).

12   In this chapter, I am speaking particularly about images of middle-class authoresses. For a discussion of the relationship between middle and working-class authoresses, see Julia Swindells, *Victorian Writing and Working Women* (Cambridge: Polity Press, 1985).

development of a professional and commercial identity for the middle-class woman writer. If these writers had come to adopt key elements of this modern and public identity, this was in part because of their own literary negotiation of this problematic position in response to a largely conservative reading public. Greenwell herself enacts this process when she attempts to defuse the element of personal exposure implicit to her description of the modern woman writer. 'To women who can so feel and write', she argues with an autobiographical edge, 'life … may be a nobler, but must be a less easy thing'.[13] But Greenwell starkly opposes the suffering of the woman writer to the Romantic trials of male genius. Whereas Carlyle's *Lecture on Heroes* acquiesced with the Romantic conception of the obsessive and single-minded male poet, Greenwell describes a distinctively female place for women in the world of work that shuns competition with men in any profession and carves out a space for female writing (including her own) in which success for the female author lies in the application of a style that expresses a 'pathos exclusively feminine – feminine not in weakness, but in strength'. 'A woman's best praise', she argues, 'can no longer exist, as it has done hitherto, in being told that she has written *like a man*'.[14] According to Sandra Gilbert and Susan Gubar's notion of the nineteenth-century woman writer's fragmented subjectivity, Greenwell's disavowal of a conventional poetic identity for women might seem symptomatic of the woman writer's anxiety about the inappropriateness of working in what was considered to be predominantly masculine cultural territory.[15] Janet Gray, however, describes it as a part of Greenwell's attempt to mediate between the expanding public role that women were demanding and conventional notions of the feminine sphere. '[S]he regarded', Gray argues, 'women's writing as texts about changes in women's essence – occurring within women's sphere but indicating a need for that sphere's expansion'.[16]

In 'Our Single Women', Greenwell attempts such mediation in relation to the items she reviews, which include, among others, Anna Jameson's *Sisters of Charity and the Communion of Labour* (1859), a publication by the *English Woman's Journal* entitled *Thoughts on some Questions Relating to Women* (1861), and recent *Transactions of the National Association for the Promotion of Social Science*, whose connections with the Society for Promoting the Employment of Women were already well-established. Greenwell supports the general theme of the defence of sisterhood and women's labour that runs through the pieces she reviews, but she qualifies their more controversial aspects, arguing, for instance, that more opportunities for work in the industrial sphere should be made available to women '*so long as they are provisional and exceptional*'.[17] Rather than endeavouring to enter the fields of men's

---

13   Greenwell, 'Our Single Women', p. 63.

14   Ibid., p. 68 [italics in original].

15   Sandra M. Gilbert and Susan Gubar, *The Madwoman in the Attic: The Woman Writer and the Nineteenth-Century Literary Imagination*, 2nd ed. (New Haven: Yale University Press, 2000).

16   Janet Gray, 'The Sewing Contest: Christina Rossetti and the Other Women', *a/b: Auto/biography Studies* 8 (1993), p. 248.

17   Greenwell, Our Single Women', p. 71 [italics in original].

work, she argues, women need '*more perfect freedom and expansion*' in that field of work which is properly their own.

Greenwell does not question the gendered separation of spheres or try to redefine the elemental understanding of feminine nature. She does, however, attempt to modernise and broaden the image of work that can be considered feminine, and she distinguishes what she sees as the development in women's writing, as well as her 'less sustained and exalted … accomplishments':

> Her attainments are no longer like the flowers in a child's garden, stuck in without a root to hold by, but living blossoms, unfolding from principles – those everlasting 'seeds of things'. If we listen to her music, we hear no more of that vague and brilliant skirmishing over the keys – 'execution', we believe, it used to be called – which not many years ago was held in general esteem. If we inspect her drawings, even her finer needlework, we shall perceive a recognition of law, an obedience to Art's unchangeable canons.[18]

In this passage, Greenwell describes the change in women's traditional domestic work from 'attainment' to 'Art'. Moreover, the imagery of growth she uses to illustrate this change implies that this progression is the natural and desirable improvement of an innate, though previously undeveloped, artistry. The connection she makes between writing and other attainments such as needlework identifies authorship as another form of domestic accomplishment that, like drawing and playing, has blossomed from a womanly root. Rather than immodestly publicising the female author's personal life, this description implies that the open secret that a woman's writing reveals is the moral principles that were supposed to form the centre of a woman's being. In this way, the image of writing is transformed from a dangerous public display to a suitably natural feminine occupation.

Greenwell's attempt at mediation between writing and domesticity thus reflects her own process of negotiation as a woman writer discussing subjects that were popularly supposed taboo. Her description of artistic development serves her well since it cloaks the controversial elements of her own writing, crediting female accomplishment with the high culture status of art, within conventional feminine terms. Such a concerted effort to downplay the claims for artistry, however, registers her own anxiety about, or at least an awareness of, what the *Saturday Review* describes as 'a sort of faint dislike, not perhaps to women who write, but to women turning authors'.[19] The distinction that the *Saturday Review* makes between women who write and women turning authors is also one which was made two years later by Charlotte Yonge in her novel, *The Clever Woman of the Family* (1865), when her rather staid military man Colonel Keith argues that, 'The withholding of the name prevents well-mannered people from treating a woman as an authoress, if she do not proclaim herself one; and the difference is great between being known to write,

---

18   Ibid., p. 68 [italics in original].
19   'Authoresses', *Saturday Review* 16 (1863), p. 484.

and setting up for an authoress'.[20] While Yonge expresses her own authorial anxiety about the disapprobation of the educated, serious-minded, and principled middle-class male of the type who would read the *Saturday Review* (of which Colonel Keith is a prime example), she also reveals the underlying process of negotiation that makes all the difference to public perception. The implication is that the difference between being known as a likable woman who writes rather than an unwomanly authoress lies less in what she writes or how she writes it, and more in what she proclaims herself to be. In proclaiming herself to be merely a 'woman who writes', the woman writer could attempt to minimise the degrading effect of publicity on her personal identity. As with the discourse of compatibility, however, such negotiation had an ambivalent effect on the image of the woman writer. While it allowed her greater freedom in pursuing a literary career, it also confined her sphere of action within the domestic. Even before Greenwell argued for the expansion of this sphere, women writers were using the figure of the female author in their writing in order to explore the complexities and contradictions of the process of negotiation.

Teaching and Learning: Negotiating Authorial Identity and *Aurora Leigh*

As I have argued in relation to the artist, women were often regarded as proficient and graceful copyists without the power of imagination to envision original subjects. For the woman writer, it was similarly argued that her imaginative work was nothing more than the faithful reconstruction of her daily life and her own emotional experiences. This, for instance, is one of the main reasons Greenwell gives for the futility of competition between men and women in art. Between men and women, she claims, there is 'an essential radical, organic difference, which makes her fail where he excels, and excel where he would fail most greatly … In imaginative strength she has been proved deficient … In her whole nature we trace a passivity, a tendency to work upon that which she receives, to quicken, to foster, to develop'.[21] This gendered distinction that Greenwell describes reflects wider cultural assumptions about the qualities associated with women's writing. When reviewing a selection of Dinah Craik's novels for the liberal, though Christian-oriented, *North British Review* in 1858, for instance, R.H. Hutton uses this distinction to describe why the novel is a more suitable genre for women than poetry:

> Poetry is concerned, it is true, mainly with the creation of living and breathing life, yet it certainly requires a power akin to the power of abstraction … Though women have usually finer spiritual sympathies than men, they have not the same power of concentrating their minds in these alone, and living apart in them for a time, without being disturbed by the intrusive superficialities of actual life and circumstances. Their imagination is not separable, as it were, in anything like the same degree, from the visible surface and form

---

20   Charlotte M. Yonge, *The Clever Woman of the Family* (London: Macmillan, 1892), p. 101. Further references to this edition will be given in the text.

21   Greenwell, 'Our Single Women', pp. 72-73.

of human existence; and hence, such poetry as they do usually write, is apt to be mere personal sentiment without any token of true imaginative power at all.[22]

Throughout the nineteenth century, critics such as Hutton increasingly identified novels as a feminine form. The intricate delineation of mundane detail and daily domestic activity as well as the insightful and sympathetic representation of human emotion and personal sentiment was thought to be not only natural to the prosaic quality of women's imagination but also particularly suited to the realist properties of the novel. 'It is clear', Hutton claimed, 'that, hitherto at least, feminine ability has found for itself a far more suitable sphere in novel writing than in any other branch of literature'.[23]

The difference Hutton notes between the novel and poetry and between men's and women's imaginations also marks the distinction between what was considered the masculine and the feminine style of writing. As Nicola Thompson has shown, writing designated as feminine, or 'womanly', dealt chiefly in the realistic representation of the intricacies and vicissitudes of human life and emotion.[24] Identified more with the popular than the artistic, the cultural definition of feminine style served ideologically to tie the female author to supposedly feminine qualities of didacticism, morality, and altruism, on the one hand, and notions of the everyday and the popular, or mass-market, on the other. This critical conception of a gendered difference in writing, Gaye Tuchman argues, contributed to a cultural hierarchy that 'identified men with ideas capable of having an impact upon the mind – with activity and the production orientation associated with high culture. Women were identified with mass audiences, passive entertainment, and flutter – popular culture'.[25] While this was not, as Gary Kelly makes clear, a specifically Victorian distinction, it remained a pervasive cultural projection that was determinative for women writers.[26] 'The Victorians', Elaine Showalter notes, 'expected women's novels to reflect the feminine values they exalted, although obviously the woman novelist herself had outgrown the constraining feminine role'.[27] But as Valerie Sanders has shown, this challenge to gender convention was far from obvious for many 'anti-femininst' women novelists of the time.[28]

---

22   [R.H. Hutton], 'Novels by the Authoress of *John Halifax*', *North British Review* 29 (1858), p. 467.

23   Ibid., p. 466

24   Nicola Diane Thompson, *Reviewing Sex: Gender and the Reception of Victorian Novels* (London: Macmillan, 1996).

25   Gaye Tuchman, with Nina Fortini, *Edging Women Out: Victorian Novelists, Publishers, and Social Change* (New Haven: Yale University Press, 1989), p. 78.

26   Gary Kelly, *Women, Writing, and Revolution: 1790-1827* (Oxford: Clarendon Press, 1993).

27   Elaine Showalter, *A Literature of Their Own: From Charlotte Brontë to Doris Lessing*, rev. ed. (London: Virago Press, 1999), p. 7.

28   Valerie Sanders, *Eve's Renegades: Victorian Anti-Feminist Women Novelists* (London: Macmillan, 1996).

The gendered schema, Thompson contends, was beneficial for those women, like Charlotte Yonge, who 'conformed so closely to the ideal and idealized view of feminine writing that she is chivalrously excepted from more critical examinations of intellectual content'.[29] As with the female artist, though, critical chivalry had the tendency to descend into critical condescension. The sentimental and earthly qualities that were identified as the defining characteristics of feminine writing were viewed from a less chivalrous perspective as unimaginative and mundane, and a pedestrian imagination, distracted intellect, and superficial experience were all proposed as markers of women's inferior literary production. Even those women who did produce literature in the masculine genres of poetry or history could not escape the stifling chivalry of the patronizing critic.[30] Eric Robertson, for instance, chose to preface his collection of poetry from well over 30 female poets from all periods of English literary history with the qualification that 'Women ... have produced a great quantity of beautiful poetry that is worthy of a place in any rank but the very first'.[31] Keeping them out of this first rank, according to F.T. Palgrave, were the very things that defined their writing as feminine. 'It appears to me indisputable', he writes, 'that the introduction of a definite, frequently indeed of a directly religious, moral is not only a mark or note of poetry by women, but is one chief reason why they have not carried their poetry to greater excellence'.[32] In indicating that great poetry requires a genius that women are incapable of possessing, these men, like Hutton, essentially devalue women's poetry and imply that there is something intrinsically unfeminine about a vocation for writing. To achieve greatness of the first rank in either poetry or prose, a woman would have to possess a masculine mind, and such intellectual cross-dressing would be unseemly, if not impossible.[33]

For those women whose writing did not conform to the feminine form, the critical result was often derision or disbelief. Infamously, when Anne Brontë's *The Tenant of Wildfell Hall* appeared in 1848, many reviewers refused to believe that such coarse characters and shocking incidents could be imagined, let alone written

---

29   Thompson, *Reviewing Sex*, p. 6.

30   For a discussion of the contributions made by women to the writing of history and the reasons these contributions were ignored or disparaged by mainstream critics see Rosemary Mitchell, '"The Busy Daughters of Clio": Women Writers of History from 1820-1880', *Women's History Review* 7 (1998), pp. 107-34.

31   Robertson, *English Poetesses*, p. xvi.

32   F.T. Palgrave, 'Women and the Fine Arts', *Macmillan's Magazine* 12 (1865), p. 219.

33   Although there was a tradition of feminine poetics in circulation, these three men privilege a mainstream Romantic definition of great poetry which favoured supposed masculine forms of experience. Robertson, for instance, writes, 'The poet gives us experience sublimed ... He is a child of the universe. For him there is a feeling of everlasting mystery. He is always looking beyond' [*English Poetesses*, p. xii]. For an explanation of the models of Victorian feminine poetics see especially Isobel Armstrong, '"A Music of Thine Own": Women's Poetry', *Victorian Poetry: Poetry, Poetics and Politics* (London: Routledge, 1993), pp. 332-57, and Angela Leighton, *Victorian Women Poets: Writing Against the Heart* (London: Harvester Wheatsheaf, 1992).

down and published, by a woman. As I noted in the previous chapter, the sex of Acton Bell was, for some reviewers, undoubtedly male. The reviewer for *Sharpe's London Magazine*, for instance, insisted that 'there is a bold coarseness, a reckless freedom of language, and an apparent familiarity with the saying and doing of the worst style of *fast* men, in their worst moments, which would induce us to believe it impossible that a woman could have written it'.[34]

The real difficulty for the reviewer, though, occurred when the sex of the author was known and her writing did not conform to the expected feminine style. J.M. Ludlow addressed this problem in his review of *Ruth* when he compared the first work of Charlotte Brontë with that of Elizabeth Gaskell:

> Even if we contrast the two names more immediately before us, those of the authoresses of "Jane Eyre" and "Mary Barton", many of us at least can hardly repress the feeling, that the works of the former, however more striking in point of intellect, have in them a something harsh, rough, unsatisfying, some say all but unwomanly, as compared with the full, and wholesome, and most womanly perfection of the other.[35]

Although, like *Mary Barton, Jane Eyre* is a love story that ends in the conventional marriage of the heroine, *Jane Eyre* was seen as a 'protest against social conventionalisms and inequalities'.[36] While *Mary Barton* included the improper flirtation between Mary and the upper-class Harry Carson, it ultimately validated the existing social order through Mary's humiliation for her transgression and through the union of the two working-class lovers, Mary and Jem. Conversely, Jane's self-determinacy, pride, and discontent, along with the differences in class and station between Jane and Rochester, offered a challenge to the social orthodoxy and prompted Lady Eastlake to brand the book an 'anti-Christian composition'.[37] Although *Jane Eyre* attracted much critical admiration when it was first published, Charlotte Brontë is criticised by Ludlow for being unwomanly because her novel failed to reproduce the ideal of feminine writing. Rather than consider that the problem lies in a flawed definition of womanly writing, Ludlow prefers to believe that the fault is Brontë's, and before the true sex of Currer Bell was known, there was, as a reviewer for the *Christian Remembrancer* notes, a social urgency in proclaiming "him" to be male: 'We cannot wonder that the hypothesis of a male author should have been started, or that ladies especially should still be rather determined to uphold it. For a book more unfeminine, both in its excellences and defects, it would be hard to find in the annals of female authorship'.[38]

---

34   'Unsigned review', *Sharpe's London Magazine* 7 (1848), rpt in *The Brontës: The Critical Heritage*, Miriam Allott, ed. (London: Routledge & Kegan Paul, 1974), p. 265.

35   [J.M. Ludlow], 'Ruth', *North British Review* 19 (1853), p. 169.

36   *Athenaeum* no. 1149 (3 Nov. 1849), p. 1107.

37   Lady Elizabeth Eastlake, '*Vanity Fair* – and *Jane Eyre*', *Quarterly Review* 84 (1848), p. 173.

38   *Christian Remembrancer* (1848), rpt. in *The Brontës: The Critical Heritage*, p. 89.

This reviewer's observation that, regardless of the author's actual sex, women have a particular interest in identifying Currer Bell as male implicitly acknowledges the female reading public's investment in the paradigm of gendered writing. In the interest of feminine propriety, argues the reviewer, it had become necessary for unfeminine creations to be identified as the work of male authors. In doing so, critics and readers not only reinforced gender stereotypes, but also supported their own gender identities along feminine or unfeminine lines. For a woman to declare *Jane Eyre* unfeminine is to declare her own womanliness. In this way, the image of the feminine authoress offered a cultural benchmark against which the female readers, including those who were women authors themselves, could publicly assert the measure of their own femininity. When discussing in print the feminine or unfeminine qualities of other authoresses, women writers could also negotiate their own authorial identities. The spectrum of such identifications can be seen by looking briefly at the strategies employed by the writers Anna Maria Hall, George Eliot, and Dinah Maria Mulock Craik.

A novelist and miscellaneous writer, Anna Maria Hall, who was also a regular contributor to the *Art Journal*, of which her husband was the editor, addressed the issue of her own authorial identity by defining those of her more celebrated predecessors. In a series of signed sketches of women writers that she compiled for the journal in the 1850s and 1860s, Hall blends biography with personal memoir as she describes the lives of various authoresses as well as her own experiences of meeting and corresponding with those she knew personally. In 'Memories of Miss Jane Porter', for instance, which was published in the *Journal* in 1850, Hall describes the happiness of the 'celebrated' woman who retains an '*un*public' life.[39] The truly celebrated women, she argues, are those mothers and wives who 'have watched over, moulded, and inspired our "celebrated" men':

> But if we have few 'celebrated' women, few, either who impelled either by circumstances or the irrepressible restlessness of genius, go forth among the pitfalls of publicity, and battle with the world, either as poets – or dramatists – or moralists – or mere tale-tellers in simple prose – or, more dangerous still, 'hold a mirror up to nature' on the stage that mimics life – if we have but few, we have had some, of whom we are justly proud; women of such balanced minds, that toil they ever so laboriously in their public and perilous paths, their domestic and social duties have been fulfilled with as diligent and faithful love as though the world had never been purified and enriched by the treasures of their feminine wisdom; yet this does not shake our belief, that, despite the spotless and well-earned reputations they enjoyed, the homage they received (and it has its charm), and even the blessed consciousness of having contributed to the healthful recreation, the improved morality, the diffusion of the best sort of knowledge – the *woman* would have been happier had she continued enshrined in the privacy of domestic love and domestic duty.[40]

---

39   Anna Maria Hall, 'Memories of Miss Jane Porter', *Art Journal* 2 (1850), p. 221 [italics in original].

40   Ibid.

Hall portrays the most desirable model of female authorship, that of the truly 'celebrated' woman of whom society can be justly proud, as primarily domestic. While she is driven to write (or even act), either through necessity or vocation, what she produces, because of her domestic feeling, will be edifying and invigorating for the national character. Writing is imagined less like a profession and more like a calling that the woman undertakes from a sense of duty rather than desire. Hall's admirable female author is a unwilling celebrity who would prefer to remain private.

Drawing on the lives of a number of female authors along with Porter, such as Hannah More, Maria Edgeworth, Felicia Hemans, and Maria Jane Jewsbury, Hall finds further support for this position, claiming 'perhaps of all this list, Maria Edgeworth's life was the happiest; simply because she was the most retired, the least exposed to the gaze and observation of the world, the most occupied by loving duties towards the most united circle of old and young we ever saw assembled in one happy home'.[41] She returned to the same theme (and some of the same authors) almost 15 years later when, as part of a series of 'Memories of Authors of the Age', again written from personal recollection, she offers extended sketches of the lives of Felicia Hemans, Letitia Landon, Mary Russell Mitford, and Maria Edgeworth. Each of these biographies consistently stresses, like that of Jane Porter, the domestic qualities and the desire for privacy evinced by each subject. Even the rather unconventional and sometimes scandal-ridden history of Letitia Landon is dismissed as unfounded slander against an unfortunate girl whose devoted attentions to her grandmother attest to her modesty and propriety. As Hall remembers:

> I have seen the old lady's "borders" and ribbons mingled with pages of manuscript, and know her to put aside a poem to "settle up" grandmamma's cap for Sunday. These were the minor duties in which she indulged, but her grandmother owed the greater part if not the entire of her comforts to the generous and unselfish nature of that gifted girl.[42]

In her memories of Miss Jane Porter, Hall had established her own likeness to such a model of successful, but private, authorship by emphasising her own connection to Porter: 'Miss Porter never told me she was an Irishwoman, but once she questioned me concerning my own parentage and place of birth; and … she observed *her own circumstances were very similar to mine*'.[43] Hall's description of these domestically-minded yet talented and successful authors as her friends and mentors who were in circumstances similar to her own suggests that she is identifying herself with their private as well as their professional lives. As a wife writing with and for her husband, and by using her biographical sketches to teach the lesson that woman 'must look for her happiness to HOME', Hall implies that her own public work can be as domestic in character. In doing so, she tacitly accommodates herself to her description of the

---

41   Ibid.

42   S.C. Hall and Mrs. S.C. Hall, 'Memories of Authors of the Age: Letitia Elizabeth Landon', *Art Journal* 17 (1865), p. 91.

43   Ibid., p. 222 [italics in original].

truly celebrated woman and embodies her own image of the admirably feminine author.[44]

In contrast to Anna Hall, George Eliot attempted to separate herself from the general rabble of female and feminine authors by aligning her literary production with that of men through her self-identification as a producer of high-culture novels.[45] In order to give force to this identification, Eliot consistently positioned herself through her own writing in a dominant and authoritative posture in relation to other women writers. The most notable example is her essay 'Silly Novels by Lady Novelists' which she wrote for the *Westminster Review* in 1856. Published at the time when Eliot began writing her first story, this article was instrumental to Eliot's concerted effort to establish her own high-cultural authorial identity. In this article, she articulates her disgust for the various species of silly novels she felt many women authors were producing. The basis for this, she explains, stems not merely from them being badly written. She finds them offensive because they are the products of vanity, written by women whose motives lie in their desire to exercise and exhibit their intellectual achievements. Such posturing, she argues, corroborates cultural assumptions about the futility of educating women and misrepresents the 'really cultured woman' who she describes as 'simpler and less obtrusive for her knowledge':

> She neither spouts poetry nor quotes Cicero on slight provocation; not because she thinks that a sacrifice must be made to the prejudices of men, but because that mode of exhibiting her memory and Latinity does not present itself to her as edifying or graceful. She does not write books to confound philosophers, perhaps because she is able to write books that delight them. In conversation she is the least formidable of women, because she understands you, without wanting to make you aware that you *can't* understand her. She does not give you information, which is the raw material of culture, – she gives you sympathy, which is its subtlest essence.[46]

Eliot depicts the cultured woman with an intellect that makes her understanding superior to the silly lady novelists and the common social crowd, including men. Eliot's description of this woman, however, suggests that this superiority is cloaked in an appearance of conventional feminine behaviour – she does not contradict men in public; nor does she crassly display her intellect either in society or in print. She does, however, seek to educate men through a womanly sympathy that instructs without cajoling. Along with education and talent, then, the truly cultured woman must also know how to control the public perception of her private identity.

---

44   Ibid.

45   Alexis Easley, 'Authorship, Gender and Identity: George Eliot in the 1850s', *Women's Writing* 3 (1996), pp. 145-60.

46   George Eliot, 'Silly Novels by Lady Novelists', *Westminster Review* 66 (1856), pp. 442-61, rpt. in *Essays of George Eliot*, Thomas Pinney, ed. (London: Routledge and Kegan Paul, 1963), p. 317.

Through her description of the difference between the silly novelist and the cultured woman, Eliot initiates her career in fiction by negotiating a distinct authorial identity. In her disdain for these silly examples of female intellectual posturing, Eliot offers a critical standpoint from which these epitomes of feminine writing are denigrated and dismissed. She explains that the harshness of her judgment stems not from a prejudice against women authors, but from a special interest in their success because, she notes, 'every critic who forms a high estimate of the share women may ultimately take in literature, will, on principle, abstain from any exceptional indulgence towards the productions of literary women'.[47] In this article Eliot condemns the traditional condescension handed down by critics to all female writers. Her own critical chivalry is reserved only for those writers, unlike herself, who she finds pitiful, namely, 'lonely women struggling for a maintenance, or wives and daughters devoting themselves to the production of "copy" out of pure heroism, – perhaps to pay their husband's debts, or to purchase luxuries for a sick father'.[48] Before she has published her first novel, then, Eliot anticipates the critical complaint about her own failure as a writer of fiction to reproduce the feminine style and establishes, through her own anonymous contribution, a critical voice that answers such a complaint and identifies authors such as 'George Eliot' as truly cultured women.

One such complaint is made by Dinah Craik when she discusses Eliot's *The Mill on the Floss* in her appeal 'To Novelists – and A Novelist' that was published in *Macmillan's Magazine* in 1861. In this article, Craik finds Eliot's novel intellectually and artistically brilliant and her depiction of Maggie Tulliver to be true to nature. Craik's major criticism, though, is that the story is morally flawed: 'Ask, what good will it do? – whether it will lighten any burdened heart, help any perplexed spirit, comfort the sorrowful, succour the tempted, or bring back the erring into the way of peace; and what is the answer? Silence.'[49] What is missing from Eliot's depiction of Maggie, she argues, is the feminine element of the heart – the potential for the characterisation to teach a transgressive woman the error of her ways and show her the path back to true womanly behaviour. In her comments on the disappointing didacticism of *The Mill on the Floss*, Craik reproduces the standards that define female writing as fundamentally moral in order to evaluate the worthiness of Eliot's tale, and as if to prove this point, when writing about George Eliot, she retains the pronoun 'he' because, she writes, 'we prefer to respect the pseudonym'.[50] In respecting Eliot's pseudonym, Craik asserts a degree of distance between the masculine style of George Eliot and her own writing. Eliot, in fact, also made a particular point of distancing herself from Craik when, in response to an article which compared the two novelists, she wrote in a letter, 'The most ignorant journalist in England would hardly think of calling me a rival of Miss Mulock – a writer who is read only by

---

47   Ibid., p. 322.

48   Ibid., p. 303.

49   [Dinah Craik], 'To Novelists – and a Novelist', *Macmillan's Magazine* 3 (1861), p. 444.

50   Ibid.

novel readers, pure and simple, never by people of high culture. A very excellent woman she is, I believe, but we belong to an entirely different order of writers'.[51] Under the discreet disguise of mutual respect – Craik's for the work, Eliot's for the woman – both authors nonetheless seem interested in keeping their distance.

Arguably, this effort to keep their distance could be seen to stem from the fact that both women were still unmarried in 1861 and quite likely concerned with the perception of their public personae. Although the critical explanations of George Eliot's use of a masculine pseudonym vary greatly, all seem to agree that its perpetuation signals a serious attempt to separate the author George Eliot from the woman Marian Evans.[52] Similarly, Eliot seems concerned to assert her remoteness from the 'excellent woman', Dinah Craik. By contrast, Craik's anxiety surfaces in a traditionalist element in her criticism that lauds the standards of feminine writing. But, as Shirley Foster argues, the superficial conventionality of Craik's attitude toward the form of expression proper for women's fiction is subverted throughout her writing by an underlying ambivalence toward 'gender-oriented concepts of behaviour'.[53] Truly good writing, Craik contends, would combine the artistic and the imaginative with the 'ministering spirit' of Christian doctrine.[54] Thus, good writing is associated with notions of the common good; at stake was not only the quality of the prose but its altruistic potential. For Craik, such writing was the product of '"the brain of a man and the heart of a woman", united with what we may call a sexless intelligence'.[55] On the one hand, the aesthetic theory she articulates in her review of Eliot's novel assumes a gendered division between masculine and feminine qualities of literature; on the other, her definition of the greatest novelists does not admit this gendered schema.

Craik's notion of the kind of 'sexless intelligence' exhibited by the best writers attests to her perception of the standards of masculine and feminine writing as models of authorship rather than biological prescriptions. It also reveals her understanding of the female author's capacity for constructing her own public identity in relation to that of other woman authors. By 'respecting' Eliot's chosen pseudonym and the gender identification associated with it, Craik maintains the association with the masculine form that Eliot herself initiated. This, in turn, supports her position that while Eliot's work may approach the heights of artistic genius, it does not occupy a position as the very best kind of writing. Indeed, Craik's evaluation has little to do with this description of genius. Instead, the best writing is shown to correspond with the more traditional feminine qualities, for which Craik herself had been praised. Writing three years earlier, Hutton had characterised her as an artist of the

---

51   George Eliot, Letter to Francois D'Albert-Durade, 7 June 1860, *The George Eliot Letters*, G.S. Haight, ed., 9 vols (London: Routledge and Kegan Paul, 1954-78), 3, p. 302.

52   For a discussion of Eliot's pseudonym as a serious attempt to hide her identity, see Ruby Redinger, *George Eliot: The Emergent Self* (New York: Alfred A. Knopf, 1975).

53   Shirley Foster, *Victorian Women's Fiction: Marriage, Freedom, and the Individual* (London: Croom Helm, 1985), p. 66.

54   Craik, 'To Novelists', p. 446.

55   Ibid.

'deeper feminine school of modern fiction', observing that she combined the 'power of exhibiting the gradual growth of character' with 'giving, in the widest sense, *purpose* to her fictions, without in anyway making them didactic'.[56] In her appeal 'To Novelists', then, Craik, like Eliot, uses an anonymous critical essay to suggest that the best kind of writing is, in fact, the kind that she herself had been credited with producing.

In their negotiations between images of female authors, Hall, Eliot, and Craik also attempt to control the public perception of their own authorial identities. However they choose to establish their work in relation to conventions of womanly writing, each manipulates the principles of feminine authorship in order to find a legitimate critical voice that supports their choice. Elizabeth Barrett Browning also engages in this type of manipulation when, using a series of basic conflicts in the structure and narrative of *Aurora Leigh*, she defines her own image of the best writing. One of the fundamental critical debates that has occurred over at least the last 20 years, for instance, is whether *Aurora Leigh* plays out 'revolutionary impulses', or 'conservative sexual politics'.[57] While many of these studies tend to read the poem as the exploration of the conflict between being a woman and a poet, I would like to re-define slightly these categories in order to establish Aurora's central conflict as one between masculine and feminine forms of writing. Aurora thus embodies the conflict of authorial identity negotiated by Eliot, Greenwell, Craik, and other female writers and offers a coded reflection on this process of negotiation. Regardless of her conservative or revolutionary credentials, we can argue, Barrett Browning's representation of Aurora brings the negotiation of female authorial identity directly into question. In order to expose this dialogue between supposed masculine and feminine modes of creativity and determine Barrett Browning's critical response to it, we must begin by readdressing the other, better known, conflicts within the work.

The first of these conflicts is the ambiguity created by the incompatibility of the traditional love story with the female *Kunstlerroman*.[58] Indeed, the struggle between love and vocation is embodied by the argument between Romney and Aurora in the garden that comprises most of Book Two. It also initiates and justifies Aurora's aesthetic manifesto. In this dialogue, Romney voices the conventional critical position on the inferiority of feminine writing. In particular, he calls upon the evidence of women's sentimentality and pedestrian imagination:

---

56 Hutton, 'Novels by the Authoress of *John Halifax*', pp. 472, 480.

57 Gilbert and Gubar, *The Madwoman in the Attic*, p. 579; Deirdre David, *Intellectual Women and Victorian Patriarchy: Harriet Martineau, Elizabeth Barrett Browning, George Eliot* (Ithaca: Cornell University Press, 1987), p. 143.

58 For a full discussion of how Barrett Browning negotiates this conflict see Linda M. Lewis, 'The Artist's Quest in Elizabeth Barrett Browning's *Aurora Leigh*', *Images of the Self as Female: The Achievement of Women Artists in Re-envisioning Feminine Identity*, Kathryn M. Benzel and Laura Pringle De La Vars, eds (Lewiston, NY: The Edwin Mellor Press, 1992), pp. 77-88.

> Your quick-breathed hearts,
> So sympathetic to the personal pang,
> Close on each separate knife-stroke, yielding up
> A whole life at each wound, incapable
> Of deepening, widening a large lap of life
> To hold the world-full woe. The human race
> To you means, such a child, or such a man,
> You saw one morning waiting in the cold,
> Beside that gate, perhaps. (*Aurora Leigh*, II.184-92)

His description of women's emotions as both superficial and specific seems proof enough to him that Aurora cannot produce 'the Best in art', and he suggests instead that she should marry him and 'Write woman's verses and dream woman's dreams' (*Aurora Leigh*, II.148, 831). In Aurora's rejection of Romney's marriage proposal and the traditional womanly role he offers her, Barrett Browning sets aside the issues of love and marriage, those events which were supposed to complete a woman's life, in order to pursue a masculine 'vocation plot'. To this end, she separates Aurora entirely from Romney, when, as Aurora is leaving to pursue her career in London, she declines to accept the money that he thinks, as a cousin and her only male relative, it is his duty to give her.

Besides depicting Aurora's commitment to an idea of masculine vocation, Barrett Browning uses the scene in the garden to establish a parallel image of Aurora's authorial identity in relation to the feminine model. She might not be an archetypal feminine writer, but by setting this exchange in an idyllic June garden on her twentieth birthday, Barrett Browning employs imagery of nature and growth to justify Aurora's choices. Rejecting Romney, Aurora proclaims:

> But certain flowers grow near as deep as trees,
> And, cousin, you'll not move my root, not you,
> With all your confluent storms. Then let me grow
> Within my wayside hedge, and pass your way! (*Aurora Leigh*, II.848-51)

Barrett Browning casts Aurora's rejection of Romney and her poetic aspiration as a natural expression of her womanly development. Responding to the image of woman as a flower – beautiful but shallow-rooted – the youthful Aurora steadfastly commits herself to a permanent and ongoing education that will give her deep intellectual roots. Her first lesson teaches her how to negotiate her own authorial identity for public consumption.

Aurora begins from a position of naïveté about the realities of a literary career when she imagines that her growth as a poet will take place in a private, sheltered place, a wayside hedge. Her experiences in London, however, prove effective lessons in the difficulties experienced by women writers. Aurora's early publications, for instance, enable Barrett Browning to explore the problem of critical chivalry. Aurora's early series of ballads prove popular and are praised as examples of the feminine form. That they are read as conventional feminine work is made clear by the fan mail she receives. Such letters come 'With pretty maiden seals – initials twined / of Lilies, or a heart marked *Emily* / (Convicting Emily of being all heart)' (*Aurora Leigh*, III.212-14). Barrett Browning illustrates the failure of critical chivalry to please the true artist through Aurora's disappointment in her work and her realisation that 'the very love they lavished so, / Proved me inferior' (*Aurora Leigh*, III. 231-32). From this experience Aurora learns the difficulties of publicity for the woman writer and the value of publishing anonymously. This is a lesson that serves her well when she is forced to write in order to earn money. Rather than associate her name again with what she sees as inferior work, Aurora publishes her popular prose anonymously in order to safeguard her artistic identity:

> In England no one lives by verse that lives;
> And, apprehending, I resolved by prose
> To make a space to sphere my living verse.
> I wrote for cyclopaedias, magazines,
> And weekly papers, holding up my name
> To keep it from the mud. (*Aurora Leigh*, III.306-12)

In this episode Barrett Browning renders the economic lessons of necessity. Aurora's refusal to be contained within Romney's essentialist view enables her to pursue conscientiously the independence she needs for self-determination. But her resolution to devote herself to art without any guaranteed income is shown to be rather idealistic. In her need to earn money, her commitment to her art is compromised by the undeniable wrench of necessity. Because of necessity, then, she can never be completely free to pursue her writing according to her own artistic design. In Aurora's need for compromise, Barrett Browning negotiates between images of self-determining and dependent authorship. While the image of self-determining authorship is here associated with a masculine form of intellectual verse, the problems of necessity are shown to be as detrimental to masculine authorship as critical chivalry was to the feminine.

The conflict between the love plot and the female *Kunstlerroman* that seems to be set aside in the garden scene thus resurfaces in the tension between self-determination and dependency. This tension underlies Aurora's artistic development throughout the narrative and is also played out in another of the central conflicts of the piece – the generic ambiguity of the narrative's classification as a novel-poem. Writing in the high culture and masculine domain of epic poetry, Barrett Browning presents her work as a combination of the masculine and the feminine that she calls the poet's 'double vision' (*Aurora Leigh*, V.183). The book is constructed as both a masculine and poetic searching exploration of the nature of art and a feminine and novelistic examination of the realistic representation of daily life. The text thus becomes a compromise between conventionally gendered genres and provides something of an object lesson on the result of the woman writer's process of negotiation. In this negotiation, Barrett Browning defines a new form of female poetry that combines the moral power of the realist novel and the intellectual power of the epic, which 'constitutes a radical marriage that affirms, even at the structural level, the synthesis of woman and a poet she desired to achieve, both for her heroine and for herself'.[59] But the construction of this work as a novel-poem goes beyond establishing an authority for the female poet or combining 'poetic passion with other psychological and emotional imperatives, none of which are finally subordinated to the others'.[60] It also corresponds with Aurora's definition in Book V of poetry as 'living art':

> Never flinch
> But still, unscrupulously epic, catch
> Upon the burning lava of a song
> The full-veined, heaving, double-breasted Age:
> That, when the next shall come, the men of that
> May touch the impress with reverent hand, and say
> 'Behold – behold the paps we all have sucked!
> This bosom seems to beat still, or at least
> It sets ours beating: this is living art,
> Which thus presents and thus records true life. (*Aurora Leigh*, V.213-22)

This description suggests that it is the woman writer that is best suited to represent the modern age. And both Aurora and Barrett Browning claim the realist-epic novel-poem not just as an acceptable form of poetry, but also as the ideal. This, they argue, is art that lives. In the compelling image of the modern age, and the art produced from it, as a woman's breast, feeding and nurturing the next generation, Barrett Browning reserves the power of giving life to, educating, and sustaining the future for the female artist.

Her earliest critics, however, disagreed. Coventry Patmore, for instance, noted that 'a very large portion of this work ought unquestionably to have been in prose'.[61] And the reviewer for *Blackwood's Magazine* argued that Barrett Browning had failed in 'establishing her theory' that 'the chief aim of the poet should be to illustrate the age in which he lives':

> We could wish – though wishes avail not for the past – that Mrs. Browning had selected a more natural and intelligible theme which would have given full scope for the display of her extraordinary power; and we trust that she will yet reconsider her opinion as to the abstract fitness for poetical use of a subject illustrative of the time in which we live … [The] universal repugnance to the adoption of immediate subjects for poetical treatment, seems to us a very strong argument against its propriety.[62]

---

59   Chris Vanden Bossche and Laura Haighwood, 'Revising the Prelude: Aurora Leigh as Laureate', *Studies in Browning and His Circle* 22 (1992), p. 39.

60   Meg Tasker, '*Aurora Leigh*: Elizabeth Barrett Browning's Novel Approach to the Woman Poet', *Tradition and Poetic of Self in Nineteenth-Century Women's Poetry*, Barbara Garlick, ed. (Amsterdam: Rodopi, 2002), p. 26.

61   [Coventry Patmore], 'Mrs. Browning's Poems', *North British Review* 26 (1857), p. 450.

62   'Mrs. Barrett Browning – *Aurora Leigh*', *Blackwood's Magazine* 81 (1857), pp. 34, 41.

This reviewer appeals to conventions of gendered authorship divided along novelistic and poetic lines. Having offended 'propriety', as this review significantly expressed it, it fell to Barrett Browning to reject the epic treatment of everyday themes. However, she had already proposed an answer to the supposed 'universal repugnance' to such genre-busting poetry. In creating a poem akin to Wordsworth's *The Prelude*, Barrett Browning recalls Wordsworth's project in his poetry to 'choose incidents and situations from common life, and to relate or describe them throughout, as far as was possible, in a selection of language really used by men'.[63] Her evocation of the seminal work by the former Poet Laureate, then, exposes the complicity between popular constructions of gender and genre that formed the basis of such 'universal' opinions. But Barrett Browning also updates Wordsworth's work by shifting from his interest in everyday life of the rustic, pastoral poor to that of the degraded urban poor, and in doing so, distances herself from her prestigious predecessor and from Romantic solipsism.[64] Also, idealism is superseded by pragmatism as Aurora learns how to manage her writing career. Dividing her time between her pursuit of art and the work of necessity, between living poetry and popular prose, Aurora is able to avoid both endangering the commitment she has made to her vocation and passively falling victim to the feminine model, as she does when she publishes her popular ballads. In deliberately holding her name up, she shows she is aware of the possibility for the woman writer to exert control over her own authorial identity. Aurora's compromise between feminine and masculine models of authorship thus results in a new model of female authorship as a form of self-mastery. Through her negotiation, Aurora perceives the possibility for the conscious manipulation of public perception.

Aurora's most important lesson in self-mastery comes from Marian Erle. Watching Marian's light-heartedness as she plays with her son, Aurora sighs over her own childlessness and regrets what she now sees as the cause of the inadequacy she has always felt as a poet:

> Passioned to exalt
> The artist's instinct in me at the cost
> Of putting down the woman's, I forgot
> No perfect artist is developed here
> From any imperfect woman. (*Aurora Leigh*, IX.645-49)

Aurora seems to be regretting the fact that she has not followed a conventional feminine path. Looking at it from this perspective, it seems that, as Mairi Calcraft Rennie argues, the division between Marian and Aurora could be expressing the

---

63   William Wordsworth, 'Preface to Lyrical Ballads (1802)', rpt. in *Romantic Poetry and Prose*, Harold Bloom and Lionel Trilling, eds (London: Oxford University Press, 1973), p. 595.

64   Vanden Bossche and Haighwood, 'Revising the Prelude', p. 34.

conflict Barrett Browning felt in her own life between being a woman and an artist.[65] Indeed, the poem does end, as Kathleen Blake argues, with 'a reconciliation of love and art' in the coming marriage of Aurora and Romney.[66] But it is not Romney who has taught Aurora that 'Art is much, but love is more' (*Aurora Leigh*, IX.656). It is the purity and fervency of Marian's self-sacrificing love for her son that impresses Aurora. Given purpose through motherhood, Marian appears to Aurora as 'Dilated, like a saint in ecstasy' (*Aurora Leigh*, IX.188). And by the end of the story, Marian comes to epitomise the conventional wisdom that motherhood brings untold joy and womanly fulfilment.

But her state of motherhood is not one of conventional domestic happiness – there is no husband or father-figure to complete the domestic scene. While Aurora learns the beauties of sisterhood and self-sufficiency, she also, through witnessing Marian's reawakening to life, sees the woman's power of creation and self-expression that is facilitated by female forms of experience. Cora Kaplan argues that, in *Aurora Leigh*, Barrett Browning, 'embittered' by her father's despotism, 'denies any role and influence to the father in the life of the adult poet, by writing him out of the narrative'.[67] Although, as Kaplan notes, the figure of the father still lingers in the poem, Barrett Browning sidesteps the issue of masculine influence over the creative woman by introducing a critical voice that defines a distinctive female space in literature for the modern woman writer. And the space Aurora creates to 'sphere [her] living verse', literalised by her and Marian's isolated home in the Italian countryside, is constructed around the image of the woman as mother. In defiance of the demands of feminine 'propriety', Aurora, and Barrett Browning, enact a form of self-mastery and artistic control in which female strengths and virtues, particularly the sustaining quality of the mother's breasts and the woman's nurturing role, are at the root of a successful and public life for the female writer. Aurora's regret, therefore, is not that she is childless, but that she has not yet become the perfect artist. In choosing Marian rather than Romney as the source of Aurora's lessons about love, Barrett Browning appeals to conventional ideas of naturalness and biological destiny to support this position. In light of such a powerful defiance, it is not surprising that metaphors of motherhood took an increasingly prominent and complex role in representations of female writers from the 1860s. Indeed in her representation of Marian Erle, Barrett Browning offers an early example of motherhood as a distinctively feminine expression of both creativity and necessity.

---

65 Mairi Calcraft Rennie, 'Maternity in the Poetic Margins', *Studies in Browning and His Circle* 19 (1991), pp. 7-18.

66 Kathleen Blake, 'Elizabeth Barrett Browning and Wordsworth: The Romantic Poet as a Woman', *Victorian Poetry* 24 (1986), p. 397.

67 Cora Kaplan, *Sea Changes: Culture and Feminism* (London: Verso, 1986), p. 209.

Child-Rearing, Writing and Metaphors of Mothering

By acknowledging Marian Erle as a kindred spirit and an admirable model for the woman writer, Barrett Browning suggests that the woman writer could learn the lessons of freedom and self-sufficiency evinced by the fallen woman without experiencing the negative aspects of her outcast state. By making this lesson one of motherhood's redemptive power, she participates in a common nineteenth-century strategy of legitimising women's writing through metaphors of mothering. Motherhood proved a significant paradigm throughout the nineteenth century for imagining the work of women writers because motherhood was identified as the most obvious and efficient means through which a woman author could learn proper feeling and the methods necessary to produce truly moral and uplifting literature. The analogy between writing and motherhood, which Margaret Homans has termed, 'bearing the word', equated reproduction with representation, literal creation with linguistic production, in the work of the female author.[68] This notion of writing as reproduction is evident, for instance, in Dinah Craik's *A Woman's Thoughts About Women* when Craik uses motherhood as a metaphor for literary production. As I argued in the previous chapter, Craik's identification of the woman author's 'shelvesful of books', as 'the errant children of our brain' suggests a conception of domesticity that, although alternative to the traditional structure of private life, mimics the mother/child relationship at the heart of the domestic sphere. For the professional female author, she argues, books can be like children, and the process of writing them is legitimised as a natural (pro)creative act.

Children and language, however, were not merely represented, as they are in Craik's *A Woman's Thoughts About Women*, as exchangeable products of womanly creation. In fact, the rather ambivalent metaphor of child-bearing, which denotes a purely corporeal process, was often supplanted in discussions of women writers by metaphors of child-rearing. The cult of motherhood, which understood maternal love as 'the apex of feminine purity', also deemed child-rearing and development as a woman's ultimate form of work.[69] The earliest transmission of knowledge, inculcation of moral standards, and development of language in the child all rested under the control of the mother. As exemplar, moral guardian, and private angel for her children, the duties of the mother were far removed from the self-promoting, self-defining, and public work of authorship. By 1859, however, the *English Woman's Domestic Magazine* could comment about the author Mrs. Johnstone that 'she cultivated the profession of authorship with absolutely no sacrifice or loss of feminine dignity ... with as much benefit to her own happiness as to the instruction and amusement of her readers'.[70] No longer simply denoting the private relationship

---

68   Margaret Homans, *Bearing the Word: Language and Female Experience in Nineteenth-Century Women's Writing* (Chicago: University of Chicago Press, 1986), p. 158.

69   Lynda Nead, *Myths of Sexuality: Representations of Women in Victorian Britain* (Oxford: Basil Blackwell, 1988), p. 26.

70   'Literary Women of the Nineteenth-Century', *English Woman's Domestic Magazine* 7 (1859), p. 342.

of the woman with her literary work, metaphors of mothering began to reflect on the public relationship between the female writer and her readership. As such they may be regarded as a logical extension of Barrett Browning's concern with the female author's identity and her control of her public image. Indeed, as the *Saturday Review* suggested in 1862, such control had resulted in the transformation of the woman writer in the popular imagination:

> Novels, for 50 years, were never read without an apology. It was customary for the youth of more than one generation to blush when caught in the act of reading them, and to disown with a certain shame the entrancing interest they excited. It, therefore, marks an era, and shows to what point we have arrived, when a great didactic part is claimed for these frivolous misleaders, and when these wasters of time and enervators of feeling are divided into schools, and claimed as trainers of mind and educators of the imagination.[71]

As this reviewer grudgingly acknowledges, women writers could be seen to 'train' and 'educate' their readership in a way deemed impossible for the 'frivolous misleaders' of earlier generations. Although some critics, like the author for the *Saturday Review*, continued to question this educative value of female authorship, the metaphor of child-rearing contributed to an image of female authorship that, beyond being an acceptable form of work, was seen to be an expansion of a woman's domestic duties.

The potential for the metaphor of child-rearing to affect this image can be seen in J.M. Ludlow's review of Elizabeth Gaskell's *Ruth* for the *North British Review.* When *Ruth* appeared in 1853, the story of the poor seamstress who is seduced and abandoned was not a unique one, but Ruth's re-entrance into respectable society and eventual restoration to womanly virtue defied the mid-Victorian bourgeois morality that equated fallenness for the middle-class woman with social death. Ruth's story, although causing initial shock among its audience, was qualified and explained by more sympathetic reviewers, such as Ludlow, who justifies such a scandalous story by the moral lessons it teaches.[72] In his review, Ludlow argues that although the book contains obvious moral flaws, it also teaches important lessons derived throughout the novel from Ruth's own moral education. Ruth's lessons are learnt from a variety of sources: the model of Christian charity and humility evinced by the Bensons; the example of the selfless love and independence of their devoted servant Sally; and, most importantly, the joy and moral responsibility of motherhood. It is particularly through her love for her son, Ludlow argues, that 'the seduced girl is made a noble Christian woman by the very consequences of her sin'.[73] In fact, Ludlow goes so far as to suggest that Ruth's 'new sense of responsibility' after her son's birth is 'the means of her sanctification'.[74] Thus, through the education provided by domestic

---

71 'English Women of Letters', *Saturday Review* 14 (1862), p. 718.

72 For an overview of this debate, see Angus Easson, ed., *Elizabeth Gaskell. The Critical Heritage* (London: Routledge, 1991), pp. 200-39.

73 Ludlow, 'Ruth', p. 155.

74 Ibid.

felicity and motherhood, Ruth is re-established within a respectable social position as she is transformed from the fallen woman to the saintly nurse. In Ludlow's estimation, the experience of motherhood possesses powerful redemptive qualities, and even that most irredeemable Victorian figure, the fallen woman, can be said to be purified by her motherly experience.

The power of motherhood is further emphasised by Ludlow when he grants Gaskell a greater ethical and moral understanding of Ruth's sin and redemption because, as a mother herself, the 'duties of hallowed motherhood have taught her own pure soul what its blessings may be to the fallen'.[75] Although Ludlow marks the difference between Gaskell and Ruth as the difference between the pure and the fallen, he also calls attention to what they have in common, namely their experience of the sanctifying power of motherhood. As well as insight into the fallen woman, this common experience allows Gaskell a basis upon which she can address all members of society. It is this experience, he argues, that makes 'wives and mothers the greatest novelists', because, 'If the novel addresses itself to the heart, what more natural than that it should then reach it most usefully and perfectly, when coming from the heart of a woman ripe with all the dignity of her sex, full of all wifely and motherly experience?'.[76] According to Ludlow, Gaskell's role as an actual mother automatically surrounds her, her motives for writing, and the story she produces in a sanctifying haze of maternal goodwill. Her own motherly experience, mediated through the experience of her central character transforms the scandalous story of a fallen woman into a narrative of Christian repentance and reformation, maternal devotion, and womanly self-sacrifice, and the author's motives for composing such a story escape critical condemnation as salacious and materialistic efforts to interest and excite a dissolute public. Instead, Ludlow declares the purpose of *Ruth* to be a distinctly maternal effort to expound moral lessons, urge Christian behaviour, and exemplify bourgeois propriety. To be both a great writer and a good mother signalled a form of authorship that transcended issues of respectability and publicity because a mother, Ludlow argued, would only take the time away from her family to write when she felt she had something important that she must share with the world. This type of publication, he concludes, would proceed only from a woman's sense of duty to use the lessons of her domestic experience to educate and improve society, rather than from any selfish or unworthy motives such as greed or intellectual exhibitionism. Such a model of motherly writing could offer a fertile scope for self-expression, with room to be both 'womanly' and imaginative, to be a public figure while maintaining the respectability of a private woman.

The scope of such motherly writing was explored by Eliza Meteyard in a short story she wrote for the *English Woman's Journal* entitled 'A Woman's Pen'. Published in 1858, the story features a successful manufacturer who, while visiting a remote country village on a fishing trip, comes across an old authoress, Mary Cresset, whose work of homely truths and noble sentiments influenced him when

---

75   Ibid.
76   Ibid., p. 169.

he was a child and set him on his path to rise up from a 'poor forge lad' to 'one of the richest iron masters in the world'.[77] This impressive success, the iron master believes, is largely attributable to the woman whose 'power of leading the minds and giving comfort to the souls of others, has been one of her highest gifts' (*Woman's Pen*, p. 251). Although at one time famous and prosperous, the woman now lives in honest retirement and genteel poverty and expends her talent in managing a small teashop to support her widowed sister-in-law and niece. When offered an annuity by the iron master, her refusal is a testimony to a noble humility, a just independence, and a patient faith. Finally rewarded when the republication of her writings meets extraordinary success, she closes her shop in order to dedicate herself to helping establish a cooperative society for literary women. This woman is presented as a model of respectability, as a dutiful and traditional 'old maid', and as a successful and famous authoress. This success, however, is not measured in economic terms. As with the iron master who learned the right way to live from reading her works, the beneficial effect her truthful writing has had on her readers is the true marker of Mary's success. Monetary reward comes to her only after a lifetime of using her woman's pen with 'the purest hand, the purest purpose, for the advocacy of truth in all its shapes' (*Woman's Pen*, p. 258).

This 'truth', the lessons of Mary's writing, however, is curiously shapeless throughout the text. There is no description of Mary's writings or the truths she advocates, almost as if the concept of such truth is unimaginable for Meteyard herself. Described instead is Mary's parlour, the scene of her work, which attests to the fact that she knows 'nothing of the meanness or vulgarity of common life' (*Woman's Pen*, p. 252). In her parlour, 'perfect order, exquisite cleanliness, the scholar-like method with which books are set, papers laid, all bespeak habits of refinement, and the quiet daily round of lettered life' (*Woman's Pen*, p. 252). The 'truth' of Mary's writing is not some intellectual quality; it is instead identified with the purity and domesticity contained within the material items of her sitting-room. The order and cleanliness with which she arranges the tools of her trade around her provide concrete proof of the domestic capability she has fostered in the face of a professional career. The representation of her sitting-room marks Mary as a domesticated author, and her public self is irrelevant, being buried in 'so remote a place, and surrounded by so few substantial marks of either fame or prosperity' (*Woman's Pen*, p. 253). Mary's earthliness is literalised through the synecdochic function of her 'woman's pen' when this commonplace object comes to represent what is admirable in her writing. Her writing is true and pure because she conforms to the image of the proper motherly author who works to support her brother's family and only writes what she believes to be beneficial for mankind. As an author as well as a woman, Mary's intellect and imagination are firmly bounded within the domestic sphere and her work is defined by those who read her books and admire them as the pure and didactic creations of a feminine author. This characterisation corresponds with a conventional gendered

---

77 [Eliza Meteyard], 'A Woman's Pen', *English Woman's Journal* 1 (1858), pp. 252-53. Further references to this story will be given in the text.

division between female earthliness and male transcendence – men manipulate words and ideas in the achievement of abstract ends whereas women merely manipulate objects in the course of quotidian duties.

In Meteyard's representation of Mary, the literal boundaries of Mary's drawing room symbolise the metaphorical boundaries created by her gender and by the standards that define the characteristics of the 'proper' woman writer. In this way, Meteyard illustrates the constraining influence that metaphors of mothering could have on the perception of female authorship. While contributing to the notion of women as creatures ruled by earthly and sentimental concerns, the application of this metaphor also reinforced ideas about the primacy of motherhood in all women's experience. Some contemporary discussions of the female author marked biology rather than talent, education, or opportunity as the factors determining her ultimate literary failure. In his introduction to *English Poetesses: A Series of Critical Biographies* in 1883, for instance, Eric Robertson went so far as to identify motherhood as a woman's chief barrier to being a great poet. This volume, which includes biographies of a large number of female poets from Katherine Phillips and Charlotte Smith to Christina Rossetti and Emily Brontë, offers a record of the contributions that women had made and were making to the English poetic tradition, but the quality of their work, he argues, is hampered by a 'sexual distinction lying in the very soul'.[78] 'All that the greatest poet has felt over his most perfect thought', he writes, 'the mother feels through her first-born ... What woman would not have been Niobe rather than the artist who carved the Niobe? More than poetry, and more than man, woman loves the children who fall from the heavens'.[79] In Robertson's estimation, the greatest poetry is characterised by an indefinable quality of searching and reaching that lifts it beyond the physical world, a quality, he argues, that can only be attained by the male poet.

What Robertson highlights is a disparity between the concept of the male poet who could immerse himself in a world of pure intellect and imagination and the female who was tied to the material world, for, as he phrases it, 'Children are the best poems Providence meant women to produce'.[80] Clearly, he contends, woman's biologically determined role as mother is a disadvantage for the female poet. A woman would always be mother first, poet second, and the primacy of her role as mother tied her to Nature and to an earthly love. Robertson's insistence on the absolute supremacy of motherhood over poetry was mocked by the *Englishwoman's Review*, which responded to his query about Niobe by stating, 'As Niobe's only claim to fame is as the desolate mother who mourned the death of her 14 children, we think most women would prefer to forego this domestic distinction'.[81] Although such denials were scarce, one is implied in 'A Woman's Pen' when Meteyard uses the metaphor of mothering to suggest a function for Mary's writing that reaches beyond her cramped

---

78   Robertson, *English Poetesses*, p. xiii.
79   Ibid., pp. xiii-xiv.
80   Ibid., p. xiv.
81   'English Poetesses', *Englishwoman's Review* 15 (1884), p. 372.

drawing room. Meteyard portrays a woman whose motherly influence, because she does not have a child of her own, extends beyond her immediate domestic sphere into the world at large. Not only does the iron master express his indebtedness to her teaching, but also various similar stories are related. Among those affected by Mary's writing are a railway master, who gained the courage to bear difficulty and to set his life upon the proper path, and a wealthy lettered lady who is inspired to establish a scheme of self-help for literary women of all ranks and ability. As an author, therefore, her power to shape people's lives is broad even while her sphere of action is narrow.

Meteyard uses the image of the proper motherly author to expand the scope of the cultural power wielded by the woman writer. She also illustrates the way the metaphor of mothering could prove useful to women writers who wanted to maintain the appearance of femininity while perhaps suggesting more controversial ideas about female authorship. One novelist who uses such a strategy is Charlotte Yonge, whose work was repeatedly praised as the height of feminine writing.[82] As June Sturrock observes, Yonge uses the figure of the female author in her fiction to help reconcile her successful professional career with her private, domestic life when 'literary ambitions are represented as permissible, even laudable, in a woman if they are duly subordinated'.[83] In *The Clever Woman of the Family* (1865), Yonge overtly depicts the benefits of the motherly model when she compares two women authors – the proper, womanly author Ermine Williams and the 'clever' bluestocking Rachel Curtis.[84] As a regular and anonymous author of essays like 'Country Walks' for a well-established journal, Ermine's essays are intelligent, educative, and morally sound. Unable to achieve womanly fulfilment in motherhood because of an accident that has crippled her, Ermine turns to a motherly style of writing in order to experience the domestic joy from which she is debarred. As a result, she is revered, valued, and trusted by all who know her, and her invalid's drawing-room, the scene of her work, is also a haven and a valuable resource for her family and friends as they go to her for advice and comfort.

Rachel, on the other hand, writes, but never gets published, essays with titles like 'Helplessness', 'Female Folly', and 'Female Rights'. Rachel's efforts to improve society are earnest, but unlike Ermine who publishes in order to support her sister and niece, Rachel's motivations for writing stem from her desire to have 'influence over people's minds' (*Clever Woman*, p. 52). This, however, is not the motherly or domestic influence of the feminine writer. As Rachel bulldozes her way through the

---

82 For a discussion of the conventional critical judgment of Yonge's work, see Thompson, *Reviewing Sex*, esp. pp. 96-7.

83 June Sturrock, 'Literary Women of the 1850s and Charlotte Mary Yonge's *Dynevor Terrace*', *Victorian Women Writers and the Woman Question*, Nicola Diane Thompson, ed., p. 120.

84 Other women writers in Yonge's fiction include Elizabeth Merrifield in *Two Sides of the Shield*, Ethel May in *The Daisy Chain*, Authurine Arthuret in 'Come to her Kingdom', and Geraldine Underwood in *The Pillars of the House*. But the woman writer features most centrally in *The Clever Woman of the Family* and *Dynevor Terrace*.

local community, foisting upon them her opinions on everything from homeopathic medicine to the true meaning of heroism, Yonge repeatedly shows Rachel to be mistaken in her assumptions and ineffective in her efforts because she believes she can educate her audience with her intellect rather than letting her natural, womanly morality guide them to right-mindedness. Her vanity, pursuit of male ambitions, claims of literary genius, and boasts of religious doubts all contribute to a social and physical degradation that exposes her to charges of unwomanly behaviour.

Ermine and Rachel are relatively traditional examples of the benefits of the motherly style and the inadequacy and impropriety of the masculine style for the female writer respectively. Indeed, they might seem to typify Colonel Keith's distinction between being known as a woman who writes and setting up as an authoress. However, Yonge ensures that this distinction also serves to interrogate the comfortable attribution of authorial identity for these two women. The final statement of the novel that it was not Rachel but Ermine who is the clever woman of the family can be read as an indication that Ermine's cleverness stems from her successful manipulation of the metaphor of mothering. After all, it is she who successfully secures for herself a literary career and a respectable domestic identity. If this is the case, then Rachel's problem is not that she tried to write according to a masculine model of creativity. Instead, Rachel's mistake lies in her ignorance of cultural conventions and of her power to write her own authorial identity into being. Both writing and setting up as an authoress involve a woman performing the same activity, but only motherly writing offers to readers domesticity as a distraction from that problematic activity.

Representing two women authors allows Yonge to address acceptable and improper images of female authorship in uncomplicated isolation and to imply that such images might ultimately be exploited by the genuinely clever female writer. In *Dynevor Terrace* (1857), though, Yonge had already used the woman author, Isabel Conway, to examine the contradictions of the literary life for the individual woman writer. When introducing Isabel, Yonge describes 'two worlds in which she lived' – the 'cramped round of her existence' and her poetic fantasy world.[85] Peopled by characters such as the knight Sir Hubert, the world Isabel creates in her poetry is one of romance, chivalric valour, and courtly love. While Isabel is single, her writing is mostly treated as an activity that is compatible with the rest of her life, especially when it remains just a hobby she pursues in order to entertain her two younger sisters. It is even presented as a 'refuge' from the empty life of London society to which her age and class have resigned her. After Isabel is married to the clergyman, James Frost, Yonge continues to suggest domestic uses for her writing. The publication of her first piece, for instance, is only prompted by a philanthropic gesture. When James expresses his regret that he has no money to donate to the Blind Asylum, she offers one of her small pieces of travel writing for sale. Through little incidents such

---

85   Charlotte M. Yonge, *Dynevor Terrace*, 2 vols (London: John W. Parker and Son, 1857), I, pp. 287, 193. Further references to this edition will be given in the text by volume and page number.

as these, Yonge defines Isabel's writing as largely an extension of her domestic work – entertaining her sisters, helping her husband.

This positive representation of Isabel's writing and imaginary life, however, is increasingly identified with Isabel's point of view, while an alternative, less generous perspective is voiced by the ladies of the neighbourhood who take her abstraction in her work as aloofness: 'The calm, lofty manners that had been admired in Miss Conway, were thought pride in Mrs. James Frost' (*Dynevor Terrace*, II.148). In the opinion of her neighbours, the detrimental effect of her writing is obvious. Isabel's writing is solace and companionship for her, so she does not make the effort to engage in society or to appease the local parish as would befit the wife of a clergyman. But the clash between her two worlds becomes unavoidable and insupportable in the face of inflexible cultural presuppositions concerning the all-consuming duties of child-rearing. The birth of Isabel's twin daughters highlights the incompatibility of her real and imaginary lives because living in two worlds often leads her to neglect the rather dull duties of domestic life. Her work as a mother comes into conflict with her work as an author:

> Of all living women, Isabel was one of the least formed by habits or education to be an economical housewife and the mother of twins. Maternal love did not develop into unwearied delight in infant companionship nor exclusive interest in baby smiles; and while she had great visions for the future education of her little maidens, she was not desirous to prolong the time spent in their society, but in general preferred peace and Sir Hubert. (*Dynevor Terrace*, II.177)

The conflict created by her competing roles does not immediately resolve itself into the neat model of the motherly writer. Instead, the dreaminess that made Isabel charming and inscrutable in her early life leads to the ruin of her family. Yonge lays the responsibility for James's failing health, social difficulties, financial problems, and uncomfortable home on Isabel's neglect and so fully corroborates cultural preconceptions of feminine influence. Only through the intervention of James's cousin Fitzjocelyn, who is himself learning the joys of domestic life and the rewards which come with doing one's duty, does Isabel even realise that her family is in serious distress. After her awakening, Isabel's first impulse is to turn to her writing, exclaiming, 'I may be able myself to do something towards our maintenance' (*Dynevor Terrace*, II.218). But once again, Fitzjocelyn, embodying the voice of social convention, reminds her of her proper feminine role by asking, 'to your home, would *any* remuneration be worth your own personal care?' (*Dynevor Terrace*, II.219). His hints to Isabel of her husband's unhappiness, although offered by Fitzjocelyn in the kindest of tones, act as a severe condemnation of her domestic failings. Not only has she been neglecting her husband's comfort, but she has also been adding to his difficulties with thoughtless and spendthrift habits. But Isabel is not, for Yonge, irredeemably unfeminine. Her chief flaws are her imagination and her ignorance, and Fitzjocelyn's words have an epiphanic effect on her. This standard reading of the lessons of Yonge's novel is supported by June Sturrock when she concludes, using *Dynevor Terrace* as her primary example, that Yonge ignored 'the transgressive claims to power and freedom voiced in precisely contemporary representations of the woman writer'.[86] But the story of Isabel cannot be so readily contained within this apparently unambiguous morality tale.

Although Yonge's story does conclude with Isabel's domestic awakening and her cheerful performance of the harassing and fatiguing duties she had once thought of as 'devoid of poetry', it does not do so without first raising questions about the nature of motherhood and the self-expressive qualities of writing (*Dynevor Terrace*, II.233). The maternal instinct is not natural to Isabel, and for her, 'maternal love' does not translate automatically into the wholesale devotion of her time and interest to her children. While she is reported to care about them, she prefers the peace of her writing and imaginary world to their company. Significantly, however, this failing is not presented as a defect in Isabel herself; instead, the narrator suggests that it corresponds to a failing in her education. Besides money, Isabel lacks 'true' feminine instinct because she has not been properly taught how to behave like a mother.

Rather than teaching the lessons of domesticity, Isabel's early education has been conducted through the single piece of writing she has worked on throughout her development from daughter to wife and mother. Her epic poem about the romance of her medieval lovers, Adeline and Roland, remains pertinent for Isabel through her early social life and her isolated marriage because the story itself changes dynamically according to her situation in life. She, herself, does not know the ending, and she invents new characters based on the people she meets. Moreover, she often changes her plans for the story, or even what she has already written, as the people around her show new and unexpected sides of themselves. For instance, she models a rather foppish and foolish character on the '*nonchalant*' Fitzjocelyn, but when he leads her through the barricades while in Paris during the Revolution, she considers 'the amends to be made' to her poem to change the fool into a 'resolute, high-minded Knight' (*Dynevor Terrace*, I.339). This transformation of life into fiction, whilst completely at odds with cherished principles of privacy in feminine writing, also enables Yonge to depict a woman writer gaining an unprecedented measure of control over her life. It is Isabel's fiction, for instance, which leads to her choice of a husband. While most of her family and the neighbourhood think that she should and will marry Fitzjocelyn, she falls in love instead with the more romantic figure of the well-born but poor clergyman whose middle name just happens to be the same as her hero, Roland. Controlling her story allows Isabel a precarious independence, unavailable to most upper-middle class young women, to direct the story of her own life. Yonge's morally conservative novel seems to harbour subversive tendencies focused on the liberating potential of fiction and the possibility for writing women to re-imagine the world. As Isabel ties her own life into the characters of her romance, she escapes cultural determinations of feminine roles in a way sometimes deemed positive:

---

86   Sturrock, 'Literary Women of the 1850s', p. 130.

Isabel was always ready to give warm aid and sympathy in all his higher cares and purposes, and her mild tranquillity was repose and soothing to him. She was like one in a dream. She had married a vision of perfection, and entered on a romance of happy poverty, and she had no desire to awaken; she never exerted her mind upon the world around her, when it seemed oppressive; and kept the visionary James Frost before her, in company with Adeline and the transformed Sir Hubert. (*Dynevor Terrace*, II.149)

Isabel's biographical strain of fiction filters into her relationships in a way that Yonge seems to both ridicule and admire. Her ambivalence is perhaps unsurprising given Yonge's own personal and public position as a female writer. Isabel's story resists the essentialising discourse of the metaphor of motherhood and instead begins to describe an image of feminine authorship as an imaginative capacity which opened new horizons for creative work beyond those supposedly defined by female biology and inclination. Isabel's writing offers a passage to alternative forms of propriety whose advantages, however, are ultimately outweighed when her conventions of family life are endangered. Isabel's (and Yonge's) ambivalence eventually resolves itself as the competing parts of Isabel's identity are reconciled into an acceptable model of womanly behaviour. When she realises that her husband is unhappy and her household is suffering from her neglect, she literally hands over her manuscript to Fitzjocelyn, saying, 'It has been a great tempter to me … But I can have only one thought now – how to make James happier and more at ease' (*Dynevor Terrace*, II.220). All the motherly uses for authorship are ultimately rejected in favour of the duties of actual motherhood, and the primacy of the domestic over the literary appears as a cultural certainty at the close the novel.

But putting aside her manuscript does not mean that Isabel has stopped writing. In fact, her reward for her eventual compliance to conventional notions of femininity is a successful literary career. When she places her domestic work first, the writing she does compose is 'far more terse and expressive than anything she used to write when composition was the object of the day' (*Dynevor Terrace*, II.275). She even gets her long poem published, and the proceeds are added to the family budget. In putting aside her manuscript, Isabel immediately redefines her self-image from authoress to woman, without making any long-term material changes in her behaviour, through a simple reorientation of perspective. Furthermore, the professionalism she newly brings to the practice of writing is reflected too in the successful marketing of her new identity to the public. The power Yonge grants Isabel to manipulate her public image is usefully obscured from this public by an image of motherliness that surrounds the characterisation of Isabel in a haze of domestic propriety. The fact that Isabel has no real knowledge of what her domestic duties are, that she lacks the feminine instinct that should come naturally to a woman, is swept away in her one lofty, symbolic gesture. She need not write this change into her romance because the text of her epic poem has been replaced by the text of her life. Isabel will create her domestic identity the same way she created the story of Adeline and Roland, writing it as it happens.

In Isabel's story, Yonge shows the contradictory impact the metaphor of mothering could have on the image of female authorship. While it enables Isabel as a professional author to maintain the appearance of respectable domesticity, it also requires that she subsume her authorial identity in the domestic. The triumph of the domestic over the literary may just be one of perception, but it still entails a level of compromise that undermines the autonomy of self-representation her writing allows her. Some women authors, as Nina Auerbach argues, were able to break free of the limitations of this metaphor.[87] But, in obscuring the assertions of self-sufficiency supported by the female-centred interpretations of the feminine form, the figure of the motherly writer also contributed to an image of the authoress as a vulnerable and innocent participant in the public world of the literary marketplace.

Vulnerability and Degradation: The Woman Writer and the Marketplace in *The Way We Live Now* and *Diana of the Crossways*

Despite repeated assertions of the domestic character of women's writing, increasing attention was paid after the 1850s to their participation in the literary marketplace. The number of anonymous contributions to journals from the pens of women was revealed by the *English Woman's Journal*, which noted that 'Literature is followed, as a profession, by women, to an extent far greater than our readers are at the moment aware'.[88] Discussions of literature 'as a means of subsistence' and 'Literature Regarded as a Profession' appeared in the women's magazines that were interested in promoting work for women.[89] But at the same time, they also highlighted the vulnerability that was increased by this contact. An article in *Work and Leisure*, for instance, warned women of various unscrupulous schemes that preyed upon the desperation and naïveté of women who wanted to make money by writing for periodicals. The author describes a scheme in which a journal insisted that women purchase a subscription before the editor would consider their contributions. 'For a month or two', the author explains, 'the magazine came as promised; then it ceased, and we heard no more of either the Editor or of the MSS., except that the former had disappeared, and that an immense number of letters addressed to him had been received at the Windsor Post Office'.[90] While journals like *Work and Leisure* were worrying about the gullibility of the trusting woman, others, like the conservative journal the *Saturday Review*, were lamenting the degrading effect this contact with the marketplace had on womanliness: 'Young ladies who write and correspond with publishers and writers and exert themselves as in business to do a little stroke of

---

87   Nina Auerbach, 'Artists and Mothers: A False Alliance', *Romantic Imprisonment*, pp. 171-83. Auerbach is speaking specifically of Jane Austen and George Eliot, neither of whom had children of their own.

88   'The Profession of the Teacher', *English Woman's Journal* 1 (1858), p. 8.

89   'Employment for Educated Women', *Englishwoman's Review* 6 (1867), p. 312; 'Literature Regarded as a Profession', *Work and Leisure* 6 (1881), p. 40.

90   'To Amateur Authors', *Work and Leisure* 6 (1881), p. 362.

profit, lose some of that virgin absence of publicity and that engaging helplessness which as a matter of fact, have attractions for men'.[91]

These conceptions of the vulnerable female author suggested her degradation lay not in the publicity that attended publication but in her contact with a heartless commercial world. This was the fear expressed by a writer for Emily Faithfull's publication *Women and Work*, who worried about the possibility of pecuniary reward leading women to write immoral sensation novels in order 'take advantage of this base and easy method of making money'.[92] For this writer, the baseness of such writing stems as much from the sensational authoress's knowing engagement with the economic laws of supply and demand as it does from the unfeminine genre in which she writes. Writing which engages with the market in this way is severely criticised because, among other reasons, it is 'filled with artificial emotion'.[93] In other words, participation in the market economy is seen to subvert the supposed correlation between personality and production and as such is especially disruptive of the feminine model of writing. This author's disapproval of such a disparity is echoed in William Thackeray's *Pendennis* (1850) when his bluestocking, Miss Bunion, who describes herself in her volume of poems, *Passion-Flowers*, as 'A violet, shrinking meanly' and 'a timid fawn, on a wild wood lawn', is perceived by Pen to be 'a large bony woman in a crumpled satin dress, who came creaking into the room with a step as heavy as a grenadier's'.[94] The difference between her poetic portrait and the real Miss Bunion is explained by Pen's friend Wenham, who observes, 'You know passion-flowers, like all others, will run to seed'.[95] Whatever the degeneration in her physical appearance, however, Thackeray shows obvious sympathy and respect for Miss Bunion through Pen's appreciation for her work and references to their continuing acquaintance.

For Thackeray, Miss Bunion is not a character to be despised because she is a bluestocking and unattractive. Although she comes into the room dragging straw on her skirt and proclaiming the benefits of the omnibus, nobody laughs at these obvious social blunders. What does come in for censure, though, is the difference between her public image and her private appearance. By casting herself in her poetry in more feminine terms, Miss Bunion has shown her knowledge of how the marketplace works and has, as a result, fostered the success of her poems. But Thackeray criticises this knowing manipulation of public perception when he shows that this difference exposes her to public derision in a way neither her authorship nor her poverty does. Any disapproval of Miss Bunion results from Pen's disappointment that the timid and fawn-like Miss Bunion, who writes 'lines on the christening of Lady Fanny Fantail', is not the retiring and feminine woman her public identity

---

91 'Authoress', *Saturday Review*, p. 484.

92 *Women and Work* no. 37 (13 Feb. 1875), p. 4.

93 Ibid.

94 William Makepeace Thackeray, *The History of Pendennis*, John Sutherland, ed. (Oxford: Oxford University Press, 1999), p. 433.

95 Ibid.

seems to suggest.[96] In Miss Bunion's public/private disparity, Thackeray suggests that the difficulty experienced by readers in correctly identifying the authentic authoress behind a work is tied to a general mid-century discomfort with the idea of the woman writer's divided subjectivity. For Pen, this kind of disparity, and the duplicity it seemed to herald from female writers, is considered abnormal and troubling. However, subsequent representations of the woman writer throughout the 1850s and 1860s would repeatedly use this division as an opportunity for female-self expression. The notion of the divided self could ultimately be justified so that a new kind of professional relationship between writer and work and between writer and public became naturalised.

The cultural acceptance of the notion of the woman writer's divided subjectivity not only expanded the possibility for female self-expression, but also contributed to the continuing development throughout the second half of the nineteenth century of the image of literature as a purely professional and commercial pursuit because it enabled authors, both male and female, to challenge the assumption that their personality was unavoidably invested in their work. The division in the woman writer's subjectivity was matched in the male writer with what Mary Poovey describes as the '"problem" of the literary man's social status'.[97] In her discussion of *David Copperfield*, Poovey notes that the literary man occupied a highly problematic position in mid-Victorian society because of the opposition he embodied between, on the one hand, the professional demands of the capitalist marketplace and, on the other, the belief in masculine genius as a high-culture pursuit above the mundane concerns of market relations. Representing the woman writer's divided subjectivity, then, could be a self-reflexive action for the male authors. It enabled them to shed light on the general problem of literary identity in an industrial marketplace without themselves becoming implicated in its troubling consequences. In combining the competing ideological preconceptions of the public writer and the private woman, writers interested in exploring the problems of self-image and public image could thus develop a conception of the professional authoress that coupled the capability for sophisticated manipulation of the public consciousness with naïve understanding of the realities of the literary marketplace. Two authors who participated in this type of displaced introspection were Anthony Trollope and George Meredith. By examining their representations of women writers, we can begin to see how the figure of the degraded authoress proved useful to those male authors who sought to refute the Romantic model of writing and embrace a new professionalism as the embodiment of the author's emotional and imaginative interaction with the world.

Trollope, John Sutherland notes, constructed in his *Autobiography* an authorial identity as the consummate professional.[98] In Sutherland's analysis of Trollope's

---

96   Ibid.

97   Mary Poovey, *Uneven Developments: The Ideological Work of Gender in Mid-Victorian England* (London: Virago, 1989), p. 102.

98   John Sutherland, *Victorian Fiction: Writers, Publishers, Readers* (London: Macmillan, 1995), pp. 114-32.

manuscript work on *The Way We Live Now* (1875), he makes two points about Trollope's construction of the novel that are particularly relevant to this discussion. The first is that the novel was written 'at the time when Trollope was formulating his views on the art of writing fiction for the *Autobiography*'.[99] The second is that Lady Carbury, a writer, was initially supposed to be the chief character. Although Melmotte eventually took over as the chief character, Lady Carbury's initial centrality points to an affinity between her characterisation and Trollope's theorisation of his own writing in his autobiography. Lady Carbury may be read as a reflection, to some extent, of Trollope's feelings about the nature of his own professional identity.

Trollope describes Lady Carbury as a rather conventional woman who is nonetheless perceived as unconventional by the public. Even before her book is published, she is already a public figure because she is a wife whose life infamously does not embody the domestic ideal. The victim of an unhappy marriage to a brutal man, she escapes from him only to find her reputation tainted rather than his. Even her self-sacrificing and devoted attention to her children is not enough to protect her from public disdain. Whatever the realities of her life, her failure to maintain the appearance of respectability is represented as her true transgression. She is, as R.D. McMaster argues, a thoroughly unromantic character and an inauthentic woman.[100] Trollope thus uses the image of the vulnerable woman writer to investigate the hypocrisy of a public who are both voyeuristic and conventionally moralistic. This is a society in which the waxing and waning of public approval for Lady Carbury is shown to be prompted not only by her distance from or reproduction of the ideals of womanly behaviour, but also by the amount of public interest her private life generates. For instance, while Trollope quickly points out the injustice of the double standard that exposes her to censure rather than her debauched and cruel husband, he also describes the social cachet generated by her scandalous past. Lady Carbury's reputation piques the curiosity of the London literary circles, and as a result her regular Tuesday literary soirees are well-attended.

Privately, Lady Carbury may be a passive subject of public interest, but professionally, she is represented as an active and knowing participant in the literary market. As the novel begins, she is writing to three editors of popular papers, Mr. Booker of the *Literary Chronicle*, Mr. Broune of the *Morning Breakfast Table*, and Mr. Alf of the *Evening Pulpit*, in order to win from them favourable reviews for her book, 'Criminal Queens', a historical review of murderous and treacherous queens from Cleopatra to Marie Antoinette. Not only does her book lay claim to masculine and high culture associations through its efforts to be an intellectual study, but like the morally suspect sensation novels, it is also full of 'adultery, murder, treason, and all the rest of it'.[101] Her letters, then, are an attempt to win for her book the

99 Ibid., pp.114-15.

100 R.D. McMaster, 'Women in *The Way We Live Now*', *English Studies in Canada* 7 (1981), p. 77.

101 Anthony Trollope, *The Way We Live Now*, John Sutherland, ed. (Oxford: Oxford University Press, 1982), Book I, p. 2. Further references to this edition will be given by book

chivalrous treatment that often attended the publication of a typically feminine work. Because it is intellectual, though, the subject itself is immediately identified as a topic beyond her ability, and the book, Mr. Booker presumes, must be full of 'the numerous historical errors into which that clever lady must inevitably fall in writing about matters of which he believed her to know nothing' (*Way We Live*, I.6). This evaluation is later supported by the review in the *Evening Pulpit* in which each historical error is detailed and corrected. But Lady Carbury seems blissfully unaware of her own or her book's failings, and although she thinks herself eminently winning and subtle in her letters, the editors are fully aware of her machinations. Mr. Booker even goes so far as to think of her as a 'female literary charlatan' (*Way We Live*, I.6). This pronouncement of Lady Carbury as a fraud is primarily derived from her duplicitous letters, but she is more precisely a *female* literary fraud because her book does not conform to accepted conceptions of feminine writing.

In her letters, Lady Carbury trades on her femininity, flirting with Mr. Broune, flattering Mr. Booker, and appealing to Mr. Alf for protection and support in her efforts to provide for her children. And, not surprisingly, her pleas for sympathy are heeded by the editors who eventually give her book good reviews, except Mr. Alf who is more concerned with sales than chivalry and knows that a 'crushing review is the most popular' (*Way We Live*, I.97). While the narrator obviously disapproves of Lady Carbury's schemes, branding her letters 'detestably false' and her tactics 'abominably foul', the entire system of literary review is also being criticised (*Way We Live*, I.11). It is not only authors who are affected by this corrupt system. Through these editors, Trollope shows the degrading effect of the professional marketplace on all those who participate. Mr. Booker, for instance, is a talented, intelligent, and hard-working professor of literature, but he is compelled by economic necessity and a family of daughters to praise 'Criminal Queens' and by doing so to 'descend so low in literature' (*Way We Live*, I.99). His hypocrisy stems from self-interest – he repays the 'rubbish' that Lady Carbury wrote about his book by conjuring up some meaningless praise for hers, 'knowing that what he wrote would also be rubbish', because he 'knew that even the rubbish was valuable' (*Way We Live*, I.99). Mr. Broune gives her a glowing review because she has solicited his promise to do so with her soft eyes and sad voice. Even Mr. Alf, who is unaffected by her charms, bases his review on his own selfish motives rather than the merits or defects of the work.

The interaction between Lady Carbury and the three editors shows the extent to which literary success depends on personality rather than talent in the corrupt literary marketplace. By creating a situation in which Lady Carbury feels she must employ her femininity in order to secure professional success, Trollope suggests the personal degradation that emerges from this corrupt and opportunistic system. The immodesty that Lady Carbury's letters display, particularly her flirtatious appeal to Mr. Broune, indicates a sexual impropriety that is capitalised upon by Mr. Broune when he seizes the opportunity when they are alone to kiss her. While she quickly

---

and page number in the text.

escapes from his embrace and admonishes him, she retains her composure 'without a flutter, and without a blush' (*Way We Live*, I.4). Even this degree of self-possession suggests that she has an improper amount of experience in dealing with unwanted sexual advances. But whereas Lady Carbury thinks this interview successful because she has solicited his promise that he would publish one of her articles, the narrator points out that this judgment of success is relative; she may have won a professional concession, but she has lost socially and personally. 'The lady who uses a street cab', he explains, 'must encounter mud and dust which her richer neighbour, who has a private carriage, will escape. She would have preferred not to have been kissed; – but what did it matter?' (*Way We Live*, I.5).

This degradation is further demonstrated in a positional metaphor that is played out throughout the novel. At the beginning of her 'career' and the novel, Trollope initially places Lady Carbury in a position of mastery as she writes her letters with a confident flourish of self-possession. This mastery is particularly influential over Mr. Broune who is persuaded by her feminine flatteries and helplessness to propose to her. But the degrading effect of the literary world on Lady Carbury slowly pulls her down from her height of sexual and social dominance and reorients her relationship to Mr. Broune. At the beginning of the novel, she stands over him, admonishing him for his attempt to kiss her and refusing his proposal, but by the end of the narrative, she has been reduced to kneeling at his feet, arguing her unworthiness. As he raises her from her kneeling position, it becomes clear that the strongly self-confident woman at the beginning of the novel has been reduced to an image of wifely obedience and self-denigration who, like Rachel Curtis, realises that 'After all, then, she was not a clever woman, – not more clever than other women around her' (*Way We Live*, II.461).

The degradation of Lady Carbury's literary career may pull her down from the heights of social dominance and masculine intelligence, but it also has the contradictory effect of raising her to into a proper feminine role as she is literally raised off her knees by Mr. Broune and figuratively raised to respectability through their marriage. Her metaphorical descent through the narrative is quietly matched therefore by her growing domestic fortunes as Mr. Broune provides the solution to problems created by her unwise mothering of her feckless son. The promise of respectability, though, is not the motivating factor for Lady Carbury's second marriage. She is forced to relinquish the independence she has cherished and steadfastly protected since the death of her first husband primarily because she has no money. Although she had hoped to maintain her economic independence through her literary career, she is unsuccessful, in part, because she cannot manage her son, and, in part, because she writes in the masculine style while still trading on her femininity in order to secure critical chivalry. The result is a literary androgyny that gives her neither the authoritative power of George Eliot's critical persona nor the conventional power attributed to Charlotte Yonge, and her marriage is a conscious decision to abandon the masculine author for the feminine woman. The contradictions of Lady Carbury's character, her intense maternal devotion and her manipulative and opportunistic femininity, are not resolved into an acceptable model of the womanly author as they are, for instance, in Isabel Conway. In fact, the moments at which she uses her private identity in order to support her professional work are shown to add significantly to her degradation.

Through the corruption which touches all those in *The Way We Live Now* who participate in the literary marketplace, Trollope expresses his concerns about the degradation brought on by a system that he, as an editor of periodicals himself, intimately knew. But, while showing his own insider knowledge of this corrupt system, he distances himself from it through his disdain for it and all those who take part in it. Trollope describes a marketplace where talent is often second to professionalism and where key undertones of sexuality are often more persuasive than creative, fully-realised work. His representation of the degraded female author enables Trollope to exploit the well-rehearsed schema of gendered authorship in order to confront the apparent contradiction that the modern author must work in and for the marketplace, yet somehow remain untainted by it. While women authors trapped between the commercial and domestic spheres might seem to typify this difficult relationship, Trollope also demonstrates that Lady Carbury's apparent naïveté is an effective answer to an otherwise intractable problem. Feigning ignorance of both the critical condemnation that greets her work and the sexual implications of her professional machinations, Lady Carbury gains currency in a marketplace that will not permit her to be both professionally promiscuous and lady-like. Although short-lived, her success is achieved primarily through her understanding and manipulation of the marketplace. Through Lady Carbury, then, Trollope demonstrates the inadequacy of traditional masculine Romantic individualism for the modern professional author.

The difficulties and opportunities of the gendered schema of authorship for the woman writer are further investigated by George Meredith in his representation of Diana Warwick in *Diana of the Crossways* (1885). Meredith places Diana in a difficult social position when, falsely accused of adultery, she is separated from her husband and thrown upon her own resources. Unsurprisingly, then, necessity is the motivating circumstance that turns Diana to writing. But Diana supports no one but herself, and without the mitigating circumstance of domestic duty to qualify her economic motives, her connection to the literary marketplace is more obvious and damaging. As a result, the pinch of poverty, which should spur the impoverished authoress to action, has a debilitating effect on Diana:

> The slow progress of a work not driven by the author's feeling necessitated frequent consultations between Debit and Credit, resulting in altercations, recriminations, discord of the yoked and divergent couple. To restore them to their proper trot in harness, Diana reluctantly went to her publisher for an advance item of the sum she was to receive, and the act increased her distaste. An idea came that she would soon cease to be able to write at all.[102]

---

102   George Meredith, *Diana of the Crossways* (London: Virago, 1985), pp. 221-22. Further references to this edition will be given in the text.

In this passage, the narrator mitigates the degrading effect of economic exchange on Diana by emphasising the importance of her personal feelings and personal investment in her work to her success. The assumptions about a woman's personal relationship with her writing serve to place her within the range of respectable models of feminine authorship. Her first two novels are models of feminine writing – stereotypical romances filled with mundane detail, unimaginative incident, and 'superficial discernment' (*Diana*, p. 221). As a result, they are both popular successes that inspire critical praise and public admiration. But this feminine style also reveals personal secrets of her woman's heart. The publication of her second book, *The Young Minister of State*, engenders a frenzy of gossip intent on discovering the model for the hero of the title. The obvious choice is her intimate friend, the politician Percy Dacier, and while Diana admits to her friend Emma that he did form her model, she does not see the implications of the resemblance. Her book, through the character of the young minister, allows her to declare openly her admiration for him, but it also, unbeknownst to her, reveals what is seen as her love for him, and the romance of the novel's hero and heroine is taken by the public as proof of a romance between Diana and Percy. Ironically, the personal elements in Diana's fiction, the marker of her feminine style, which should secure the respectability of her public image, expose her to charges of impropriety where no real impropriety has taken place. The feminine style fails to safeguard Diana's respectability, and Meredith uses the romance to subvert the conventions of feminine writing even while Diana follows them; it is, after all, the 'transformative potential of romance', Diane Elam argues, that enables Diana to create for herself a new image and 'new positions of subjectivity'.[103]

Like Isabel Conway, Diana draws directly from her own life in creating characters for her work, and Meredith implies that this inclusion of personal detail is also an assertion of independence and self-determination. The relationship with Percy that Diana imagines for herself in her fiction is not sexual, but one in which she assumes the position of his confidante and political advisor with 'the wiles of a Cleopatra' (*Diana*, p. 200). In order to maintain for herself the relationship she has created in her mind, Diana refuses to allow Percy to talk for himself of his love for her. When shortly after the publication of the novel he follows her to France on a desperate mission to declare his love for her, Diana silences him, thus preventing him from stepping outside of the fiction and into what is described as an 'abyss' (*Diana*, p. 214). For Percy, this abyss is the social and professional consequences of an ill-

---

103 Diane Elam, '"We Pray to Be Defended from Her Cleverness": Conjugating Romance in George Meredith's *Diana of the Crossways*', *Genre* 21 (1988), pp. 187, 189. In some ways, Diana can be seen as an early form of the New Woman, or at least a version of the 'girl of the period'. Her efforts at self-determination and independence reflect the feminist goals that were defined and codified over the succeeding decade into the emerging figure of the New Woman. But, as Rita Kranidis argues, Diana's ultimate surrender to the conventional romantic resolution of marriage and motherhood significantly reduces any contribution she could have made to feminist ideals [Rita Kranidis, *Subversive Discourse: The Cultural Production of Late Victorian Feminist Novels* (London: Macmillan, 1995)].

advised affair. For Diana, the abyss marks the gulf between fiction and reality. The image of their romance that Diana creates is implicit, unspoken, and non-physical, and in order to protect this cherished vision, Diana must prevent him from expressing a different version of the relationship. Her effort to control an image of Percy is also an attempt to control her own sexuality and to mend a public image damaged by the scandals that have plagued her since her marriage. This control, however, lasts only as long as she conforms to the image of feminine authorship offered to her by the romance genre.

In composing her third novel, her former ambition and productivity are lost and she becomes subject to 'heavy musings' and irregular habits. She also adopts what she considers a perverse approach to her writing: aiming for a more realistic portrayal of both plot and character, she knows as she is writing that the book will be a professional failure. This wilful disregard for the marketplace, however, could also be described as artistic integrity. 'She had the anticipatory sense of its failure'; the narrator comments, 'and she wrote her best, in perverseness; of course she wrote slowly; she wrote more and more realistically of the wooden supernumeraries of her story, labelled for broad guffaw or deluge tears' (*Diana*, p. 221). In other words, she attempts in her third novel to move from the popular, emotional romances of her first two novels to a more realist form of writing that, by the 1880s, had acquired considerably more intellectual capital. This movement toward the intellectual form suggests another effort at reorienting her authorial identity. Diana claims for her writing an artistic integrity that seeks to align her work with the productions of high culture, to divorce herself from the feminine and its problems for female sexuality. But Diana cannot escape the fact that her primary reason for writing is money. When she says, 'Ink is my opium, and the pen my nigger, and he must dig up gold for me', she applies metaphors of both mastery and forgetfulness to this motivation (*Diana*, p. 115). She needs to control money in order to retain her independence and respectability, but she must also deny this economic imperative in order to maintain the complex image she projects of unconventional respectability. Diana treads a narrow and shifting path between financial and domestic security that, when properly negotiated, offers her social opportunities normally denied to the outcast woman.

The popular and critical failure of her third and fourth books, though, denies her this masterful position, and she finds her authorial identity denuded of masculine genius and of feminine propriety. The loss of control over her authorial identity undermines her power to control the image she has constructed of her relationship with Percy, and she can no longer keep him from changing the nature of their relationship. When Percy literally begins to manipulate her, grabbing her in his arms and kissing her, the fiction of her vision of their relationship becomes evident. In her fictional image of their romance, Diana exerted control over Percy, shaping an image of him through her book and granting or denying him her attention. But when forced to comply in the actual physical consummation of this visionary romance, 'she felt humiliated, plucked violently from the throne where she had long been sitting securely, very proudly' (*Diana*, p. 311). Like Lady Carbury, Diana's participation in a literary life leads to the physical degradation of unwanted sexual advances. But this is not a process of degradation that leads to self-definition. The crucial difference between the two women lies, unsurprisingly, in their experience of actual motherhood. Without having had any children, Diana's body still represents sexual promise rather than a promise fulfilled, and without the purifying power of motherhood, sexual indiscretion initiates the fall without the redemption.

The image of authorial mastery that Diana attempts to project is doomed to fail because this is her 'dreamed Diana', an image which is merely a public projection of the 'half-known, half-suspected, developing creature claiming to be Diana', that she thinks herself to be (*Diana*, p. 97). From the beginning, then, Diana's self-image is fractured and indeterminate, and as such, it puts Diana in the contradictory position of being able to create, yet powerless to control, her own self image. Losing the power to control the image of herself and her relationship with Percy that she has created endangers her ability to redefine herself within a new, equally beneficial position. Lady Carbury's seamless transformation into Mrs. Broune suggests a calculated decision and self-determination to trade independence for financial security. Diana, on the other hand, seems carried along by forces beyond her control when she decides at the end of the novel to marry her unromantic and stalwart friend Tom Redworth. Like the tireless Captain Dobbin of Thackeray's *Vanity Fair*, Redworth's sheer patience eventually seems to wear Diana down and constitutes the method through which 'a barely willing woman was led to bloom with the nuptial sentiment' (*Diana*, p. 402). Self-determination is denied Diana because she refuses to pander to conventional dictates and popular demands, but this artistic integrity is also her downfall when it leaves her without a clearly defined identity.

Diana's degradation, her artistic failure, and her unwilling capitulation to marriage all seem the result of a self-inflicted crisis created by what the narrator identifies as Diana's 'perverseness'. From one perspective, this perverseness could be seen as Diana's effort to define her work as masculine; her motivation to write could be seen as a vocational drive as she seeks a level of genius which, according to the conventional model of female authorship, it would be impossible for her to achieve. From another, her perverseness appears as the wilful desire to defy the critics and readers who have enjoyed the 'womanly' vacuity of her first two novels. This perspective is given credence by Gillian Beer's suggestion that there is a close affinity in this novel between Meredith and his heroine. Through Diana, she argues, Meredith depicts the 'relationship between writer and reader in action – that relationship which troubled him throughout his career and which in his own work contained always a large element of antagonism'.[104] Her degradation is a direct result of her refusal to compromise, an indication of the artistic integrity she had hoped to achieve. In this way, Diana can be seen as the embodiment of Meredith's own problems of integrating artistic integrity and popular success. In choosing the degraded female author as his representative, though, Meredith exhibits his own 'perverse' drive to emphasise his vulnerability within the popular literary marketplace.

---

104 Gillian Beer, *Meredith, A Change of Masks: A Study of the Novels* (London: Athlone Press, 1970), p. 142.

This perverseness is described by Allon White as Meredith's 'masochism', his compulsive need to relive the experience of shame brought on by the public exposure of writing.[105] In his representation of Diana, Meredith carefully obscures this sense of shame by projecting onto a female author, for whom the adoption of high-cultural discourse represented a substantial problem, an impersonal, artistic, masculine style of writing likely to antagonise its intended audience.

The belief in literature as a revelation of personality was repeatedly denied by writers throughout the second half of the nineteenth century not only because it destabilised private respectability; it also undermined the perception of literature as a professional occupation for both men and women. The principle of compatibility that had worked so well for the seamstress and the artist was more complicated for the authoress because the presumption of her personal involvement with her work exposed the domestic sphere to untenable public scrutiny. While the metaphor of authorship as a (pro)creative act, for instance, suggested that writing itself could be an essentialist act for women, it also emphasised the female author's need to balance her writing with her domestic life. The feminine, motherly writer could only maintain her private respectability at the cost to her professional identity. What the image of the woman writer emphasises in writing by both men and women is the process of negotiation between the public and the private in which all authors participated. For male authors, this figure gave them a benchmark against which they could define the qualities that constituted their work as masculine and, therefore, intellectual and artistic.[106] The figure of the female author could also be a repository for their professional anxieties without exposing male authorship to risk of public exposure.

That the clash between the professional and the domestic, between the public and private, the artistic and the mundane, in the construction of authorial identity was framed within models of female experience, however, highlighted the vulnerability inherent in the supposed private nature of writing for all authors. And the contested subjectivity and unstable social status of the figure of the woman writer made her an effective symbol of the alienation of the private individual in the capitalist marketplace. For female authors, the process of negotiation enabled them to use the qualities of feminine writing to define a specifically female space in the professional, public sphere in terms that were not likely to become socially prejudicial to them. The woman writer's alienated position in the marketplace therefore represented a viable professional space wherein the identity of the female author could develop and flourish.

---

105   Allon White, *The Uses of Obscurity: The Fiction of Early Modernism* (London: Routledge and Kegan Paul, 1981), chap 4.

106   Mark Turner describes, for instance, Trollope's effort to create a separate and self-contained male space in the 'feminine' world of the periodical press by recreating the intellectual atmosphere of the gentleman's club in the non-fiction prose of the *Cornhill Magazine*, Mark W. Turner, *Trollope and the Magazines: Gendered Issues in Mid-Victorian Britain* (London: Macmillan, 2000).

Chapter 4

Unceasing Industry:
Work and the Female Performer

The interest in creative work as a revelation of personality was not only a phenomenon encountered by authors in the second half of the nineteenth century. Writing in 1867 about the actress Helen Faucit, the *Art Journal* noted the priority given to the personal attributes of the performer over her performance when it commented that 'it is not of the art we think, while she is before us, but of the perfect picture of an ideal woman'.[1] Victorian critics were well aware of the cult of personality which determined the public's relationship with both male and female performers; it was, as Mowbray Morris argued in 1883, the defining characteristic of the art of acting:

> It is less the art than the artist that we admire and applaud. The poet, the painter, the sculptor, the musician – it is their work that attracts and charms us; but of themselves – the workmen, often we know little or nothing, save their names as title-page or catalogue may have preserved them. But with the actor, the man himself, the individual is all in all.[2]

Although Morris overestimated the public's indifference to discovering the personality behind a poem, he points out a crucial distinction between the stage and other artistic professions. As the other chapters have shown, the propriety of women working in other artistic professions could be demonstrated by the assertion of compatibility between their work and their domestic duties. Arguments for this compatibility depended on two closely related factors. Firstly, compatibility relied upon the convenience of work that could be done at home. Needlework, painting, and writing could all be quietly and privately produced in the drawing room in between the demands of the household duties. As the *English Woman's Journal* noted in 1859, 'The writer, the painter, any other artist in fact, can work independently'. But, because of the nature of theatrical work, the *Journal* added, 'the dramatic artist cannot'.[3]

Secondly, the artistic items produced by such 'independent' female workers could be proof of their domestic qualities. A painting, a book, or a tapestry could be considered as a concrete testimony to the propriety, or impropriety, of the

---

1   'The Art of the Stage', *Art Journal* 19 (1867), p. 20.

2   Mowbray Morris, 'On Some Recent Theatrical Criticisms', *Macmillan's Magazine* 48 (1883), p. 321.

3   'A Few Words About Actresses and the Profession of the Stage', *English Woman's Journal* 2 (1859), p. 393.

woman who created it. But since the female performer did not produce anything as tangible as a book or a painting, the product of her artistry was not so easily evaluated. Every person who read *Jane Eyre* had access to the same text, but on the stage, each performance was different and specific to the time and place of its production. An actress could be identified with a particular role – 'We speak of Lady Macbeth', Morris noted, 'while we are in reality thinking of Mrs. Siddons'.[4] But the transience and intangible nature of a single performance made it unreliable as a measurement of feminine respectability. Even the most celebrated performance produced no substantial artefact, and reviewers were forced to look outside the actual representation onstage in order to determine the propriety of a woman's performance. Much of the critical work of recent years has discussed this issue of the Victorian female performer's propriety by focusing on the visual aspect of her performance. Whether erotic, sculptural, or dramatic object, the performer is identified by these studies as a commodity available for public consumption.[5] This chapter draws on this formulation of the female performer as commodity in so far as it defines the Victorian theatre as another kind of work space ultimately designed to offer commodities to a paying audience. Rather than seeing her merely as a sexual object for sale, however, this chapter will show that the woman's body could also be defined mechanistically as one of a number of working components in a labour-intensive profession. This chapter traces what Kerry Powell calls the 'familiar narrative in which women of the theatre achieved social acceptance gradually over the Victorian period'.[6] What it makes clear is that, within popular representations, the performer's work was often portrayed not as an obstacle to be overcome on this path to social redemption, but rather as one of the crucial sources of this acceptance. The propriety of the female performer, I argue, was often measured by the variety of activities that constituted her work in the theatre, and many credited her with respectability by citing the long hours and selfless dedication to work that her profession required.

The World of the Stage

Some reviewers, particularly those writing for women's magazines such as the *Lady's World*, asserted the propriety of a particular actress by focusing on those aspects of her role that could be considered the most feminine. A detailed description of an admired costume could take up paragraphs of print, and the critical estimate of her work

---

4   Morris, 'On Some Recent Theatrical Criticisms', p. 321.

5   See, for instance, Michael Booth, *Victorian Spectacular Theatre, 1850-1910* (London: Routledge & Kegan Paul, 1981); Tracy Davis, *Actresses as Working Women: Their Social Identity in Victorian Culture* (London: Routledge, 1991); Gail Marshall, *Actresses on the Victorian Stage: Feminine Performance and the Galatea Myth* (Cambridge: Cambridge University Press, 1998); Martin Miesel, *Realizations: Narrative, Pictorial and Theatrical Arts in Nineteenth-Century England* (Princeton: Princeton University Press, 1983).

6   Kerry Powell, *Women and Victorian Theatre* (Cambridge: Cambridge University Press, 1997), p. xi.

often involved a survey of the emotional responses it elicited. *The Times'* review, for instance, of Ellen Terry's performance as Juliet in the 1882 Lyceum production of *Romeo and Juliet* focuses more on her costume than performance, noting that 'Miss Terry has never been more exquisitely dressed than in her first robe of pure white satin bordered with gold, and in the lovely pale blue brocade that forms her second costume'.[7] The review then continues its critique of Terry's Juliet by noting that 'Foremost among all the requisites for a Juliet is the physical requisite, – she should look the part; and that Miss Terry does this to perfection, her admirers need not be told. In the tender passages; in the exquisite, unapproachable balcony scene; in the farewell with her husband, in the first love scene of all, she completely commands her audience'.[8] Her dramatic talent, while credited with showing through in 'several minor touches', gets the merest mention at the end, almost as an afterthought in the review.[9] As in this review, sentiment, fashion, and beauty, all traditionally feminine interests, were regularly referenced in descriptions of the actress's performance.

The womanliness of a single performance or performer had a wider significance for arguments over the acceptability of the theatre as an entertainment for the moral middle classes. Indeed, the propriety of actresses was identified as one of the central issues in discussions concerning the legitimacy of the stage. In the first half of the century, much of what was written about the theatre did not distinguish between actors and actresses; they were judged equally as either moral or immoral, respectable or disreputable.[10] But, as Christopher Kent argues, from the 1850s, differences between actors and actresses were asserted with increasing frequency.[11] This double standard is criticised in an article written for the *Saturday Review* in 1862:

> The objection to the theatre which most good people make is, that actors and actresses are not virtuous characters, or rather, although modesty and prudery may forbid them saying so plainly, they do not so much care about the men, but they think the women are bad ... The objection to theatre is therefore really, in the main, an objection to the character of the women.[12]

In this passage, the character of the actress is identified as an issue not only of personal morality, but also of institutional legitimacy, and the figure of the actress is shown to be the target of the public's disapproval of the stage in general. The connection

---

7   'Romeo and Juliet at the Lyceum', *The Times* (9 March 1882), p. 6.

8   Ibid.

9   Ibid.

10   For a general overview of theatre criticism throughout the nineteenth century see George Rowell, *Victorian Dramatic Criticism* (London: Methuen, 1971). Although Rowell's compilation is not comprehensive, it does provide a good collection of the writings of the most prolific and well-respected critics such as William Hazlitt, G.H. Lewes, and William Archer.

11   Christopher Kent, 'Image and Reality: The Actress and Society', *A Widening Sphere: Changing Roles of Victorian Women*, Martha Vicinus, ed. (Bloomington: Indiana University Press, 1977), p. 95.

12   'The Army and the Stage', *Saturday Review* 13 (1862), p. 321.

between the reputation of the actress and the theatre in general was satirised by *Punch* in 1884 in an article commenting on the publication of a speech on 'The Drama' given by Madge Kendal to the Congress of the National Association for the Promotion of Social Science that included a portrait and autograph of the actress:

> For let it be once known far and wide that a lovely woman, exhibiting in classic drapery the exquisite gifts of Nature touched up for Stage purposes by theatrical Art, is in her private life a model of all the virtues, and this will serve as an attractive advertisement to many goody-goody people who might otherwise have avoided what would have appeared to them, when forming their opinion of the piece and Actress from the photographs, to be merely the assumption of a certain character on account of the opportunity afforded by it for suggestive display ... The strictest virtue, cleverly advertised, is a greater attraction than the most notorious reputation for profligacy. The latter will attract some: the former all. And so, nowhere more than on the Stage, is Virtue its own reward.[13]

In this article, the author censures not Kendal's participation in self-publicity, but the hypocrisy of 'an Actress [who] preaches self-effacement, in the matter of advertisements, as a professional duty', yet allows her speech to be published with a portrait and autograph which 'become a *réclame* for the talented Actress'.[14] The complex and deferential manner in which actresses were obliged to promote themselves suggests their essentially contradictory status as professional women performers. The publicity inherent to the acting profession strongly transgressed social sanctions prohibiting female self-publicity, always leaving successful actresses, such as Kendal, to answer, somehow, for their success.

Discussions concerning the respectability of the stage had specific resonance for the female performer, and the general 'objection to theatre' impacted on them most significantly because of the threat such open, and often celebrated, female commodification posed to the middle-class ideals of private femininity. This threat is most clearly emphasised in frequent comparison between the actress and the prostitute because, whatever her talent or character, it was difficult for an actress to escape the fact that she worked in a very conspicuous occupation and was paid for what many considered to be merely a form of sexual display.[15] Actresses were thus an easy target for the vehement objections against women working not only because of the highly public nature of their work, but also because this work lacked clear domestic associations. In fact, as Michael Baker observes, 'The position of the professional actress ran directly counter to the prevailing view of womanhood'.[16]

---

13   'The Flame Once Kendal'd', *Punch* 87 (25 Oct. 1884), p. 193.

14   Ibid.

15   For further discussion of the association of the actress with the prostitute see Tracy Davis, 'Actresses and Prostitutes in Victorian London', *Theatre Research International* 13 (1988), pp. 221-34.

16   Michael Baker, *The Rise of the Victorian Actor* (London: Croom Helm, 1978), p. 97. For a discussion of how this idea of the actress as different from normal womanhood was used to moderate the threat that actresses posed to the patriarchal power structure see Kerry Powell, *Women and Victorian Theatre*.

The strangeness of the actress to ordinary womanhood was also compounded by the fact that, more than any other occupation, the acting profession was often presented as a homogeneous 'institution'[17] existing in a strange and clannish 'world within a world'[18] commonly referred to as 'the stage'. Far from demonstrating compatibility, the actress was identified with the prostitute instead of the domestic woman, with public work instead of private accomplishments, and with the public institution of the stage instead of the home. This distance was emphasised throughout the first half of the century even in those novels in which the actress appears only as a minor character. The provincial leading lady Miss Snevellicci of Dickens's *Nicholas Nickleby* (1839), the grasping and selfish Miss Costigan of Thackeray's *Pendennis* (1850), and the exotic and tragic Stella of Benjamin Disraeli's *Coningsby* (1844) are portrayed almost exclusively as women of the stage. In fact, the distance between the world of the stage and the domestic sphere forms the central focus of many early theatre novels. Mrs. E.J. Burbury's *Florence Sackville, or Self-Dependence* (1851) and Annie Edwards's *The Morals of Mayfair* (1858) both take the incongruity between these two spheres as their subject. While Burbury's novel features a modest, self-controlled, and genteel actress with a theatrical temperament, Edwards tells the story of an actress whose corrupt and selfish nature leads her to beguile wealthy lovers and drink heavily until she loses her job and dies penniless in the back streets of the Haymarket. Although their plots differ considerably, both stories feature as their actress-heroines reduced middle-class gentlewomen who turn to the stage in order to earn money, and the transition they make from the home to the stage dramatises the gulf between these two ways of life.

Like all institutions, though, the stage had its own highly systematised structure of rules and relations and its own hierarchy of social and economic organisation. There were 'various classes of theatres' as well as 'gradations and sections' in the kinds of theatrical employment.[19] A London engagement was better than a provincial tour, and appearing at Her Majesty's Theatre was more lucrative than performing at the Garrick. A leading role was more respectable than a part in the chorus, and Shakespearean tragedy was more desirable than a Dion Boucicault melodrama.[20] In relation to the performers, this hierarchy translated into the distinction between the small theatrical 'nobility' comprised of the most popular and successful actors such as Henry Irving, Squire Bancroft, and Herbert Beerbohm Tree (all of whom received knighthoods), the large middle class of ordinary performers, and the under classes that staffed the chorus and ballet lines.

---

17   'Peace and Good-Will: The Pulpit and the Stage', *Era* (27 Jan. 1867), p. 10.

18   'On the Adoption of Professional Life by Women', *English Woman's Journal* 2 (1858), p. 7.

19   'A Few Words About Actresses', p. 395; Eliza Lynn Linton, 'The Wild Women as Social Insurgents', *Nineteenth Century* 30 (1891), pp. 596-605.

20   For a description of the social and economic hierarchy of the nineteenth-century theatre, see Michael Booth, *Theatre in the Victorian Age* (Cambridge: Cambridge University Press, 1991).

In this social and economic stratification, the theatrical hierarchy mimicked the hierarchy of Victorian society. Physical separation, for instance, accompanied social distinction in the theatre just as it did in the country house. The principal actress had her own dressing room even though, as Mrs. Mowatt describes in her *Autobiography of an Actress*, it was usually only 'a small closet-like apartment' furnished with little more than a 'dingy looking-glass, a couple of super-annuated chairs, a rickety washstand'.[21] Although only a rude apartment, Mowatt explains, this 'star dressing-room' served to separate the leading ladies from the 'despised, persecuted, and often misjudged race' of the ballet girls.[22] In its quest for legitimacy, the theatrical institution attempted to adopt the social structures of mainstream society. Such separation was necessary because, like their working-class counterparts, the women of the vulnerable theatrical under class were often the object of suspicions of sexual and moral impropriety, and their low pay, long hours, and virtual anonymity left them unable to defend themselves against such insinuations.[23] While the ballet girls were most often considered to be 'the perpetrators of "beastly excesses"', Jan Macdonald notes, there were people who were sympathetic to the vulnerable reputations of the 'lesser ladies' of the stage.[24] In many periodical articles discussing the plight of these less fortunate performers, actresses were frequently cast as the unwitting victims of profligate husbands, unscrupulous managers, and malicious moralists.[25] It was also often suggested that they were merely misunderstood.[26]

---

21   Mrs. Mowatt, *Autobiography of an Actress*, rpt. in *Eliza Cook's Journal* 7 (1854), p. 361.

22   Ibid., pp. 361, 186.

23   See, for instance, A.T. Davidson, 'The Clergy and the Theatre', *Macmillan's Magazine* 37 (1878), pp. 497-503.

24   Jan McDonald, 'Lesser Ladies of the Victorian Stage', *Theatre Research International* 13 (1988), p. 239.

25   For an example of the first see 'Actresses' Husbands', *Athenaeum* (4 April 1874), pp. 469-70, and 'The Music Hall', *The Cornhill Magazine* 13 (1889), pp. 68-79; this is also the theme of a story by Mary Braddon entitled 'Her Last Appearance' (1877). For an example of the second see 'Woman's Work in Public Amusements', *Work and Leisure* 6 (1881), pp. 129-32, 159-64 (this article also contains an argument against the condemnation of the stage by the church). A good example of the third can be seen in a series of articles and letters written to the *Era* in January of 1867. These letters objected to the statement of one Rev. Dr. Walker of Cheltenham who was said to have preached against the theatre as nothing but a 'robbers' den and the ante-chamber of Hell'. See especially Silas Sunbeam, 'Church and Theatre', *Era* (13 Jan. 1867), p. 7, and 'Peace and Good Will: The Pulpit and the Stage', *Era* (27 Jan. 1867), p. 10. Juliet Pollock argues against 'ecclesiastical persecution' ['For and Against the Play', *Nineteenth Century* 1 (1877), p. 618], and *The Times* accuses clergymen of exaggeration [(7 Oct. 1879), p. 7].

26   See, for instance, [H.B. Baker], 'Our Old Actors: Mrs. Jordan', *Temple Bar* 51 (1877), pp. 174-88, and 'Going on the Stage', *Saturday Review* 22 (1866), pp. 602-604. This was also a theme included in a story published by Henrietta Stannard entitled 'Stage Effects', *Cornhill Magazine* 6 (1886), pp. 490-503.

But no actress's reputation was ever really safe from moralistic attacks. Although well-known performers and middle-class actresses had the resources to deflect such criticism, even the best publicised stage personalities could find themselves subjected to bourgeois censure. 'When aspersions were aimed at a low status group', Davis argues, 'a ripple effect implicated all other female performers: the distinctions between chorus singers, ballet-dancers, supernumeraries, and principal players that were so important to the profession were of little concern to the general public'.[27] Although the stage's internal system of social stratification mimicked that of Victorian society, it lacked the public/private distinction that gave force to the claims of the middle-class domestic woman's modesty. The professional hierarchy that separated actresses of higher standing from those of the chorus did not offer the same protection as conventional class barriers. Actresses not only shared the same environment, they also shared the same set of associations, and, therefore, the distance between the various 'classes' of actresses could be asserted but not sustained. What the figure of the actress demonstrated most clearly was the inadequacy of the existing social structures to protect the working woman from unwanted and objectionable associations.

For those sympathetic or concerned with the image of work as a respectable pursuit for women, then, redeeming the image of the actress was a necessary project. Even the stars of the Victorian stage found that protecting the reputation of ballet girls was important for maintaining their own respectability. And while representations of the actress in the first half of the century had generally highlighted the distance between the stage and the domestic sphere, many began to recognise the importance of arguing the opposite. Unsurprisingly, then, this is precisely what Mrs. Mowatt sets out to do in a story included in her autobiography about a ballet girl named Georgina. Mowatt uses Georgina's story as exemplary of her position that 'there is nothing in the profession *necessarily* demoralizing or degrading, not even to the poor ballet girl'.[28] This argument consists of the lengthy description of the continuous work and domestic attention that occupies every moment of Georgina's life. A short excerpt is given here:

> Georgina's parents kept no servant; she discharged the entire duties of the household – cooking washing, sewing, everything. From daylight to midnight not a moment of her time was unemployed. She must be at rehearsal every morning at ten o'clock, and she had two miles and a half to walk to the theatre … Her ten o'clock rehearsal lasted from two to four hours, more frequently the latter … From rehearsal she hastened home to prepare the midday meal of her parents and attend to her mothers wants. After dinner she received a class of children, to whom she taught dancing for a trifling sum. If she had half an hour to spare, she assisted her father in copying law papers. Then tea must be prepared, and her mother arranged comfortable for the night. Her long walk to the theatre must be accomplished at least half an hour before the curtain rose … Not to be ready for the stage

---

27 Davis, 'Actresses and Prostitutes in Victorian London', p. 222.

28 Mrs. Mowatt, 'Ballet Girls', from *Autobiography of An Actress*, rpt. in *Eliza Cook's Journal* 7 (1854), p. 186.

would have subjected her to a forfeit. Between the acts, or when she was not on stage, there she sat again, in her snug corner of the green-room, dressed as a fairy, or a maid of honour, or a peasant, or a page, with a bit of work in her hands, only laying down the needle, which her fingers actually made fly, when she was summoned by the call-boy, or required to change her costume by the necessities of the play.[29]

As only a portion of Mowatt's longer description of Georgina's endless domestic and professional duties, this excerpt shows the importance Mowatt placed on the intricate detailing of Georgina's daily life. Mowatt uses her constant work and almost saint-like self-abnegation as a shining testament to her virtuousness and feminine propriety. Drawing on religious imagery to this description, she concludes:

[T]his flower blossomed within the walls of a theatre, was the indigenous growth of that theatre; a *wallflower*, if you like, but still sending up the rich fragrance of gratitude to Him by whose hand it was fashioned. To the eyes of the Pharisee, who denounces all dramatic representations, while with self-applauding righteousness he boldly approaches the throne of mercy, this 'ballet girl', like the poor publican, stood 'afar off'. To the eyes of the great Judge, which stood the nearer?[30]

Mowatt's discussion of Georgina describes the uplifting influence of the variety of activities that surround the actual performance. By focusing on Georgina's duties off stage as largely determinative of her life as a performer, Mowatt locates Georgina's respectability in the overall execution of both her domestic and professional work. Georgina's respectability as a woman is tied to her life as a performer. She comes from a family for whom 'it was difficult to define their position in the social scale', but her patient submission to her domestic duties and the 'duties of her profession' is described by Mowatt as something which 'elevates and purifies the spirit'.[31] By articulating the *business* of Georgina's theatrical and domestic work, Mowatt not only dismisses the moral ambiguities associated specifically with the ballet girl's public display, but also turns this performer into an example of ideal femininity for all women.

The possibility of the performer to act as an example for all women was further explored by the author of 'A Few Words About Actresses and the Profession of the Stage' for the *English Woman's Journal*. In this article, the author argues that recording the minutiae of the activities comprising the days of most actresses was a necessary enterprise because, 'The life of an Actress is to the world at large a curious *terra incognita*, peopled by forbidding phantoms of evil, or seductive visions of pleasure and success'.[32] Recording these details, the author argues, will show that this *terra incognita* is a public misconception of what is, at its heart, a rather more familiar existence. The public would often find, the author argues, 'an amount of sober purpose and heroic faithfulness to duty' in 'irreproachable women and patient

---

29   Ibid., p. 187.
30   Ibid.
31   Ibid.
32   'A Few Words About Actresses', p. 385.

workers'.[33] But, according to this author, the world of the stage is not only a place where virtuous women could exist; it is also a place where the best women are created:

> When temptations from without, and dangers within the theatre are escaped – the chief amongst the latter being that of losing her moral entity in a confusion of easy sympathies and temporary unions of interest, a danger arising out of the very nature of her work itself – when these are overcome, very helpful and satisfactory women are the result of an actress's training. Their larger experience of life, the way in which they have had to grapple with real, hard facts, to think and work and depend upon themselves, their quiet battles for order and purity, and the constant use of the higher faculties of taste and imagination, raise them far above those women who are absorbed by the petty vanities and trifles and anxieties of a woman's ordinary life.[34]

One of the chief protections against the temptations and dangers of the theatre, this author argues, is attention to the business of the profession. The busier a performer is, the less time she would have to get into trouble: 'Study, acting, rehearsing, and preparing her dresses, leave her with scarcely a moment's rest, and week after week, month after month, if she is so fortunate as to obtain a long engagement, this strain upon mind and body goes on ... So, unless she neglect her work, or degenerate into a slattern, she must be unceasingly industrious'.[35] Unceasing industry and long engagements were necessary for the actress to survive and were prerequisites for success. Beauty and self-publicity can get you onto the stage, the author argues, but true success comes from professional commitment: 'It is in the rough hard work itself that the real service lies'.[36]

Statements such as this were derived especially from principles of Thomas Carlyle's 'gospel of work' and were concerned with the growing rationalisation of labour as a spiritual and moral enterprise. The public image of the actress benefited from the use that was made by the women's movement of the Protestant work ethic (expressed in sentiments such as Dinah Craik's assertion that 'Labour is worship'[37]) in order to support the arguments for expanding the opportunities for work for women. In consequence, as the rest of this chapter will show, the actress's respectability grew as did the bulk of writing repeatedly detailing the actual work she completed and the intricate details of her every day life. Shifting attention from the mere physical display of an actress's body onstage to the work she was doing also shifted the issue of the commodification of the actress from the sexual to the industrial economy. To focus on acting as a form of work rather than sexual display, then, meant redeeming the image of the actress in the eyes of the middle class. In Mowatt's story, for

---

33 Ibid., pp. 386, 387.

34 Ibid., pp. 398-97.

35 Ibid., p. 394.

36 Ibid., p. 390.

37 Dinah Craik, *A Woman's Thoughts About Women,* (London: Hurst and Blackett, 1858), p. 18.

instance, Georgina's good character is confirmed by her prohibitive work schedule and her domestic feeling, and Mowatt's concluding question even goes so far as to place the moral integrity created by such work above simple religiousness as the path to grace. Georgina's good character, though, is also corroborated by less conventional means. The ultimate confirmation of her innocence is garnered from the information that she had, in effect, been born and raised on the stage, that she had 'literally grown up behind the scenes of a theatre'.[38] Although such domestic deprivation would be seen as disastrous for most women, in representations of the actress, it often had the opposite effect.

Natural Acting and Unconscious Emotion: Unsexing the Professional in Geraldine Jewsbury's *The Half Sisters*

A theatrical upbringing was seen by many as a natural bulwark to respectability for the working actress. As outlined by the *English Woman's Journal*, the acceptable motivations attributed to those who applied themselves to the 'Art of Acting' were much the same as those cited for other artistic women: 'a gifted woman's devotion to art, or the honest and laborious means by which she earns her bread'.[39] But the standard appeal to vocation and necessity in order to secure respectability is significantly modified in this article, Mowatt's story, and other discussions of the actress throughout the mid-Victorian period, by the presence of a third motivation which set the actress apart from her other artistic contemporaries: some women were destined for the stage by the circumstances of their birth and 'drifted into it as their natural and inevitable course'.[40] Daughters of the dynastic acting families, like Fanny Kemble, Madge Kendal, or Ellen Terry, performed from the earliest years of their childhood, appearing on stage and beginning their careers as a matter of course in what was considered by many to be the obvious and natural development of the life of a stage child. Terry, for instance, who was, as she described herself, a 'child of the stage', made her debut in *The Winter's Tale* when she was nine and continued acting throughout her life.[41] The particular benefit of this circumstance, Sandra Richards notes, was its resemblance to conventional domesticity: 'The flourishing of theatrical dynasties throughout the century paved the way to respectability for the actress by making possible, for the first time, a family life as stable as any that could be found in the middle classes outside of the profession'.[42] Richards here is writing specifically about the domestic life of actresses as wives, but the theatrical dynasty provided shelter for actresses, regardless of whether they were born into or married into the family.

---

38 'Ballet Girls', p. 187.
39 'A Few Words About Actresses', pp. 387, 385.
40 Ibid., p. 386.
41 Ellen Terry, *The Story of My Life* (Woodbridge: Boydell Press, 1982), p. 1.
42 Sandra Richards, *The Rise of the English Actress* (London: Macmillan, 1993), p. 113.

Although some performers tried to keep their children away from the stage in order to protect them from the difficulties of life in the theatre,[43] for many there was a sense of destiny about the future of stage children. In the case of Fanny Kemble, this sense of destiny even seemed to overwhelm her inclination. As the daughter of Charles Kemble and the niece of Sarah Siddons, Fanny Kemble (1809-93) had an impeccable theatrical pedigree. But the story of her artistic life as it is told by friends, biographers, and even herself through her autobiographical writings, is repeatedly depicted as a constant struggle between what is described as her family's expectations and her histrionic personality on the one hand and her intellectual interests and conventional womanly feeling on the other.[44] It was this contradiction between nature and inclination that Henry James, in his obituary for her in 1893, identified as the most formative influence on her life and her career. 'One had to take her career, the juxtaposition of her interests', he argued, 'exactly as one took her disposition, for a remarkably fine cluster of inconsistencies'.[45] However, James recognised these apparent contradictions as part of a broader strategy that had been responsible, in large measure, for Kemble's successful creation of a respectable public persona. Her theatrical disposition, he argues, produced the appearance of 'submission to the general law', while her independent thought in fact granted her freedom from conventionalities.[46] As she served the theatre, theatricality served her.

What James calls theatrical, though, Kemble terms the dramatic, and in doing so, she steps back from the institution of the theatre to identify herself with what she considers to be a more natural form of performance:

> That which is dramatic in human nature is the passionate emotional humorous element, the simplest portion of our composition, after our mere instincts, to which it is closely allied, and this has no relation whatever, beyond its momentary excitement and gratification, to that which imitates it, and is its theatrical reproduction; the dramatic is the *real*, of which the theatrical is the *false*.
>
> Both nations and individuals in whom the dramatic temperament strongly preponderates are rather remarkable for a certain vivid simplicity of nature, which produces sincerity and vehemence of emotion and expression, but is entirely without the *consciousness* which is never absent from the theatrical element.[47]

---

43 William Macready, for instance, wrote to *The Times* insisting that his daughter was not going to become an actress and that she has no 'intention to quit the sphere of private life to which she had been educated', W.C. Macready, *The Times* (8 May 1860), p. 5.

44 Alison Booth argues that the homogeneity in the public perception and biographical accounts of Kemble's life is the result of the force of Kemble's own assertions about her life in her writing, Alison Booth, 'From Miranda to Prospero: The Works of Fanny Kemble', *Victorian Studies* 38 (1995), pp. 227-54. Her autobiographical writings mainly comprise a series of journals covering most of her life. These journals include: *Journal of a Young Actress* (1835), *Journal of a Residence on a Georgian Plantation in 1838-1839* (1863), *Records of Girlhood* (1879), and *Records of Later Life* (1882).

45 Henry James, 'Frances Anne Kemble', *Temple Bar* 97 (1893), p. 506.

46 Ibid.

47 Frances Anne Kemble, 'On the Stage', *Cornhill Magazine* 8 (1863), p. 733.

The form of dramatic acting that Kemble describes in this passage was defined by many theatre critics as 'natural' acting. Natural acting, which was also known as the Kemble school after Fanny Kemble's father, was generally thought to consist of a performance that did not seem to be a performance at all. Opposed to the Kemble school was the Garrick. This form of acting, named after the famous eighteenth-century actor David Garrick (1717-1779), was characterised by the highly stylised acting in which the performer expressed the emotion of the character through a codified system of facial expressions. Both schools of acting were regarded as legitimate working methods whose practice lent an air of professionalism and propriety to the stage. However, as theatrical fashions changed in the nineteenth century, the Garrick school was increasingly ridiculed.[48] An 1859 article in *All The Year Round*, for instance, lightly satirises the Garrick school, parodying an acting manual in its descriptions, for instance, of how to act grief and joy:

> Grief, sudden and violent, expresses itself by beating the head and forehead, tearing the hair, and catching the breath, as if choking; also by screaming, weeping, stamping, lifting the eyes from time to time to heaven, and hurrying backwards and forwards ... Joy is expressed by clapping of hands and exulting looks; the eyes are opened wide, and on some occasions raised to heaven; the countenance is smiling, not composedly but with features aggravated.[49]

In opposition to the natural school, the Garrick school in the middle of the century was identified as both overly theatrical and insincere, and the natural school was preferred by most critics. Along with the appearance of greater sincerity, natural acting, as it was defined by G.H. Lewes, also entailed a 'treatment which is *true to the nature of the character represented under the technical conditions of the representation*'.[50] Lewes's formulation called for not only a natural style, but an individualistic emotional response. He argued that in representing Hamlet, for instance, an actor must not react as just anyone would upon seeing a ghost, but as Hamlet would. Such a style of acting called upon performers to abandon standardised emotional representation that was recognizably 'theatrical' and advertised skilled acting performances as 'natural'. Madame Ristori, for instance, is praised because she practices an 'art so perfect that it is wholly hidden, that its products appear spontaneous, effortless. Never for a single moment does she *act*'.[51] And Madame

---

48   For a discussion of the Victorian dislike of performance that seemed too visibly rehearsed, see Rebecca Stern, 'Moving Parts and Speaking Parts: Situating Victorian Antitheatricality, *ELH* 65 (1998), pp. 423-44.

49   'Appalling Discloure for the Lord Chamberlain', *All The Year Round* 1 (1859), p. 263.

50   G.H. Lewes, 'On Natural Acting', *On Actors and the Art of Acting* (New York: Greenwood Press, 1968), p. 108 [italics in original].

51   [H.B. Baker], 'The Theatres', *Temple Bar* 39 (1873), p. 550.

Modjeska's Juliet is criticised because 'Her art is evident; she is all actress; self-conscious, inconsistent, disappointing'.[52]

Discourses concerning natural acting described an actual practice of performance wherein the labour of natural acting was conducted by the actress 'throwing herself into the role', in effect, temporarily becoming the character she performed. But this presumed transformation suggested attendant dangers for the actress. In becoming Lady Macbeth or Juliet, the actress would have to assume passions and experiences of that character. The actress could be seen as a tried and experienced woman without ever leaving the stage. Such danger, however, could be diffused by the idea of the innateness of the dramatic temperament that the term 'natural' acting implied. This, for instance is the argument used by Fanny Kemble in 'On the Stage' when she claimed the ability for natural acting as an inborn characteristic, an essential trait that could not be developed or learned. A person must inherit such a trait, she argues, as she had inherited it from her father. By simply reiterating her theatrical pedigree and asserting the innateness of her own dramatic nature, Kemble constructs an image of herself as the 'unconscious' actress who can transmit an emotion without knowing it. Like Sybil Vane of Oscar Wilde's *The Picture of Dorian Gray*, who can pour all her passion and sexuality into her stage performances while she remains ignorant of real love, Kemble appears as the innocent ingénue who does not recognise the sexuality at the heart of her theatrical performance. Kemble's claims that the stage was 'repugnant' to her seem to be at odds with both her theatrical career and her dramatic nature, but such a rhetorical strategy balances the career born out of necessity with the desire for respectability. It is obvious, to a writer for the *Daily Telegraph* at least, that 'The innate modesty of a woman rebels against the difficulties of the position of an actress, and few save women of the world or with minds of a genius have strength to pass through the ordeal'.[53] With a disingenuous innocence, Kemble locates her strength in her ignorance.

Such presumed ignorance is the central focus of the journal she kept from 1832-1834 while on tour in America with her father. She completed the journal before her marriage in July 1834, and throughout the journal she maintains an air of sexual innocence appropriate to the modest maiden. Even her portrayal of Juliet is devoid of conscious emotional display when she must rely on 'rouge' to simulate 'the startled life-blood in the cheek of that young passionate woman'.[54] In this journal, acting is not an outlet for any unspoken passion or natural pouring forth of a feminine soul, it is a mere job, an occupation which she pursues in order, she writes, 'to earn my bread, – and verily it was in the sweat of my brow'.[55] The image of the actress Kemble

---

52 'Court Cards', *Punch* 80 (1881), p. 165.

53 'Women and the Stage', *Daily Telegraph*, rpt. in *Women and Work* no. 31 (2 Jan. 1875), p. 5.

54 Fanny Kemble, *Journal of a Young Actress* (1835), Monica Gough, ed. (New York: Columbia University Press, 1990).

55 Fanny Kemble, *Journal of a Young Actress*, 2 vols (Philadelphia: Carey, Lea & Blanchard, 1835), p. 109. Quoted in Booth, 'From Miranda to Prospero', p. 234. Booth notes that there are certain differences between the 2 volume edition and Gough's reprint, including the absence of the section from which this quote is taken.

creates in her 1835 journal resonates interestingly with Mrs. Mowatt's story of the life of Georgina. Both are hard working, consistently busy, theatre born, and sexually innocent, and they also share a love of home. Off stage, Kemble presented herself to public inspection as a model of womanly virtue, never being seen in public without a chaperone and visibly maintaining, and recording for public view, her devotion to traditional womanly pursuits such as visiting, sewing, and reading.[56] Although her reiteration of her attention to domestic pursuits highlights the effectiveness of society's pressure to adhere to the domestic ideal, James argues that Kemble was able to use these conventions of womanhood consciously in order to fortify her claims to respectability.[57] Mrs. Mowatt's story also uses the details of a conventional domestic life as proof of proper feminine feeling. Georgina, although a ballet girl, is not only a virtuous and hard-working performer, she is also a model domestic woman whose 'devotion to her parents was the strongest impulse of her nature'.[58] The domestic instincts of these women, however, are fostered within their natural environment of the theatre. As actresses themselves, both Kemble and Mowatt used the image of the virtuous performer to protect their own respectability and stressed the domestic qualities that a life in the theatre can preserve, or even enhance.

In her theatrical novel, *The Half Sisters* (1848), Geraldine Jewsbury offered an early representation how the stage can function in this way in her depiction of her heroine, Bianca. By casting Bianca as the illegitimate daughter of a respectable, middle-class English father and a passionate Italian mother, Jewsbury creates a heroine who, while outcast from conventional society, possesses a dramatic temperament that grants her a natural place in the society of the stage. Italians, after all, were, as Fanny Kemble argued, 'nationally and individually ... dramatic'.[59] Even her humble and anonymous beginning as the 'Dumb Girl' for the local circus cannot hide the fact that Bianca 'had been intended by nature for an actress'.[60] Her natural capacity for dramatic art enables her to impersonate whatever character is required of her with virtually no training, and it also allows her to adapt easily to any situation that may arise. On the day of her first performance when Bianca goes out with the troop on a procession through the town to publicise the upcoming show, the narrator comments:

Bianca was stunned, bewildered, and ashamed of her conspicuous position, and of the wonder and notice they obtained from the crowd; but she had no sort of alternative, all those around her seemed to take it as a matter of course, and before the ride was over, the people she was amongst seemed the realities, and the people in the streets through which they passed appeared the show. (*Half Sisters*, p. 30)

---

56   Booth, 'From Miranda to Prospero', p. 237.

57   For a reading of actresses' autobiographies in relation to the domestic ideal see Mary Jean Corbett, *Representing Femininity: Middle-Class Subjectivity in Victorian and Edwardian Women's Autobiographies* (Oxford: Oxford University Press, 1992).

58   'Ballet Girls', p. 187.

59   Kemble, 'On the Stage', p. 733.

60   Geraldine Jewsbury, *The Half Sisters*, Joanne Wilkes, ed. (Oxford: Oxford University Press, 1994), p. 29. Further references to this edition will be given in the text.

Bianca unconsciously reorients her perception of the world in order to deal with the embarrassment she feels at this blatant exhibition. This unconscious transformation comes naturally to her and allows her to become the actress. As her fellow performers become real to her so does her own place in their conspicuous parade. Although Bianca has exposed herself in a most public fashion, appearing merely as an object to be gazed at in both the parade and as the dumb girl, she remains unaware of the sexual implications of her display because 'her sole idea of the circus was, that it was the means of earning a certain number of shillings, on which she might support her mother' (*Half Sisters*, p. 31). In giving Bianca such a compelling domestic motive for her work, Jewsbury gives force to her representation of Bianca's continuing innocence throughout her early career. Each time Bianca performs, she undergoes a transformation similar to that of her first performance. The action on the stage becomes her reality, and 'the tawdriness and paltriness of the dresses and trappings did not appear when seen from the proper point of view' (*Half Sisters*, p. 32).

Throughout the narrative, Jewsbury attempts to reorient the reader's perception of the 'proper point of view' from which Bianca's work should be seen. In the people that surround Bianca, she presents the various negative attitudes about the acting profession. For the middle-class men who are aware of the immodesty inherent in the sexual display of the actress, such as Bianca's fickle fianceé, Conrad Percy, or the middle-class industrialist, Mr. Bryant, Bianca's work as an actress is degrading and corrupt. Even her half sister Alice and her friend Lady Vernon, women who are themselves assured of her virtue and worth, think her work is dreadful and worthless, though less personally degrading. In explaining her work to Alice, Bianca exclaims:

> You cannot change my nature, I must be what I am. The stage is to me a *passion,* as well as a profession; I can work in no other direction; I should become worthless and miserable; all my faculties would prey upon myself, and I should even be wicked and mischievous, and God knows how bad, if I were placed in any other position. (*Half Sisters*, p. 134)

Bianca argues that her work is not only her means of supporting herself, it also serves to regulate her behaviour. Far from being an incitement to licentiousness, her work protects her virtue as she explains to Lady Vernon: 'I often wonder how women, who were *not* actresses, contrived to pass their time ... no rehearsal for three hours in the morning, no long performance in the evening, – to say nothing of the hard study between the times' (*Half Sisters*, p. 253-54). By devoting all her time to her work, Bianca sets herself apart from the women who are not actresses – the women who, like Alice, have to contrive ways to pass their time. It is these women, she implies, who are susceptible to wickedness because of 'the ENNUI, which eats like a leprosy into the life of women' (*Half Sisters*, p. 249).

In her comparison between Bianca and her half sister Alice, Jewsbury provides a clear example of this principle in action. Alice is a model of femininity, and the first time we see her, she is sitting with her mother, 'engaged on a large piece of household needlework' (*Half Sisters*, p. 13). Her life follows the proper and suitable path for a gentlewoman, and when she marries the eminently respectable Mr. Bryant, it seems as if she will spend a retiring life maintaining his household. But Alice, whose early domestic training should have perfectly prepared her for her role as a dutiful wife, falls victim to the boredom and frustration of her confining life and wishes for the type of excitement depicted in the romance novels she spends her copious free time reading. With no work to keep her busy, Alice falls prey to the wickedness of having too much free time and becomes the fallen woman who dies for her sexual sin, her flirtation with Conrad. Bianca, on the other hand, although an actress, fulfils the ideal role of the patient, steadfast, and trusting woman, remaining faithful to Conrad throughout their long relationship, even when he abandons her for months and despises her for her work. It is Bianca rather than Alice who fulfils the expectations of feminine virtue and is rewarded with a seemingly happy marriage to the eminently respectable Lord Melton at the end of the novel. By inverting the conventional expectations concerning the conduct and fate of Alice and Bianca, Jewsbury not only demonstrates the benefits of giving women something to do, but she also defines conventional womanly perfection as a form of emotional and sexual weakness. Meredith Cary argues that in her fiction Jewsbury repeatedly shows that women's lives are made better, more fulfilled and less dissolute, by work.[61] In this novel specifically, Lisa Surridge argues, Jewsbury 'exemplif[ies] the positive aspects of women's work … to suggest, with deep irony, that even stage life could be safer and more genuine than the false constraints of the "Mrs. Ellis" ideal'.[62] It is not simply, however, Bianca's work that ensures her virtuousness. Through the positive representation of Bianca's unconscious performance, her devotion to her mother, her natural dramatic temperament, and the vocation she feels for her work, Jewsbury shows the uncharitable judgments of the more conventional-seeming characters to be harsh and misguided.

Jewsbury thus describes work as a desirable activity for women by showing how it protects Bianca's virtue. She also further strengthens the justifications for Bianca's career by attributing to it an aspect of spiritual and social improvement. When preparing for her London debut, an old actor who has been Bianca's mentor advises her to devote herself to her work and to treat it as a sacred art form. It is only this kind of dedication to the work of acting rather than the rewards, he argues, that will neutralise the sexual associations that have historically plagued members of the profession: 'I believe you have it in you to raise it (the acting profession) from its meretricious state. It needs to be purified from the sensualism that has defaced it, before it can assume its legitimate rank' (*Half Sisters*, p. 161). The old actor appears to describe a credible image of genius for the acting profession. He holds out the rewards of art to Bianca, but insists that in order to achieve them she must sacrifice to her art her womanly nature, leaving behind in particular her love for Conrad. Bianca's mentor identifies in acting the conventional division between masculine

---

61   Meredith Cary, 'Geraldine Jewsbury and the Woman Question', *Research Studies* 42 (1974), pp. 201-14.

62   Lisa Surridge, 'Madame de Staël Meets Mrs. Ellis: Geraldine Jewsbury's *The Half Sisters*', *Carlyle Studies Annual* 15 (1995), p. 82.

genius and feminine emotion. But as an aging emblem of a traditional theatrical aristocracy, his notions of genius also seem narrow and outmoded, especially when Bianca, although awed by him, refuses to accept his pronouncements against love.

In fact, Bianca directly proves the old actor wrong in her first London performance when she chooses to play Juliet, a character who is herself passionate and ruled by love, because it is a part she associates with Conrad. The power of Bianca's representation of Juliet lies in the sexual energy behind her passion for Conrad that, when channelled into her performance, electrifies the audience. As a natural actress, though, this channelling is presented as the unconscious result of her dramatic temperament, and when Bianca steps out of character, she leaves this passion behind, collapsing on the floor in a spent heap. In this way, Bianca's unconscious performance protects her modesty, providing her with an outlet denied to conventional women, such as Alice, for her passionate feelings for Conrad. Furthermore, it also contributes to the public perception of her as a model of 'perfect respectability' (*Half Sisters*, p. 178). Her success not only brings her financial reward, it also opens the doors of London society to her and wins her the admiration of the theatre-going public.

Such popularity, however, is also shown to be a double-edged sword. Along with success and popularity come the newspaper articles, gossip columns, and public interest that seeks to discover the personality behind the actress. As a public figure, Bianca must endure her private life being open to public inspection, and while the public 'reward[s] so much virtue, by lighting it up with their "countenance"', Bianca achieves in her social life 'a *succès*, as marked in its way, as that she had achieved in her profession' (*Half Sisters*, p. 178). Such personal publicity is announced by Conrad to be not only the abhorrent condition of the actress, but also of the female author as well:

> A woman who makes her mind public, or exhibits herself in any way, no matter how it may be dignified by the title of art, seems to me to be little better than a woman of a nameless class. I am more jealous of the mind than of the body; and, to me, there is something revolting in the notion of a woman who professes to love and belong to you alone, going and printing the secrets of her inmost heart, the most sacred workings of her soul, for the benefit of all who can pay for them … You know I am not straight-laced, but in the matter of matrimony one's respectability is at stake; it is the ground in which one hopes to take root and flourish, and the profession of an actress or an authoress is not the most promising for one's credit. (*Half Sisters*, p. 214)

In Conrad's scathing indictment of the impact an authoress or actress's career could have on a marriage, Jewsbury draws attention to her own ambivalence toward her career and her fears about the influence of a professional life on a woman's domestic happiness. In a letter to Jane Carlyle in 1850, Jewsbury expressed these difficulties when she wrote:

> [W]hen women get to be energetic, strong characters, with literary reputations of their own, and live in the world, with business to attend to, they all do get in the habit of making use of people, and of taking care of themselves in a way that is startling! And yet how are

they to help it? If they are thrown into the world, they must swim for their life … In short, whenever a woman gets to be a personage in any shape, it makes her hard and unwomanly in some point or other, and, as I tell you, I am bothered to explain how it is, or why it is, or how it should be otherwise. Because, if women chance to have genius, they have it, and must do something with it … but when they are recognised – their specialty spoils them as women, and I cannot at all reconcile the contradictions into anything like a theory … And yet, I suppose I shall go on writing books, and all that, and follow the profession of an author, as long as my brain holds good for the work. I wish I had a good husband and a dozen children![63]

J.M. Hartley takes these admissions to Jane Carlyle as evidence of Jewsbury's 'energetic drive towards combination' of, but ultimate 'sense of incongruity' at, her roles as 'woman' and 'writer'.[64] Judith Rosen sees them as confirmation of Jewsbury's inability to 'comprehend a female existence outside the absolutes that define and divide the two genders'.[65]

This ambivalence she expresses in her correspondence surfaces in *The Half Sisters* as a question over the benefits of a professional life for a woman. Verbalised by the caddish Conrad, this question expresses the same fears of hardness and unwomanliness expressed in the letter: 'What is it that professional life does for women? Take Bianca, if you will, as a specimen, she is one of the best, and what has been its effect? it has unsexed her, made her neither a man nor woman' (*Half Sisters*, p. 216). In Conrad's estimation, Bianca has sacrificed her femininity by dedicating herself to her work, as the old actor predicted she would. She has been damaged, Conrad argues, by being 'neither one thing nor another; she has neither the softness of a woman, nor the firm, well-proportioned principle of a man' (*Half Sisters*, p. 217). Conrad essentially embodies a conventional strain of middle-class thinking concerning the dangers of professionalism on a woman's sexuality, expressing disgust at what he sees as the sexual impropriety of Bianca's work on the stage. He idealises, instead, the traditional model of femininity embodied in the demure, domestic figure of Alice. But Jewsbury undermines Conrad's middle-class moralising by casting him as the seducer and ruination of the very woman he idealises. Condemning him to a life of remorse as a monk when Alice dies of her sexual shame, Jewsbury juxtaposes this substantial sexual indiscretion with Bianca's supposed impropriety.

Although Conrad's negative description of the professional woman's 'unsexing' is undermined by his own hypocrisy, his pronouncements can still be seen as an exaggerated form of Jewsbury's own doubts about the effect of work on a woman,

---

63   Geraldine Jewsbury, 'Letter 101', *Selections from the Letters of Geraldine Endsor Jewsbury to Jane Welsh Carlyle*, Mrs. A. Ireland, ed. (London: Longmans, 1892), pp. 368-69.

64   J.M. Hartley, 'Geraldine Jewsbury and the Problems of the Woman Novelist', *Women's Studies International Quarterly* 2 (1979), p. 139.

65   Judith Rosen, 'At Home Upon a Stage: Domesticity and Genius in Geraldine Jewsbury's *The Half Sisters*', *The New Nineteenth Century: Feminist Readings of Underread Victorian Fiction*, Barbara Leah Harman and Susan Meyers, eds (London: Garland Publishing, 1996), p. 19.

particularly that it could unsex her. But the representation of Bianca's performance suggests it could have more positive consequences. Like Charlotte Brontë in her characterisation of Vashti in *Villette* (1853), Jewsbury explores the power exercised upon an audience by the actress who, like Vashti, possesses the quality of being 'neither of man nor of woman'.[66] On the stage, Vashti is both 'marvellous' and 'wicked', 'strong' and 'horrible', and as such prompts Lucy Snowe to ask: 'If so much unholy force can arise from below, may not an equal efflux of sacred essence descend one day from above?'[67] Vashti's performance is both dangerous and sexual, but it also possesses an inspirational and astonishing quality that lifts it above the typical theatrical experience. Although scarcely as threatening as Vashti's spectacular presence, Bianca's overt sexuality onstage creates a memorable and mesmerising performance. Her disappointment and anxiety that Conrad has not come to see her debut imbues her acting with a dramatic tension and a passionate despair that creates a sensation in the audience and a triumphant performance. Unlike Alice's romantic notions, which have no outlet, Bianca's love for Conrad is channelled into her performance, and the passions of a sexual woman become identified as the authentic outpourings of a natural dramatic temperament.

Jewsbury uses the figure of the actress in *The Half Sisters* to investigate her own questions about the effects of a public life on femininity. In doing so, she represents the working woman's divided subjectivity between the professional and domestic as a strength. Professional unsexing protects Bianca's womanly modesty from the degradation of her sexualised performance. Furthermore, like rehearsing, studying, or making her costumes, her love for Conrad can be identified as a material component of her work. In this instance, then, feminine sensibility aids genius rather than hindering it, and through Bianca's performance, Jewsbury describes a form of female genius that thrives on the supposed weakness of woman's nature. Far from being incongruous, the roles of the emotional 'woman' and professional 'actress' are shown to be compatible. Unlike other arguments for compatibility, however, in this case it is the professional that advances the respectability of the domestic. This wild Italian girl is shown to be transformed into a genteel woman by her work on the stage, and she ultimately attains, through her success as a star personality, an unassailable social legitimacy in her role as Lady Melton.

The image of the natural actress enabled those intimately involved in the acting profession and those interested in protecting the respectability of all working women to assert the innocent modesty of even this most public and sexualised figure. It supported the claim for the unconsciousness of the actress's latent sexuality by locating the authenticity of the natural performance in an inborn characteristic. With ignorance as her justification, though, the innocent actress must ultimately be stripped of her power to perform when this sexuality is awakened. Thus, Sybil Vane's genius disappears when Dorian Gray's proposal awakens her feminine passion, and, in a less

---

66   Charlotte Brontë, *Villette*, Margaret Smith and Herbert Rosengarten, eds (Oxford: Oxford University Press, 2000), p. 257.

67   Ibid., p. 259.

tragic conclusion, Bianca gives up her career when she marries Lord Melton. In *The Half Sisters*, however, conventional domesticity doesn't bring about the end of the significant relationship between successful performance and private respectability. As Lord Melton, after their marriage, watches Bianca industriously working away at crocheting a cushion, he remarks, 'I have been wonder-struck at the prudence and dexterity with which you have adapted yourself to what must be such a new order of things – the orderliness, the – what shall I say? – house-keeping qualities, which have developed in you are so marvellous' (*Half Sisters*, p. 391). In response to this praise, Bianca exclaims:

> [I]s this positively the first time you have discovered that I am a clever woman? You are like all the rest of men, and have no faith in a woman's genius, until it is shown in the practical manifestation of arranging your breakfasts, dinners, and servants. There is no wonder in the matter; the simple secret of filling any position, great or small, consists in giving your mind to see and understand what are the peculiar requirements of it, and doing them heartily. (*Half Sisters*, p. 391-92)

As Bianca sees it, neither acting nor housekeeping come 'naturally' to a woman. Both are roles that, as a clever woman, she learns and performs. Regardless of her position within theatrical and domestic spheres, the issue throughout this novel remains one of the potential for the working woman to achieve through performance a legitimate feminine existence. And this issue of legitimacy was one to which representations of the actress repeatedly returned.

The Question of Legitimacy in Wilkie Collins's *No Name*

The questioning and asserting of the respectability of the actress throughout the 1840s and 1850s highlighted the intersections between the world of the stage and the private sphere. With increasing frequency into the 1860s, these supposedly separate worlds were drawn even closer together in a number of ways. One of these ways was the increasing desire of the public to learn more about the private lives of public performers. Writing specifically about theatrical couples, Sandra Richards notes that 'Producers exploited audiences' penchant for finding parallels between the real and stage life of an acting partnership. Cults of personality centred on such talented pairs and fed on their domestic circumstances'.[68] By casting these popular couples together in plays, producers were able to market their domestic situation as well as their professional reputation to a voyeuristic public. The danger of any performer selling their private identity in this way, however, is clearly evidenced by a court case reported in the English papers involving the ownership of a photographic image of the celebrated French actress Rachel Felix. This picture was taken as Rachel lay on her deathbed in January 1858 and apparently captured the moment of death with such accuracy that Rachel's sister asked that the photograph be kept private and its

---

68 Richards, *The Rise of the English Actress*, p. 113.

clarity softened. The photographer, however, allowed Madame O'Connell to make a copy of it, and she, after having an engraving made, put copies out for sale.

In describing this picture, the *Art Journal* called it 'the last scene in the last performance of the great actress, for her own private benefit', further adding that it 'lifts, with a sacrilegious hand, the curtain behind which the stage is a death-bed and the drama a death!'[69] Even Rachel's death is portrayed in terms of a theatrical performance, and this very private moment is offered for sale as another, and perhaps the most authentic, illustration of the personality behind the actress.[70] The sale of the pictures was stopped when Rachel's sister sued Madame O'Connell, claiming that 'though her sister had been a public performer, and as such public property, she was not acting here, – and her death-bed, like her private life, was the property of her family alone'.[71] But the image had already been circulated, and Madame O'Connell had made a substantial sum of money from it. This case emphasises the difficulties caused by the actress throwing open her domestic doors to the curious public. Propriety may be proven, but the domestic life, whose privacy was supposed to be so stringently guarded, becomes another form of entertainment for the voracious masses. Privacy is forfeited, but even more importantly, as 'public property', the performer also loses the ability to control the way in which their private life is presented to public view.

Such public ownership of the performer's reputation, however, bred a familiarity between actresses and public that, according to a writer for *Work and Leisure*, gave the public a share in the responsibility of protecting the actress's precarious virtue. '[I]t should be our part', the author argues, 'to do what in us lies to support and encourage them, giving honour where honour is due instead of making their lives more difficult by censoriousness and neglect'.[72] This writer was, in effect, making the same argument that had been put forward by the *Daily Telegraph* a few years earlier in relation to actors: 'When Society does not turn its back upon a gentleman because he is an actor, the best possible encouragement is given to an actor to be a gentleman'.[73] Although the *Telegraph* claimed that the same was not true for actresses because they needed more active guidance, the basic tenet of social encouragement was elsewhere applied to the actress. As the status of actresses, of the theatrical profession, and even of the theatrical institutions themselves became closely interrelated, the 'honour' of the actress could be derived from her legitimate work within an 'honourable' theatre. One of the most conspicuous examples of this can be seen in the career of Ellen Terry, whose work, playing, among other roles,

---

69   'Mademoiselle Rachel', *Art Journal* 10 (1858), p. 253. The details of the case as told here are taken from this article.

70   Rachel's death is, in fact, still being read in this way. In her biography of Rachel, for instance, Rachel Brownstein comments, 'When Rachel actually did die on 3 January 1858, she could not but do so theatrically' [Rachel M. Brownstein, *Tragic Muse: Rachel of the Comédie Française* (New York: Alfred A. Knopf, 1993), p. 26

71   Ibid.

72   'Woman's Work in Public Amusements', *Work and Leisure*, p. 164.

73   'Women and the Stage', rpt. in *Women and Work*, p. 5.

Shakespeare's most famous heroines, with Henry Irving at the Lyceum 'turned her into a mirror of every dear Englishwoman'.[74]

The close relationship in the popular consciousness between the legitimacy of the actress and that of the stage itself, however, contributed to a general distrust of the sincerity and veracity of the actress in everyday life. In reference to the actress's respectability, for instance, Tracy Davis notes, 'The general public – accustomed to the transformative allure of theatrical illusion – distrusted what merely seemed to be'.[75] Such distrust of the actress's sincerity is clearly expressed in the small religious pamphlet mentioned earlier, *The Sempstress and the Actress, or, The Power of Prayer*. In order to decide whether she should accept the work the actress has offered her, the seamstress asks the actress to kneel with her and pray for guidance. As the actress watches the seamstress, she has a religious epiphany of her own; she realises the wickedness of her life and vows to leave the stage in order to work for God. She pleads with the seamstress, begging for her prayers and her help, but the emphatic, dramatic quality of her conversion as 'in the agony of her spirit, she threw her arms around the neck of the suppliant' rouses the suspicions of the seamstress.[76] The apparent mimicry of the seamstress's prayers in the actress's conversion calls the actress's sincerity into question:

> The praying young woman was taken by surprise. She did not know whether her visitor was in earnest or whether she was in jest. She went on in her simple prayer, telling the Lord the new doubts which were in her mind as to the sincerity of the actress; for she really thought she might be trifling with her and with the subject of prayer.[77]

The highly stylised manner in which the actress acts out her religious fervour suggests that such behaviour is unnatural to the actress, or at least it appears so to the seamstress. Whether this is the natural reaction of a dramatic temperament or the skill of a theatrical professional is unclear to the seamstress, and social prejudices about the profligacy of actresses contribute to her incredulity that such a rapid conversion could take place.

As part of a series called *The Revival: A Weekly Record of Events Connected with the Present Revival of Religion*, this story was intended to be a morality tale on the power of faith, but in the seamstress's distrust of the actress's sincerity, it also expresses a more general anxiety that the actress could use her ability for impersonation as a means of social manipulation. This same anxiety, Lyn Pykett notes, often formed the central focus for many sensation novels because, she argues, 'At times the sensation novel seems to *define* femininity *as* duplicity and to represent respectable,

---

74   Nina Auerbach, *Ellen Terry, Player in Her Time* (London: Phoenix House, 1987), p. 178

75   Tracy Davis, *Actresses as Working Women*, p. 98.

76   *The Sempstress and the Actress; or, The Power of Prayer* (London: J.F. Shaw, 1859), p. 2.

77   Ibid., pp. 3-4.

genteel femininity as impersonation, performance or masquerade'.[78] Mary Elizabeth Braddon draws on just this fear in her representation in *Lady Audley's Secret* (1862) of the 'doubly charming' Lucy Audley, whose 'soft and melting blue eyes', 'wealth of showering flaxen curls', and 'gentle voice', all hide what is described by the characters in the novel as a growing madness that leads her to commit bigamy and attempted murder.[79] Lucy is more than once referred to as an actress by both the narrator and by Braddon's representative of almost pathologically conventional masculinity, Robert Audley. As Robert uncovers the extent of Lucy's treachery, he remarks, 'Good heavens! What an actress this woman is. What an arch trickster – what an all-accomplished deceiver'.[80] While Robert's dread of Lucy is inspired by the crimes he suspects she has committed, he is more specifically revolted by her ability to maintain the outward effect of ideal femininity and to deceive all those around her. Although Lucy's treachery is ultimately exposed, *Lady Audley's Secret* creates its sensation from the fear that the domestic sanctuary could be infiltrated and poisoned by an unwomanly woman whose power of performance and dissimulation could mask unnaturalness beneath an innocent exterior.

While the sensation novel plumbed what Nina Auerbach describes as the Victorian fear of the 'dangerous potential of theatricality to invade the authenticity of the best self' in order to shock and thrill its middle-class audience, the theatre novel, Lauren Chattman argues, thematised this potential in order to 'use the concept of performance to undermine stable categories of gender'.[81] Writing specifically about *The Half Sisters* and Wilkie Collins's *No Name* (1862), Chattman notes that these novels suggest that 'gender does not emanate from a subject's inviolable core, but is part of an assumed identity and is performed according to culture's script'.[82] As a theatre novel, *No Name* represents the performative aspect of conventional femininity and describes the way in which the intelligent actress-heroine can impersonate her way back into the domestic sphere and a legitimate domestic existence. As a sensation novel, it also brings into focus the idea that any number of sins and secrets could be concealed underneath the appearance of domestic harmony. As a sensational theatre novel, then, *No Name* not only presents acting as an inherent and unavoidable part of everyday life upon which identity can be constructed and performed, but also represents this performance as a series of disguises that can hide unnatural behaviour behind masks of conventionality. In fact, Collins centres the main theme of the novel on one such system of disguise when it is revealed that the

---

78   Lyn Pykett, *The Sensation Novel from The Woman in White to The Moonstone* (Plymouth: Northcote House, 1994), p. 24.

79   Mary Elizabeth Braddon, *Lady Audley's Secret*, David Skilton, ed. (Oxford: Oxford University Press, 1998), p. 6.

80   Braddon, *Lady Audley's Secret*, p. 257.

81   Nina Auerbach, *Private Theatricals: The Lives of the Victorians* (Cambridge, MA: Harvard University Press, 1990), p. 8, Lauren Chattman, 'Actresses at Home and On the Stage: Spectacular Domesticity and the Victorian Theatrical Novel', *Novel* 28 (1994), p. 73.

82   Chattman, 'Actresses at Home and On the Stage', p. 85

recently deceased parents of Norah and Magdalen Vanstone were not married and that the girls are illegitimate.

The sharp contrast between this illegitimacy and the domestic idyll that was the Vanstone household highlights the typical sensational contrivance wherein comfortable Victorian assumptions concerning the home were punctured by the exposure of a scandalous secret. The possibility that the image of middle-class respectability could be manipulated to conceal a fundamental deception was sensational at best, and at worst, subversive of the domestic ideal. Indeed, the first section of the novel sets up one such instance of subversion when Collins uses the production of private theatricals in which Magdalen takes part to 'creat[e] a dramatic world out of a domestic chaos'.[83] By the second half of the century, drawing-room theatricals were usually considered to be a safe activity for the middle-class woman because private and amateur. But in this private production of Sheridan's *The Rivals*, Collins explores the 'domestic chaos' created by the introduction of visible theatricality into the domestic sphere. Unlike Bianca, whose experience of acting is purely professional, the lines between public performance and private life are never so clear for Magdalen. When performing the roles of both the sentimental model of conventional womanhood, Julia, and the vivacious waiting-maid, Lucy, Magdalen directly translates her domestic experiences into her performance. In one such instance of borrowing, Magdalen consciously bases her characterisation of Julia on her sister Norah, who easily recognises her own mannerisms in what the narrator describes as Magdalen's 'cool appropriation of Norah's identity to theatrical purposes' (*No Name*, p. 48). Conversely, Magdalen uses her theatrical experience to help her perform in the domestic sphere as the roles she plays in this production foreshadow the roles she plays in life as Julia Bygrave and the parlour maid, Louisa. In Magdalen's conscious performance, Collins undermines the supposed distance between the stage and the domestic sphere and demonstrates the transgressive nature of private performance. The staging of private theatricals proves enlightening because they directly expose the private sphere to public scrutiny and offer evidence that skilled impersonation could take place within the domestic space. And, by usurping her sister's personality for her character, Magdalen 'transforms her sister's body into public spectacle despite Norah's refusal to take part in the theatrical proceedings'.[84] Even before the revelation of the Vanstones' secret, then, the family's quiet, private lives are disrupted by Magdalen's newly discovered passion for acting and her innate theatrical talent. As a result, Magdalen is recast from a modest and innocent domestic woman into 'the character of a born actress' (*No Name*, p. 44).

As a 'born actress', Magdalen has a 'rare faculty of dramatic impersonation', but her theatrical skills also go beyond her talent for 'mimicry' (*No Name*, p. 48). At her very first rehearsal, she astonishes the professional manager hired to direct

---

83   Wilkie Collins, *No Name*, Mark Ford, ed. (Harmondsworth: Penguin Books, 1994), p. 35. Further references to this edition will be given in the text.

84   Helena Michie, '"There is no Friend Like a Sister": Sisterhood as Sexual Difference', *ELH* 56 (1989), p. 412.

the performance because she has an innate knowledge of the mechanics of acting: '"Curious", he said under his breath – "she fronts the audience of her own accord!"' (*No Name*, p. 42). She succeeds because she is talented, but also because she employs an 'unintelligible industry in the study of her part' (*No Name*, p. 42). While those around her fail to understand the seriousness with which Magdalen approaches this small private production, the dramatic force in her nature does not allow her to trivialise any performance, including those of the others in the play, and she spends almost as much time teaching Frank Clare, who has taken the part of Julia's jealous lover, Falkland, as she does learning her own part. As a result of her assiduous work, she earns, along with the admiration of the audience, the 'professional approbation' of the manager (*No Name*, p. 43). While Magdalen has up to this point led a life of sheltered domesticity, Collins imbues her with all the knowledge that would belong to a member of a theatrical dynasty. He also further supports such an image of Magdalen throughout her professional career by repeatedly returning to the domestic genesis for Magdalen's acting in all her acting experiences and suggests in the domestic scenes that comprise her professional entertainments that she is a 'Young Lady At Home' upon the stage (*No Name*, p. 191). In this way, while she presents herself to the audience as a domestic lady, she appears most certainly as the 'born actress', not only a natural performer, but also – importantly – a conscious and experienced professional (*No Name*, p. 48).

The confusion this creates in the public perception of Magdalen's domestic character is attested to by Miss Garth, who worries about the effect innate theatricality will have on Magdalen's modest womanliness. She frets about the impression the constant praise of her talent will have on Magdalen's vanity. And as she watches Magdalen talking to her co-star Frank Clare, she wonders, 'Had her passing interest in him, as her stage-pupil, treacherously sown the seeds of any deeper interest in him, as a man? Had the idle theatrical scheme, now that it was all over, graver results to answer for than a mischievous waste of time?' (*No Name*, p. 50). The dangers that Miss Garth imagines recall the stereotypical middle-class objections to the stage as a profession for women. Suspicions of sexual impropriety and unwomanly behaviour are suddenly attached to this domestic girl. And the emotional control she exhibits on stage may enable her performance, but it detracts from the appearance of her femininity off stage. Debra Morris, for instance, describes Magdalen's 'tearless' reaction to the news of her father's death as part of Magdalen's adoption of a 'culturally traditional masculine role'.[85] And the composure with which she reads the insulting letter from her uncle in which he disinherits her and her sister strikes their old lawyer, Mr. Pendril, unfavourably and prompts her father's old friend Mr. Clare to ask, '"What is this mask of yours hiding? ... Which extremes of human temperature does your courage start from – the dead cold or the white hot?' (*No Name*, p. 125). Mr. Clare's questions define Magdalen's domestic problems according to a metaphor of theatricality that contrasts the image of Magdalen as the

---

85   Debra Morris, 'Maternal Roles and the Production of Name in Wilkie Collins's *No Name*', *Dickens Studies Annual* 27 (1998), p. 280.

conscious and professional actress with a more shocking image of Magdalen as the unnatural sensation heroine. These questions raise fears of indiscernible motives, of extreme passions, and of immoral secrets. With the most scandalous secret revealed in the first section of the novel, though, Collins turns this sensational plot device into what contemporary reviewer H.L. Mansel described as 'a protest against the law which determines the social position of illegitimate children'.[86] Although Mansel disagrees with Collins's critique of the law, branding the logic of the story as 'dust thrown in the eyes of the reader, to blind him to the real merits of the argument', his focus in the review solely on the issue of the disposition of property fails to take into account Collins's scathing criticism of the social world, whose interpretation of the situation needn't be so inflexible.[87] In tying the idea of social illegitimacy to economic powerlessness, Jenny Taylor argues, Collins investigates the impact of the 'competitive and indifferent world' on the domestic woman.[88] Social convention is transformed into social prejudice that not only explains but also justifies Magdalen's transgressions. Collins suggests that her dissimulation isn't a product of acting, but of an unjust society that forces women to fight for legitimate status.

However scandalous its story, the sensation novel generally concluded, like most Victorian realism, with the restoration of social order, and the misbehaving sensation heroine was made to suffer severe consequences for her deceitful performance. Lucy Audley, for instance, is eventually confined within a madhouse until she dies. Magdalen, however, is not so roundly condemned as Braddon's Lucy. Like Lucy, Magdalen also takes on a false name and misrepresents herself to the man she marries. Performing the role of the innocent maiden, Julia Bygrave, Magdalen marries her cousin, Noel Vanstone, in order to take revenge for what she sees as his and his father's unjust treatment of her and her sister, Norah. But, while the deceit she plans is morally wrong, her marital scheme is the means through which she gains a legitimate domestic identity and a legal right to the name Vanstone. Her deception, Collins argues, is one in which the 'general Sense of Propriety' acts as her 'accomplice' (*No Name*, p. 259). So, even though this process through which her social position is regained is shown to be part of a progressive descent into moral degradation, Magdalen is allowed, after Noel's death and a cleansing fever, to marry again and live out her life as a conventional domestic woman. Once re-established within the domestic sphere, she bears little mark of the transgressions she has committed. Magdalen's efforts to reclaim her inheritance and a legitimate place in society, Deirdre David notes, are played out in a battle between male governance and female revenge.[89] As a result, Collins's representation of Magdalen generated

---

86 [H.L. Mansel], 'Sensation Novels', *Quarterly Review* 113 (1863), p. 495.

87 Ibid., p. 496.

88 Jenny Bourne Taylor, *In the Secret Theatre of Home: Wilkie Collins, Sensation Narrative and Nineteenth-Century Psychology* (London: Routledge, 1988), p. 135.

89 Deirdre David, 'Rewriting the Male Plot in Wilkie Collins's *No Name* (1862): Captain Wragge Orders an Omelette and Mrs. Wragge Goes into Custody', *The New Nineteenth Century: Feminist Readings of Underread Victorian Fiction*, Barbara Leah Harman and Susan Meyer, eds (London: Garland, 1996), pp. 33-43.

wide critical distaste because he failed to punish sufficiently a woman who defied the patriarchal order and 'contaminated herself' through her unnatural obsession for justice and retribution.[90]

The problem with Magdalen's contamination for many critics, however, was not so much her outrage at and fight against the injustice of her situation, but, as Margaret Oliphant argues, the way Collins legitimises her actions through her superficial social respectability and through the narrative trope of the happy ending:

> Mr. Wilkie Collins, after the skilful and startling complications of the *Woman in White* – his grand effort – has chosen, by way of making his heroine piquant and interesting in his next attempt, to throw her into a career of vulgar and aimless trickery and wickedness, with which it is impossible to have a shadow of sympathy, but from all the pollutions of which he intends us to believe that she emerges, at the cheap cost of a fever, as pure, as high-minded, and as spotless as the most dazzling white of heroines. The Magdalen of "No Name" does not go astray after the usual fashion of erring maidens in romance. Her pollution is decorous, and justified by law; and after all her endless deceptions and horrible marriage, it seems quite right to the author that she should be restored to society, and have a good husband and a happy home.[91]

Vehement reactions like Oliphant's exposed deep fears about such disruptions in the representation of the social order. Concern about the unnaturalness displayed by Magdalen, for instance, caused the reviewer for the *North British Review* to declare emphatically that 'There never was a young lady like Magdalen'.[92] But Oliphant is not only disappointed in the novel because Magdalen refuses to die from her fever like any respectable fallen heroine, but also because Magdalen, despite the connotations of her name, is never really depicted as a fallen woman. Instead, in the role of Julia Bygrave, Magdalen appears in the world of the novel as a proper and modest domestic woman. Whereas conventional middle-class wisdom held that public respectability was contingent upon private virtue, Collins dramatises the falsity of this principle and participates in what Nicholas Rance describes as the sensation novel's tendency to 'undermine domestic moralism'.[93] Collins articulates the discrepancy between morality and social propriety in Miss Garth's warning to Magdalen about the dangers of taking to the stage as a career. 'Your way of life, however pure your conduct may be', Miss Garth informs her, 'is a suspicious way of life to all respectable people' (*No Name*, p. 254). Coming from a paragon of middle-class conventionality, though, the obvious injustice of a system that privileges the appearance of respectability above true virtue undermines the value of the kind of respectability Miss Garth represents.

---

90 [Henry Chorley] '*No Name*', *Athenaeum* no. 1836 (3 Jan. 1863), p. 11.

91 [Margaret Oliphant], 'Novels', *Blackwood's Magazine* 94 (1863), p. 170.

92 Alexander Smith, 'Novels and Novelists of the Day', *North British Review*, 38 (1863), p. 184.

93 Nicholas Rance, *Wilkie Collins and Other Sensation Novelists* (Rutherford: Fairleigh Dickinson University Press, 1991), p. 38.

In fact, while Magdalen's short-lived theatrical career is the lowest social point for her, it is the height of her moral respectability during the time in which she is outside legitimate society. Even though this career exposes her to the society of shady creatures such as the manipulative, dishonest, and artful Captain Wragge, and her performance is 'stripped of every softening allurement which had once adorned it', Magdalen flourishes as a professional actress (*No Name*, p. 183). Too busy to get into trouble as she moves from town to town, performing her entertainment with a single-minded feverishness for earning money, Magdalen's life on the stage is one of unceasing industry and moral respectability. Magdalen's rapid professional success is a result of her skill as an actress, and her experience in the theatre offers a glimpse into a world in which respectability is built on talent, achievement, and hard work. This life, however, is presented in the brief inter-sections between what Collins calls the 'scenes' of the novel. In this series of letters and journal entries, Collins suggests an alternative to the 'artificial social world' that is dependent upon the skills of mimicry for maintaining the façade of respectability (*No Name*, p. 581). Where the conventionality of her domestic upbringing fails to secure her a legitimate social status, her theatrical experience succeeds.

In *No Name*, Collins betrays a fundamental anxiety concerning the legitimacy and integrity of the professional working in a populist field. The ethic of hard work that characterises Magdalen's life as a professional actress secures for her a claim to moral respectability regardless of social prejudices concerning the status of her work. As a popular writer of what was considered to be both a morally suspect and feminine genre, Collins, who 'regarded his own fictional practice more seriously than many of his fellow sensationalists', was similarly forced to confront the literary prejudice that defined the popular and the feminine as markers of low culture.[94] Collins uses the figure of the professional actress to disavow prescriptive conventions that sanctioned certain types of work as legitimate. In this light, the theatre, just like sensational literature, could have the same moral potential as that associated with high-culture artistry.

Performing as Art: The Moral Potential of the Stage and the Transcendence of Performance in George Eliot's *Daniel Deronda*

Although attempts had been made throughout the early part of the nineteenth century to represent acting as one of the higher arts, it was generally dismissed as a low form of entertainment and a 'source of amusement'.[95] Through the end of the 1870s

---

94   Lyn Pykett, *The Sensation Novel*, p. 14. For a discussion of the sensation novel as a feminine genre, see Lyn Pykett, *The Improper Feminine: The Women's Sensation Novel and the New Woman Writing* (London: Routledge, 1992).

95   William Hazlitt, 'On Actors and Acting', *Examiner* (15 Jan. 1817), rpt. in George Rowell, ed., *Victorian Dramatic Criticism* (London: Methuen, 1971), p. 3. Jewsbury's old actor in *The Half Sisters*, for instance, describes acting as an 'art which has never, in any age, been made honourable' (161).

and 1880s, however, its artistic reputation grew and was increasingly defended by books like George Henry Lewes's *On Actors and the Art of Acting* (1875), by known theatre critics such as Mowbray Morris, and by reputable art periodicals such as the *Art Journal*.[96] Writing about 'The Art of the Stage', a writer for the *Journal* noted that while 'acting is regarded by many as no art at all, but a kind of happy talent … acting is … pre-eminently an art, – an art to which all the graces and riches of a cultivated mind ought to minister'.[97] Similarly, discussing the progress that had been made in the theatre in the previous twenty years, the art critic and playwright Joseph Comyns Carr described 'the steady and marked advance of the general body of the professions, the increased respect exhibited by the actor of every rank for the serious qualities of his art, and the greater degree of intelligence and taste which the manager bring to the production of the author's work'.[98]

While this association with art helped to raise the reputation of the stage as a respectable profession, it also served, to a certain extent, to separate the work of acting from the degrading world of the commercial economy. 'The man who wants simply to make money', an author for *Temple Bar* noted in 1871, 'has no right to become an author, an artist, an actor … Let him start a national bank, a transmarine bridge, or a cosmopolitan balloon, but – not a theatre'.[99] Since the reputation of the actress was intimately connected with that of the stage, this growing artistic legitimacy was reflected in the public perception of the actress as well. For those interested in promoting theatrical work as a means to domestic and moral respectability, then, the earlier tendency to deny the legitimacy of the acting profession had to be combated. Fanny Kemble's demurral about her own career, for instance, was criticised by the *Saturday Review* which complained that 'She was never in earnest, never genuine. She had neither the intuitions of genius nor the patient striving after perfection. She thought herself above her art – it was "repugnant to her" – when she, in fact, was far beneath it'.[100] A writer for the *Quarterly Review* also commented, 'That a Kemble should disparage the actor's art, is indeed strange'.[101]

Even the much disparaged ballet girl could be an example of virtuous beauty through a connection with the stage as an artistic enterprise. Commenting on 'Stage Morality, and the Ballet', Charles Mackay argued:

---

96   See, for instance, Mowbray Morris, 'On Some Recent Theatrical Criticisms', pp. 321-27. For a discussion of the growing artistic reputation of the stage throughout the nineteenth century, see Michael Baker, *The Rise of the Victorian Actor*, esp. chap. 1.

97   'The Art of the Stage', *Art Journal*, p. 20.

98   [J. Comyns Carr], 'English Actors: – Yesterday and Today', *Fortnightly Review* 39 (1883), p. 226.

99   [Alfred Austin], 'The Present State of the English Stage', *Temple Bar* 33 (1871), p. 462.

100   'A Plea for Players', *Saturday Review* 16 (1863), p. 724.

101   [Theodore Martin], 'The English Stage', *Quarterly Review* 155 (1883), p. 384. She was defended from this criticism, however, by Mowbray Morris in 'On Some Recent Theatrical Criticisms', who sees her as a representative of a time when the theatre 'was less serious in its designs and less fortunate' (p. 322).

It cannot be asserted by the severest moralist that the ballet, though it partakes of the character of a pagan festival, is of necessity indecent or immodest, and that it may not be made the source of much innocent and refined enjoyment. It is a mistake, too, to suppose that the ballet has exclusive attractions for men. Educated and accomplished women, both young and old, love to see a handsome girl, handsomely dressed or draped, displaying herself in the graceful figures and movements of the dance, upon the same principle that they admire a picture, a poem, a flower, a tree, a landscape, or anything in the works of God or man that appeals to a sense of beauty, proportion, and harmony. And if one such woman is a beautiful sight, fifty or a hundred or more of such women dressed alike, or slightly differing for the contrast of colour, are, *pari passu*, a beautiful spectacle, when they perform their gyrations and evolutions upon the stage; and neither by gesture nor sign nor suggestion convey, or seek to convey to the mind of the beholder any impression but that which springs from the legitimate exercise of their art. [102]

Mackay's formulation of the ballet as art transforms the issue of sexuality from a component of theatrical display and performance into a characteristic of individuals. For Mackay, 'the immorality of nudity ... lies in the intent of the person who displays, and in the mind of the person who beholds it', not in the mere fact of baring one's legs to public view. Graceful and artistic dancing, therefore, could be inspiring if it was accompanied by right-minded performers and managers.

Such support for the artistic reputation of the stage and the female performer was accompanied by a change in the representation of their morality. At times, the conception of the theatre could even carry a religious undertone. Mrs. Mowatt's uplifting story of the ballet girl Georgina, for instance, draws on religious imagery to suggest that the theatre acts almost like a protective sphere in which her innate virtuousness was sown and fostered, and her sexual innocence is as much assumed as asserted. As testimony to the moral potential of the stage, Georgina is herself offered as an example worthy of emulation. The relationship between religion and the stage, however, was fraught with animosity. Although *The Times* could argue in 1877 that 'the pulpit and the stage are less engaged in open warfare than during those bad old days [of the Restoration theatre]', the relationship between religion and the stage throughout the nineteenth century was characterised by mutual avoidance.[103] Describing the religious perspective, *The Times* explains, 'the stage is about as perilous a subject for a respectable church or chapel-going Englishman to open his mouth upon as any of the topics which centuries ago brought a man under the notice of the Inquisition'.[104] From the theatrical standpoint, the playwright Henry Arthur Jones argues, 'there is no general reconciliation possible between the two ideas of religion and the theatre, and so they wish to keep them utterly apart ... from an uncomfortable feeling that if once they get face to face one of them will destroy the

---

102 [Charles Mackay], 'Stage Morality, and the Ballet', *Blackwood's Magazine* 105 (1869), pp. 358-59.

103 'Stage Decorum', *The Times* (1 Feb. 1877), p. 9.

104 *The Times* (8 Oct. 1880), p. 7.

other'.[105] No reconciliation is possible, the *Era* argues, because 'The two institutions – the Pulpit and the Stage – are antagonistic'.[106]

As opposing institutions, as well as opposed ideologies, the church and the stage also marked out separate physical spaces. Many clergymen refused to even enter theatres, and when Bishop Fraser, the Bishop of Manchester, decided to address a group of performers at the Theatre Royal and the Prince's Theatre, *The Times* commented that he 'was the first Bishop of the Church of England, if not the first Bishop of the Christian Church, who had ever addressed a congregation in a theatre'.[107] This antagonistic relationship between the church and the stage is clearly demonstrated by the theatrical historian John Doran in his 1867 article entitled 'The Saints of the Stage'. Doran chronicles the stories of various early actresses who abandoned their stage careers while they were at the height of their popularity in order to enter the convent and devote themselves to God.[108] Their reward for such devotion was eventual canonisation, but they only approached God when they left the stage behind. Doran's article, however, collapses the distance between the stage and the church at the same time that it describes their isolation. Although these women become saints, they are still identified as actresses. These women are canonised because they resisted the temptations that assailed them, the temptations of beauty and success that beset all actresses. They are not only saints of the stage, but saints for the stage – examples of modesty and morality for all actresses.

Bishop Fraser's decision to address the members of the theatre in their own environment was not merely an effort to convert or save them; it was primarily a part of a wider social agenda to 'purify' the theatre itself.[109] While the stage was considered by many to be anathema to the religious establishment, some members of the church, the theatre, and the general public recognised the stage's moral potential. Managers, playwrights, actors and actresses, and the public were charged with the responsibility of producing and attending moral productions, and the plays of Shakespeare and William Robertson were placed at the vanguard of stage respectability.[110] Such moral and respectable productions were proposed as the most direct means through which the character of the theatre and its audiences could be

---

105 Henry A. Jones, 'Religion and the Stage', *Nineteenth Century* 17 (1885), p. 158.

106 'Peace and Good-will', *Era*, p. 10.

107 'Bishop Fraser on Stage Decorum', *The Times* (3 Feb. 1877), p. 9.

108 [John Doran], 'The Saints of the Stage', *Cornhill Magazine* 15 (1867), pp. 429-39.

109 'Bishop Fraser on Stage Decorum', p. 9.

110 The drawing room comedies that Robertson wrote were deemed suitable not only for middle-class audiences to see but were also instrumental in promoting the stage as a respectable occupation for middle-class women. Some, in fact, even thought Robertson's plays too respectable. The *Saturday Review*, for instance, commented that 'The school of social comedy which Mr. Robertson brought into favour is, if not intellectually strong, at least intelligent and decorous in the extreme, and may almost be said to err on the side of insipid respectability' [rpt. in 'Stage Decorum', *The Times* (7 Dec. 1874), p. 10]. For a discussion of the respectability granted to both Robertson's plays and Shakespeare's see George Rowell, *Theatre in the Age of Irving* (Oxford: Basil Blackwell, 1981).

improved.[111] With such productions, the critic Godfrey Turner argued, the stage could be a conduit for 'wholesome truth'.[112] The moral potential of the theatre was located particularly in its 'power as an educational instrument' because, as the poet Emily Pfeiffer argued, 'the drama, being a union and concrete of all the arts, is naturally powerful beyond any single one in stirring and awakening dormant sensibilities, and that it has formed, probably ever will form, the sole appeal of art through which toiling millions of our fellow-men can be reached'.[113] While Pfeiffer focuses her claims on the emotional education of the masses, the British poet and first Viceroy to India, Edward Robert Bulwer Lytton, took an even grander view:

> The social civilization of a people is significantly indicated by the intellectual character of its popular amusements, and of such amusements the stage is one of the most important. Experience has repeatedly proved the power of the stage as an educational agency for the diffusion, not only of popular refinement, but also of those ideas and sentiments which strengthen and elevate national character.[114]

Lytton describes the theatre as instrumental in the refinement of society and the progress of the nation. Although Lytton argues that the British stage still has some way to go in its improvement, he points to the work of Henry Irving and the productions of the Lyceum as evidence that the 'present prospects of the English stage' are 'encouraging'.[115]

While writers such as Pfeiffer and Lytton wrote about the morality of those who attended the theatre as spectators, others worried about the morality of performers. In a letter to *The Times* in 1884, WM Vincent took the moral potential of the stage for granted while emphasising the importance of self-regulation within the profession:

> There are many thousands, however, who, while recognizing in the theatre a source of recreation blended with the valuable moral education it is capable of, would be most thankful to know from someone like Mrs. Kendal, speaking with knowledge and candour, whether the arrangements nowadays in connexion with a theatre are in general so satisfactory that they can conscientiously support and enjoy it. They ask, in fact, for an authoritative answer to the question, "Do the managers take such reasonable care of the moral life of the young people they employ that those who feel a taste and aptitude for the theatrical profession may be recommended to engage in it without undue fear of their

---

111 See, for example, F.B. Chatterton, 'The Church and the Stage', *The Times* (5 Oct. 1878), p. 6; and Dinah Craik, 'Merely Players', *Nineteenth Century* 20 (1886), pp. 416-22.

112 Godfrey Turner, 'Amusements of the English People', *Nineteenth Century* 2 (1877), p. 827.

113 Emily Pfeiffer, 'The English Stage' [a letter to the editor], *The Times* (8 Oct. 1879), p. 8.

114 [Edward Robert Bulwer Lytton], 'The Stage in Relation to Literature', *Fortnightly Review* 40 (1883), p. 12.

115 Ibid., p. 16.

being submitted to temptations and risks beyond what must be met with, necessarily, in the ordinary course of daily life?".[116]

The theatre could thus be defended in terms of the refinement offered through its association with art, its recreative and educative potential for audiences, and its improving qualities for society and the nation at large.

While the image of the virtuous and artistic actress contributed to the growing respectability of the profession, the perception of the moral potential of the stage was most improved by the representation of another type of female performer, the singer. As the author of 'A Few Words About Singing in Public' for *Work and Leisure* argued, a singing career was preferable to work as an actress. Discussing the naiveté of amateurs wanting to enter the profession, the author remarks:

> To sing on the stage, acting at the same time, like Patti or Nilssohn, would, they imagine, be even more delightful, but the amount of talent required for such a career as that seems a little out of reach for even the most aspiring young amateur. Besides, there would be the objections of parents and guardians to the stage to be encountered; but to sing in concerts and oratorios, what can be more dignified, enjoyable, and lucrative?[117]

The greater dignity attached to a singing career is attested to by a 1879 cover illustration for the journal, the *Woman's Gazette; or, News About Work* (Figure 4.1). This illustration frames the journal title with the names of prominent female personalities associated with all manner of achievements and professions, headed, of course, by the name of Queen Victoria, the epitome of the respectable working woman. The highly-respected professionals Rosa Bonheur, Mary Somerville, and Florence Nightingale all take their place alongside Jenny Lind, a popular and critically celebrated opera singer of the time. This elevation of the accomplishments of the female singer and musician was also generally marked within Victorian fiction, as Phyllis Weliver notes: 'women characters were often designated angels when they experienced music as a link to the divine'.[118]

This difference between the moral and religious authority of the figures of the actress and the singer was the central premise of a short story that was published in *Ainsworth's Magazine* in 1849 entitled 'The Actress and the Concert Singer'. In this story, two genteel sisters are forced to find work when their parents die. One becomes an actress, and though she has a hard time achieving success, she is rewarded finally for her hard work and perseverance when she marries a baronet. The second sister, however, had 'her eye … fixed on a prouder goal' than earning money or the kind of social status her sister had achieved:

---

116 W.M. Vincent, 'The Condition of the Stage', *The Times* (30 Sept. 1884), p. 12.

117 'A Few Words about Singing in Public, or The Profession of a Vocalist', *Work and Leisure* 5 (1880), p. 164.

118 Phyllis Weliver, *Women Musicians in Victorian Fiction, 1860-1900: Representations of Music, Science, and Gender in the Leisured Home* (Aldershot: Ashgate, 2000), p. 6.

It was in sacred music that she gained a proud eminence; and while giving embodiment, as far as sounds can do, to the creations of Mozart and Handel, she seemed like a creature who lost herself in sublime enthusiasm. Yes – her look was so ethereal, and her voice so unlike the common voices of others – she might appear to fancy something more than a warm-hearted simple girl – some incarnation of the divine spirit of Melody'.[119]

The author's comparison between these two forms of performance suggests the difference in the moral potential of each art form. While the actress conforms to the dictates of moral middle-class society and regains her social legitimacy through her marriage, the singer, even while exhibiting grand passions, transcends the confines of middle-class morality. The singer is represented as something *more* than the conventional woman, and as such remains untouched by the earthly issues that plagued the actress.

This point is also made strongly by the engraving of John Jackson's portrait of the early nineteenth-century soprano, Catherine Stephens (later Countess of Essex).[120] This portrait was printed as an engraving in the Art Journal in 1853 and was given the generic title of 'The Songstress' by the journal, suggesting a less specific interpretation of the painting's iconography (Figure 4.2). Although Jackson evokes the supposed sexual impropriety of the female performer in his songstress's direct gaze out of the canvas, the painting conveys a sense of innocence through the romanticised look of her flowing costume and soft curls and the wide-eyed simplicity of her child-like countenance.[121] Although confined to the representation of her upper body, the presence of the costume and the open music sheet suggests that the portrait has been taken during a momentary pause in the midst of a performance. The picture thus depicts her professional self-possession, and her hand grasping her heart announces her sincerity and her emotional investment in her work. In this representation, the songstress's innocent simplicity transcends the sexual implications of her direct gaze and obscures her professional position as a public performer.

---

119 Nicholas Michell, 'The Actress and the Concert Singer', *Ainsworth's Magazine* 16 (1849), pp. 329, 338.

120 The original portrait is in the National Portrait Gallery.

121 For a discussion of the woman's direct gaze as a visual sign of sexual impropriety see Lynda Nead, *Myths of Sexuality: Representations of Women in Victorian Britain* (Oxford: Blackwell, 1988), p. 178-79.

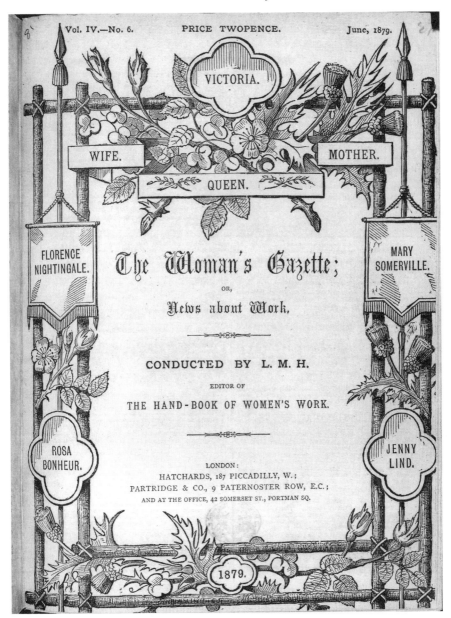

Vol. IV.—No. 6.   PRICE TWOPENCE.   June, 1879.

VICTORIA.

WIFE.   MOTHER.

QUEEN.

FLORENCE NIGHTINGALE.   MARY SOMERVILLE.

The Woman's Gazette;

OR,

News about Work.

CONDUCTED BY L. M. H.

EDITOR OF

THE HAND-BOOK OF WOMEN'S WORK.

ROSA BONHEUR.   JENNY LIND.

LONDON:
HATCHARDS, 187 PICCADILLY, W.;
PARTRIDGE & CO., 9 PATERNOSTER ROW, E.C.;
AND AT THE OFFICE, 42 SOMERSET ST., PORTMAN SQ.

1879.

Figure 4.1   Title page for *The Woman's Gazette* (1879)

Figure 4.2   J. Jackson, *The Songstress* **[engraving in** *The Art Journal***] (1853)**

The representation of the female singer thus proved useful in asserting the compatibility between artistic performance and private domesticity. Music, *The Lady's World* argued, is 'practically home employment'.[122] This compatibility was also depicted in another story published in *Eliza Cook's Journal* in 1850 entitled, 'The Singing Girl'. Exhibiting a close resemblance to Elizabeth Gaskell's irreproachable singer Margaret Legh in *Mary Barton* (1848), Patty, a working-class girl from a northern industrial town, finds fame and fortune when it is discovered that she has a beautiful singing voice. Her subsequent successful career does not corrupt her or turn her head. Instead, it allows her to support her poor parents, and it saves her from the evils of work in the factory which kept girls 'removed from those home influences which, more than anything else, tend to educate a woman, and enable her to perform her proper functions as a woman'.[123] Both Margaret and Patty are portrayed as exemplary domestic women, and far from distracting them from their duties, a singing career allows them to add to the comfort of their home and parents in a way that factory or seamstress work never could. At the centre of these representations is the relationship between their performance and the moral potential of the stage. With a professional career, Patty can 'make her beautiful gift a gladness and joy to others – now she appears as a messenger of happiness and a dispenser of pure delight'.[124] And Margaret sings her homely ballads of the working-man's distress 'with the power of her magnificent voice, as if a prayer from her very heart for all who were in distress'.[125] Following their artistic calling enables these women to extend their womanly influence outside their narrow domestic sphere. As professionals, the potential of their singing to communicate the divine extends outside the home and into the public spaces of working-class education such as the Mechanic's Institute at which Margaret begins her professional career.[126] As singers, they inspire and stir the sensibilities of all who hear them, and as women, they provide an example of beauty and purity to all who see them.

The figure of the female singer thus contributed to an image of the woman with a voice whose work, while it could be compatible with her domestic duties, could also transcend the domestic sphere. In fact, according to Susan Leonardi and Rebecca Pope, it was precisely for this reason that the figure of the singer was important to many Victorian authors. Writing specifically about the representation of the diva in Eliot's *Armgart* (1870) and *Daniel Deronda* (1876), Leonardi and Pope note that like Eliot, 'Many writers, especially women writers, seem to choose the figure of diva in order to explore what, for a woman, having a voice might mean'.[127] In Eliot's fiction, Gillian Beer argues, obtaining a voice through song signifies a woman's greater

---

122 Frederick J. Crowest, 'Music as a Livelihood', *The Lady's World* (1887), p. 174.

123 'The Singing Girl', *Eliza Cook's Journal* 2 (1850), p. 289.

124 Ibid., p. 291.

125 Elizabeth Gaskell, *Mary Barton*, Edgar Wright, ed., (Oxford: Oxford University Press, 1998), p. 39.

126 Ibid., p. 108.

127 Susan J. Leonardi and Rebecca Pope, *The Diva's Mouth: Body, Voice, Prima Donna Politics* (New Brunswick: Rutgers University Press, 1996), p. 85. See also Ellen B. Rosenman,

desire for freedom from the confines of the domestic sphere.[128] Mary Burgan takes this idea further in relation to *Daniel Deronda* and suggests that Eliot examines this notion of freedom through music not only in women who 'rise above their mundane circumstances on the wings of song', but also in the racially and socially dispossessed who, through music, '[transcend] the limitations of an English culture mired in commercialism and caste'.[129] When Eliot uses music to investigate what it means for a woman to have a voice, then, she also explores the possibility of a transcendent artistic space in which the woman's voice can be free of both the constraining force of bourgeois constructions of morality and the degrading influence of the capitalist marketplace. And through a variety of performers, Eliot demonstrates the difficulty for the woman artist to achieve and maintain such transcendence.

It is in such an idealised space, for instance, that Eliot locates the career of the grand opera singer, the Alcharisi. Unapologetic for her past and mesmerising in the present, the Alcharisi is a powerful portrait of the self-possessed and prepossessing woman. Unconcerned with her domestic duties and unhampered by the social expectations of womanly behaviour, she follows instead the demands of masculine genius and artistic vocation and frees herself from 'the slavery of being a girl'.[130] The process through which she pursues this vocation, however, is not directly represented in the text. Instead, her appearance in the novel comes after she has retired from the stage, and while she explains her reasons for pursuing her career so ruthlessly, the career itself remains the vague recollection of a time when she was a 'queen' (*Daniel Deronda*, p. 547). Through this analeptic narrative strategy, Eliot lifts the image of vocational performance embodied by the Alcharisi out of the concerns of everyday life and the realm of economic exchange by disassociating it from the material conditions of work. What is represented in the place of her professional performance is the complete integration between her person and her vocation:

> The varied transitions of tone with which this speech was delivered were as perfect as the most accomplished actress could have made them. The speech was in fact a piece of what may be called sincere acting: this woman's nature was one in which all feeling ... immediately became matter of conscious representation: experiences immediately passed into drama, and she acted her own emotions. (*Daniel Deronda*, p. 539)

In this description of the Alcharisi's manner, the components of natural acting are turned inward as all her experiences and emotions are mediated through dramatic

---

'Women's Speech and the Roles of the Sexes in *Daniel Deronda*', *Texas Studies in Literature and Language* 31 (1989), pp. 237-56.

128 Gillian Beer, *George Eliot* (Brighton: Harvester, 1986), p. 207.

129 Mary Burgan, 'Heroines at the Piano: Women and Music in Nineteenth-Century Fiction', *Victorian Studies* 29 (1986), p. 75. For a further discussion of Eliot's desire to transcend commercialism and populism through music in *Daniel Deronda* see Bruce Martin, 'Music and Fiction: The Perils of Populism', *Mosaic* 31 (1998), pp. 21-39.

130 George Eliot, *Daniel Deronda*, Graham Handley, ed. (Oxford: Oxford University Press, 1998), p. 541. Further references to this edition will be given in the text.

performance. The effect is to present her as the consummate performer, obsessed with her work and unable to leave it behind. But it also suggests the extremes of a nature formed by an all-consuming vocation. Her admission to Daniel that she could never love him is only an illustration of what she sees to be the overall truth – that loving is a talent that she lacks. She can act love, she explains, but she cannot feel it. With experience translated through drama and emotions acted rather than felt, an unbreachable distance is placed between the Alcharisi and the world. And when her son Daniel sees her, he imagines her as a variety of mythic characters – she is a princess, a sorceress, and a fairy instead of his 'human mother' (*Daniel Deronda*, p. 536).

Through the Alcharisi, Jennifer Uglow argues, Eliot expresses her ambivalence about her own sense of artistic vocation and dramatises 'her defiant yet pained awareness of what she lost in cutting herself off from her family and her background and in deciding not to have children, and her fear that her gift would vanish, never to return'.[131] The sacrifice of her domestic femininity is the price the Alcharisi pays for following her vocation, and the loss of her voice suggests Eliot's fears about the ultimate unsustainability of the life of masculine genius for the woman artist. Unfettered freedom gives way to the constraining obscurity of marriage and domestic life when, like the silenced opera singer of Eliot's dramatic poem, 'Armgart', the Alcharisi's gift deserts her. The bereavement these women endure as a result is articulated by Armgart when she laments:

> What is my soul to me without the voice
> That gave it freedom? – gave it one grand touch
> And made it nobly human? – Prisoned now,
> Prisoned in all the petty mimicries
> Called woman's knowledge ...
> All the world now is but a rack of threads
> To twist and dwarf me into pettiness
> And basely feigned content, the placid mask
> Of women's misery.[132]

The Alcharisi experiences a similar misery when the marriage she thinks will rescue her from the humiliation of failure on the stage seems a punishment for her artistic obsession. With bitter irony, the marriage becomes a hindrance to her return to the stage when she later rediscovers her voice. Locked in the false contentment of the woman's domestic existence, the Alcharisi manifests the diminution Armgart feels and appears twisted and dwarfed into pettiness. The woman who was once a queen on the stage becomes weak and 'shattered' with white hair and faded beauty (*Daniel Deronda*, p. 546). She has, as she tells Daniel, 'nothing left to give' (*Daniel Deronda*, p. 543). Both Armgart and the Alcharisi are represented as women who transcend

---

131 Jennifer Uglow, *George Eliot* (London: Virago, 1987), p. 237.

132 George Eliot, *Armgart, George Eliot: Collected Poems*, Lucien Jenkins, ed. (London: Skoob, 1989), p. 145, lines 158-62, 182-85.

women's conventional roles, but the very heights of their transcendence ensure that their falls are particularly devastating.

Eliot avoids depicting the material conditions of the professional performance in relation to the Alcharisi in order to emphasise her distance from the mundane world of everyday life. The work of the true artist is related, however, in the exchange between the musical *maestro* Herr Klesmer and the reduced gentlewoman Gwendolen Harleth.[133] When Gwendolen asks Klesmer's advice about her desire to go upon the stage in order to make money, Klesmer paints a vivid picture of the 'arduous, unceasing work' demanded by the artistic professions and the 'indignities' visited upon those who fail to do this work (*Daniel Deronda*, p. 216, 221). While Gwendolen wants to become an actress so that she might not 'need take a husband at all' and in that way, could escape the 'bondage' of marriage, Klesmer describes the stage as another form of enslavement (*Daniel Deronda*, p. 218). 'Singing and acting', he tells her, 'require a shaping of the organs towards a finer and finer certainty of effect. Your muscles – your whole frame – must go like a watch, true, true, true, to a hair' (*Daniel Deronda*, p. 219). Klesmer stresses the mechanical rather than the emotional elements of performance and suggests that the effort required for such training acts as a protection to the performer's respectability by desexualising her performance and demonstrating her vocational commitment to her work. A young woman who wants quick success, however, 'may rely on the unquestioned power of her beauty as a passport. She may desire to exhibit herself to an admiration which dispenses with skill. This goes a certain way on the stage: not in music: but on the stage, beauty is taken when there is nothing more commanding to be had' (*Daniel Deronda*, p. 221). Without unceasing practice, Klesmer contends, the actress's performance amounts to little more than a sexual display.

In Klesmer's reply to Gwendolen, Eliot dismisses the image of a performer like Collins's Magdalen who has a natural dramatic faculty. She does not deny that some, like the Alcharisi, could be born with the desire to perform, but she insists that in order to be a performer, one must 'have enough teaching to bring out the born singer and actress within' (*Daniel Deronda*, p. 542). While inclination is an important impetus to artistic performance, arduous work is placed above talent as the path to success. The true artist, Klesmer argues, surrenders egoism, self-promotion, and self-interest to the noble demands of art. This description, together with the bitter fate of the Alcharisi, implies that, in order for female vocation to be sustained, it must also be grounded in the mundane world of social, economic, and domestic concerns.

Such survival is represented in the text in the selfless and virtuous performer, Mirah Cohen. Mirah appears in the narrative as a rather ideal portrait of an unconscious performer for whom there exists a balance in the relationship between the theatre and domesticity. Her particular fitness for her work, Eliot suggests, is the natural result of a childhood spent in the theatre: 'The circumstances of her life had made

---

133 For a discussion of the connection between the Alcharisi and Gwendolen see Jeanette Shumaker, 'The Alcharisi and Gwendolen: Confession Rebellion', *George Eliot George Henry Lewes Studies* 18-19 (1991), pp. 55-62.

her think of everything she did as work demanded from her, in which affectation had nothing to do; and she had begun her work before self-consciousness was born' (*Daniel Deronda*, p. 314). It is also something she does out of filial duty. When Mrs. Meyrick asks her if she had any teaching as to what her religious duty was, Mirah answers that she was taught 'only that I ought to do what my father wished' (*Daniel Deronda*, p. 182). What her father wants for her, however, is the opposite of what she wants for herself. 'I did not want to be an artist', she explains, 'but this was what my father expected of me' (*Daniel Deronda*, p. 182). Although Mirah has only been taught to obey her father and not a higher moral power, and the world of the theatre is all she has ever known, she is imbued with an innate sense of refinement and rightness that rebels against the profligacy of the life that has been going on around her. As she tells Mrs. Meyrick, 'I hated our way of life' (*Daniel Deronda*, p. 181). Mirah does not sing because she wants a career on the stage or because she has a vocation; instead she sings in order to please other people: first her father and then her new friends. As Daniel, the Meyricks, and Klesmer all ask her to sing, her first thought is to please them, and as Klesmer makes her go through song after song, she is 'simply bent on doing what Klesmer desired' (*Daniel Deronda*, p. 415). Mirah's respectability is further enhanced by the fact that her singing, like that of Patty, has the power to uplift all who hear her, and, combined with her quiet modesty, it prompts Mrs. Meyrick to exclaim that 'She is an angel' (*Daniel Deronda*, p. 416). But rather than the divine angel of music, Mirah is represented as more the angel of the house. Even though she was raised in a rather immoral theatrical society and was almost sold into prostitution by her father, Mirah's respectability is never really questioned in the novel. Her modesty, propriety, and, most importantly, her natural performances all protect the respectability of an unprotected girl who is eventually rewarded with the conventional life she desires when she marries Daniel and joins him in his work.

Her propriety and domesticity are further strengthened by the defects in her talent. Her voice, although beautiful, is also delicate and not suited for 'singing in any larger space than a private drawing-room' (*Daniel Deronda*, p. 415). In this limited vocal power and angelic domesticity, Eliot associates her representation of Mirah with the most famous 'anti-diva' of the nineteenth century, Jenny Lind. As Leonardi and Pope explain, 'Lind had carefully constructed a public persona as an anti-diva who, unlike her sister divas, was religious and morally upright … shy and modest, reluctant of fame and longing for her Swedish home – as a singer, in other words, whose thoughts and actions were as pure as her voice'.[134] *Eliza Cook's Journal* took the popularity of Lind as a 'sign of the times' that 'mere power, and rank, and wealth, are beginning to lose ground in comparison with genius and goodness – that conventional nobility is to yield its glories to the nobility of nature – that men are becoming more ready … to recognise the inner worth rather than the outward show'.[135] In the association of Lind with Mirah, then, Eliot's representation proposes an image of the female artist

---

134 Leonardi and Pope, *The Diva's Mouth*, p. 44.
135 'A Sign of the Times', *Eliza Cook's Journal* 3 (1850), p. 408.

that, while seemingly rather conventional, imagines the participation of the woman's voice in the public sphere as a noble and powerfully moral enterprise. Ultimately, however, Mirah's potential influence is dedicated to a more conventional role when she marries Daniel: 'Indeed, we can see Mirah's career as typical of those imagined by numerous proponents of women's opportunities for work, in which a woman's work leads her to the "wider views" which will allow her to be a companion in marriage to a man who seeks to perform noble work'.[136]

Before the conventional ending of Mirah's story, though, Eliot also suggests a vision of the possibilities of feminine vocation. This occurs when the performer, becoming subsumed within the performance, is momentarily rendered transcendent. When Mirah sings for Daniel for the first time, her pathos-filled execution is described as a perfect example of a natural performance: '[It] had that essential of perfect singing, the making one oblivious of art or manner, and only possessing one with the song' (*Daniel Deronda*, p. 315). Although Daniel begins as a spectator, deliberately placing himself where he can see her as she sings, he soon feels compelled to cover his eyes in order to 'seclude the melody in darkness' (*Daniel Deronda*, p. 315). In this scene, the performance succeeds because the performer herself is effaced, becoming a disembodied voice.[137] As Delia Da Sousa Correa has shown, in Eliot's fiction, 'musical experience transcends our perception of linear sequence ... and suspends temporality'.[138] Separated from her body, Mirah's voice momentarily transcends the moral and social conventions associated with the feminised space of the drawing-room. Her voice is transcendent in that it escapes the vulnerability and earthliness that had long been identified as the essence of the female body. Crucially, moreover, she is able to accomplish this transcendence without leaving the domestic sphere. Through Mirah, Eliot offers an image of the woman artist whose voice can enter the public sphere while the woman herself remains in the private. The issues of publicity and sexuality that plagued the woman artist are thoroughly explored throughout the novel, but in this transcendent moment, Eliot manages to resolve these difficulties for at least one of her characters. Such moments, though, were to become more common in the representation of female artistry towards the end of the century.

The Public Image of Ellen Terry

This chapter has shown that representations of female performers from the 1850s through the 1870s described a number of strategies through which the *terra incognita* that was the life of the performer could be understood as compatible

---

136 Joanne Long DeMaria, 'The Wondrous Marriages of *Daniel Deronda*: Gender, Work, and Love', *Studies in the Novel* 22 (1990), p. 411.

137 Carol de Saint Victor, 'Acting and Action: Sexual Distinctions in *Daniel Deronda*', *Cahiers Victoriens et Edouardiens* 26 (1987), p. 81.

138 Delia Da Sousa Correa, '"The Music Vibrating in Her Still": Music and Memory in George Eliot's *The Mill on the Floss* and *Daniel Deronda*', *Nineteenth Century Contexts* 21 (2002), p. 556.

with domesticity. The performer's life was repeatedly laid open for inspection by those sympathetic to the working woman and was shown to be characterised by the familiar qualities of modesty, propriety, virtuousness, and unceasing industry. The result of this scrutiny in all its forms was the development of an image of the female performer who was made respectable through her association with the material aspects of her work. This image offered a useful paradigm for asserting the moral and domestic respectability of other public women at a time when working women were increasingly named as professionals. By the 1880s, Susan Barstow argues, the actress enjoyed a rehabilitated reputation and a widespread social acceptance: 'For the first time in the century, successful actresses were courted by bourgeois society ... Advertisements soon featured famous actresses endorsing a whole range of domestic products; and as the actress lent glamour to domesticity her own image was domesticated'.[139] In part, we can understand this easy acceptance as a hard won product of over 30 years of intense debate. However, as the end of the century approached, a transformation occurred in public life in which celebrity, far from detracting from a working woman's private respectability, became a resource that she might be able to manipulate and exploit.

The benefits of this modern form of celebrity are exemplified by the case of Ellen Terry (1847-1928) who was able to retain her popularity and her social respectability even while leading what could be considered, according to nineteenth-century standards, a very profligate private life. Terry's experience as a public woman on the stage was one of the least shocking aspects of her life. Terry left the stage at the age of 16 to marry the painter, G.F. Watts, but the marriage was ill-fated and short-lived, and they separated within a year. Soon after the collapse of her marriage, she ran off with the architect and stage designer, Edwin Godwin, the father of her two illegitimate children, and they lived together for six years until she returned to the stage again in 1874. Although Terry married twice more, both times for the sake of public respectability, her early life remained fresh in the public memory.[140] But even though Terry led a scandalous private life, she was able to remain one of the most popular and successful actresses on the late-Victorian stage. She could do so in part because of her association with the eminently respectable Henry Irving, which contributed a sense of artistic refinement to her public image. More importantly, though, as Michael Booth notes, she 'had such power over the press and the public' that they saw only 'her warmth and her sense of fun', and she excelled at representing 'those attributes of womanhood deemed perfect and desirable'.[141]

---

139 Susan Torrey Barstow, 'Ellen Terry and the Revolt of the Daughters', *Nineteenth Century Theatre* 25 (1997), p. 22.

140 For a discussion of the beneficial impact of her relationship with Godwin see Nina Auerbach, *Ellen Terry*, pp. 136-42.

141 Michael Booth, 'Ellen Terry', *Bernhardt, Terry, Duse: The Actress in her Time*, John Stokes, Michael Booth, and Susan Bassnett, (Cambridge: Cambridge University Press, 1988), pp. 115, 110.

The public, interested by virtue of Terry's celebrity in discovering the personality behind the famous actress, demanded ever more details of her life. A series of three films made by the celebrated early British filmmaker George Albert Smith in which Smith photographed Terry at her home explicitly sought to satisfy this demand. The films (which sadly have not survived) were produced and exhibited in 1898 when Terry was at the height of her popularity and performing at the Lyceum with Henry Irving. They are described in the trade catalogue as 'splendid likenesses of the popular actress', but, interestingly, Terry is shown engaged in various domestic activities rather than any activities related to the stage.[142] In the catalogue descriptions, the films are billed as: 'Miss Ellen Terry gathering flowers in her garden accompanied by a pet dog', and 'Miss Ellen Terry. Afternoon tea with a friend in the garden'. Significantly, the third film, which depicted 'Miss Ellen Terry appearing at her country cottage window', is described as 'Very characteristic'.[143] The films gave spectators throughout the country the opportunity to see the famous and much-loved Ellen Terry, and even those familiar with her performance on the stage were offered a glimpse of the supposedly authentic and idyllic private life of the actress.

Terry, however, did not restrict herself to this single conventional public image. Elsewhere she chose to present a public image in which her work was the defining feature. Like Kemble, Terry also described her life as a working actress as an endless, wearying round of rehearsals, performances, and theatrical obligations, and when she writes to her friend Amey Stansfield in 1907, she blames her work for her failure to write sooner: 'I am sorry you felt my silence[.] *So many* speak to me, & I try to answer all, but it is quite impossible – I am now up to my neck in business & also in other people's affairs'.[144] When she wrote her autobiography, *The Story of My Life*, in 1908, she constructed it as a record of her professional career and kept the details about her life outside the theatre to a bare minimum. For instance, her marriage to G.F. Watts is only briefly mentioned, and even then, the emphasis is shifted away from the personal aspects of her relationship in order to focus on the intellectual and artistic circle into which she, at the tender age of sixteen, was thrust. Likewise, her two subsequent marriages are barely even mentioned, and her six-year relationship with Godwin is euphemistically referred to as a time when she led 'a most unconventional life'.[145] Even her two children are talked about almost exclusively in relation to their work for the stage. Although Terry does relate some anecdotes about her children, she quickly dismisses these stories by feigning concern for the reader and exclaiming, 'I feel that if I go maundering on much longer about my children, some one will exclaim, with a witty and delightful author when he saw "Peter Pan" for the seventh time: "Oh, for an hour of Herod!"'.[146] Terry presents the

---

142 *Catalogue of Films* (Warwick Trading Co. Ltd, 1897), p. 59.

143 Nos. 3014, 3015, 3016, *Catalogue of Films,* pp. 59–60.

144 John Whitehead, ed., 'A Grain of Sand: Ellen Terry's Letters to Amey Stansfield', *Theatre Research International* 13 (1988), p. 219.

145 Ellen Terry, *The Story of My Life* (Woodbridge: The Boydell Press, 1982), p. 49.

146 Ibid., p. 51.

story of her professional career as the whole story of her life; her private identity is defined through her work on the stage.

In her autobiography, Terry manoeuvred her public image carefully away from the domestic idyll of Smith's films, but did so in such a way that fans were still left with a respectable portrait of a woman who had married three times and borne two illegitimate children. She had been able to manipulate the public's view of her – and exploited a modern world system in which clever women could reinvent themselves in and for the public eye. Whether Terry exploited the public image of the housewife as in Smith's films, or of the industrious actress as in her autobiography, she had increasingly come to embody the epitome of the transcendent performer in which the limitations of the woman's body and the vulnerability inherent in female essentialism were overcome. As a result of her grand lifelong performance, Terry exerted immense influence, Barstow notes, on the women of the Edwardian feminist movement for whom 'the dream of being an actress had a symbolic rather than a practical significance'.[147] These Edwardian daughters, Barstow argues, looked to Terry's example as 'a means of escape from conventional female expectations and identities'.[148] The figure of the actress that for so long had represented the most vulnerable of working women now made a virtue of this vulnerability. Whereas earlier representations of the actress had depended upon various associations between theatrical and domestic spaces, Terry understood and crucially was able to exploit these representations. In the public eye, she could play the part of the domestic angel or the industrious actress at will and deliberately used her expertise to control and exploit her marketplace. The legitimacy of the actress as a working woman no longer depended on an affiliation with domesticity, but was located instead in the professional mastery of public identity as performance. The issue of the woman's entrance into the public sphere through work, which had at mid-century created so many difficulties, was, by the end of the century, being used to assert the very legitimacy it had earlier jeopardised.

---

147 Barstow, 'Ellen Terry and the Revolt of the Daughters', p. 25.
148 Ibid.

Conclusion

> The woman of the middle classes has, until quite recent times, been unduly restrained from contributing her quota to the fund of socially valuable labour; she has had unceasingly impressed upon her that her chief function is maternity, but this function has not been regarded as primarily of social value, but associated essentially with her dependence on an individual ... The reawakening of the middle-class woman is now, however, altering all this. Her desire to take part in work of social value is accompanied by economic conditions and a social opinion which convert the desire into a command ... The duty of woman to labour is becoming as clearly recognised as her right to labour; neither one nor the other can be withdrawn now ... The home, whether we approve it or no, has ceased for ever to be the sole field of woman's activity.[1]

Over the 40-year period from 1848-1890, the public perception of work as a desirable activity for women changed dramatically. Working women, who in the middle of the century had been represented as either the victims of degrading circumstances or unfeminine creatures, were now by the end of the century being seen as legitimate, self-sufficient and socially valuable members of a modern workforce. Writing in 1894, the Social Darwinist Karl Pearson cast a scientific eye on this changing role of the female worker in modern society. Describing this change not as a revolt instigated by the New Woman, but rather as the 'evolutionary outcome' of 'capitalistic methods of production', Pearson identifies the processes that brought about these changes as the inevitable progress of social history.[2] Work is presented by Pearson as a duty that, like her role as mother, a woman must discharge. Significantly, however, Pearson does not see paid work as an extension of a woman's domestic duties. In fact, he cites social degeneration as the inevitable outcome of women's unlimited participation in the labour market during their childbearing years. He argues that it is best for society if those women who have a strong maternal instinct devote themselves to childbearing. In this way, through the process of evolution, the maternal instinct will be even stronger in future generations. Those women without a strong maternal instinct are therefore left to pursue other forms of socially valuable labour. Though Pearson argues that it is the social duty of the majority of women to become mothers, he also admits the value of other forms of women's labour in the progress of a civilised society.

Pearson's evolutionary perspective places the professional working woman at the centre of a social construction of normality. But Pearson could be seen as something of a radical at this time. As the organiser in the late 1880s of the innovative and

---

1   Karl Pearson, 'Woman and Labour', *Fortnightly Review* ns 55 (1894), pp. 573, 574-75.

2   Ibid., p. 570.

controversial 'Men and Women's Club', which was visited by such New Woman figures as Olive Schreiner, Mona Caird and Annie Besant, Pearson proposed to seek open, rational, and scientific discussion of issues of gender and sexuality. Pearson's proclaimed dispassionate brand of social theory, though less radical than that of the New Women with whom he associated, seemed to offer scientific justification for the ideals of a progressive feminist movement condemned elsewhere as hysterical, unwomanly, and dangerous.

Pearson's perspective was nonetheless far from isolated in the context of mainstream culture in the 1890s. Even persistent anti-feminist arguments against female emancipation, such as Eliza Lynn Linton's 1891 attack on 'The Wild Women as Social Insurgents', acknowledged, for instance, that, even in the traditionally perilous environment of the theatre, there was 'no reason why perfectly good and modest women should not be actresses'.[3] The naturalisation of women's entry to the public sphere of paid work was accomplished with personal, economic, and ethical justifications increasingly taken for granted. The perception of woman's paid work as an activity with social value was becoming obvious and accepted by all writers across the spectrum of late-Victorian social debate.

This naturalisation, though, did not simply materialise in the 1890s, but had been the result of a lengthy process. Critical discussions of the New Woman have tended to see her development in the 1890s in isolation. Rarely looking back further than the late 1880s, they see the last decade of the century as a time in which a dramatic change took place in attitudes toward women working. Those who do look back often see only the outspoken leaders of the liberal feminist movement and campaigners for women's rights, from Romantic feminists such as Mary Wollstonecraft, to Victorian figures like Caroline Norton and Barbara Bodichon. Although 'New Womanhood' was most visibly represented by increasingly aggressive political movements, progress toward this figure was being made all the time in the most everyday registers of day-to-day life. The undoubted 'newness' of the 'New Woman' movement notwithstanding, this progress had actually taken place across at least the preceding 50 years. This book has shown that such development was brought about by a concerted, though often undemonstrative, process in which cultural representation played a decisive role. Offering representations of working women who retained their femininity even while entering the marketplace and participating in economic exchange, a wide variety of authors and artists were able to bridge the gap between cherished visions of respectable womanhood and the prohibited public sphere of professional work. Writers as unconventional as George Eliot or as conservative as Charlotte Yonge all contributed – sometimes unwittingly – to the naturalisation of paid work for middle-class women, though their means of doing so varied widely.

On the surface, many argued for the compatibility of paid work with the domestic sphere. But while arguments based on domestic compatibility had great benefits for the working woman, they also detracted from the independence and

---

3   Eliza Lynn Linton, 'The Wild Women as Social Insurgents', *Nineteenth Century* 30 (1891), p. 600.

self-sufficiency she could achieve, keeping her confined ideologically within the domestic sphere. The contradictions generated by this compromised existence made the woman worker an apposite figure through which writers, both male and female, could investigate their own ambivalence about the public and remunerative aspects of their work. Appearing both vulnerable and transgressive, womanly and degraded, the woman worker embodied the difficulties for the creative individual caused by the intersection of the ideals of high culture and the demands of the populist marketplace. By combining art with forms of industrial or mass production in representations of the respectable woman worker, authors projected a form of paid creative work that was not violated or profaned by the public world of the market in which it traded. These representations offered images of female creative labour as a refined and refining experience that raised the profile of women's work in general.

Through the conjunction between femininity, art, and the marketplace in representations of female creativity, authors transformed the woman worker's compromised condition within the domestic sphere. They began to suggest that the transcendent and independent quality unproblematically accorded to aspects of male genius could also be experienced by women within a domestic space and the ideological constraints of 'proper' womanhood. Whether it was through metaphors of the screen or of child-rearing, through the refinement of standard female employments such as needlework, or through the characterisation of industrial employments as 'properly women's work', representations of women working in artistic professions challenged prevailing conceptions about the degradation associated with women's entrance into the world of paid work. Kirsteen's dress shop, Olive's drawing-room studio, Aurora's verse that lives, and Bianca's unconscious performance all dramatise instances or moments of female transcendence that defined forms of female labour that existed independently, yet operated within, the patriarchally-controlled domestic sphere and marketplace.

Feminist criticism of the last 30 years has focused on the ideology of separate spheres. But as this book has shown, a reconsideration of the 'separate-ness' of these spheres reveals that the divisions between public and private were more flexible. Homes were described as workplaces and workplaces as homes. Domesticity and work were not merely specific activities associated with particular places; rather, I have shown them to be mutable qualities that could be manipulated by working women in order to justify increasingly professional careers. By the end of the century representations of the working woman were less bound to conventional notions of domestic respectability. Indeed, as a regretful Eliza Lynn Linton wrote, '"Unladylike" is a term that has ceased to be significant'.[4] Work, refinement, domesticity, and art were no longer primarily objective markers of respectability within bourgeois culture, but could also be seen as personal attributes that could be exploited by those with the dexterity to manipulate public image to advantage.

---

4   Ibid., p. 599.

Bibliography

Editions of Novels

Barrett Browning, Elizabeth, *Aurora Leigh* (1857), Kerry McSweeney, ed. (Oxford: Oxford University Press, 1993).

Braddon, Mary Elizabeth, *Lady Audley's Secret* (1862), David Skilton, ed. (Oxford: Oxford University Press, 1998).

Brontë, Anne, *The Tenant of Wildfell Hall* (1848), Stevie Davies, ed. (London: Penguin Books, 1996).

Brontë, Charlotte, *Villette* (1853), Margaret Smith and Herbert Rosengarten, eds (Oxford: Oxford University Press, 2000).

Collins, Wilkie, *No Name* (1862), Mark Ford, ed. (Harmondsworth: Penguin Books, 1994).

Craik, Dinah, *Olive: A Young Girl's Triumph Over Prejudice* (1850), Cora Kaplan, ed. (Oxford: Oxford University Press, 1996).

Dickens, Charles, *Nicholas Nickleby* (1839) (London: Oxford University Press, 1950).

——, *David Copperfield* (1850), Nina Burgis, ed. (Oxford: Clarendon Press, 1981).

——, *Our Mutual Friend* (1865), Stephen Gill, ed. (London: Penguin Books, 1985).

Edwards, Amelia Blanford, *Barbara's History* (1864) (London: Rubicon, 2000).

Eliot, George, 'Armgart' (1870), *George Eliot: Collected Poems*, Lucien Jenkins, ed. (London: Skoob, 1989).

——, *Daniel Deronda* (1876), Graham Handley, ed. (Oxford: Oxford University Press, 1998).

Gaskell, Elizabeth, *Mary Barton: A Tale of Manchester Life* (1848), Edgar Wright, ed. (Oxford: Oxford University Press, 1998).

——, *Ruth* (1853), Angus Easson, ed. (London: Penguin Books, 1997).

Howitt, Anna Mary, *An Art Student in Munich* (1853), rpt. in *Canvassing: Recollections by Six Victorian Women Artists*, Pamela Gerrish Nunn, ed. (London: Camden Press, 1986), pp. 19-44.

Jewsbury, Geraldine, *The Half Sisters* (1848), Joanne Wilkes, ed. (Oxford: Oxford University Press, 1994).

Meredith, George, *Diana of the Crossways* (1885) (London: Virago, 1985).

Oliphant, Margaret, *Kirsteen* (1889), Merryn Williams, ed. (London: J.M. Dent, 1984).

——, *Miss Marjoribanks* (1866), Elisabeth Jay, ed. (London: Penguin Books, 1998).

Reynolds, G.W.M., *The Seamstress, or the White Slave of England* (1853) (London: John Dicks, 1853).

Rossetti, Christina, 'Speaking Likenesses' (1874), *Poems and Prose*, Jan Marsh, ed. (London: J.M. Dent, 1994).

Stone, Elizabeth, *The Young Milliner* (1843) (London: Cunningham and Mortimer, 1843).

Thackeray, William Makepeace, *The History of Pendennis* (1850), John Sutherland, ed. (Oxford: Oxford University Press, 1999).

Trollope, Anthony, *The Way We Live Now* (1875), John Sutherland, ed. (Oxford: Oxford University Press, 1982).

Yonge, Charlotte M., *Beechcroft at Rockstone* (1865) (London: Macmillan, 1893).

——, *The Clever Woman of the Family* (1865) (London: Macmillan, 1892).

——, *Dynevor Terrace* (1857), 2 vols (London: John W. Parker and Son, 1857).

Primary Sources

A.C.M, 'Industrial Art Work', *Woman's Gazette* 1 (1875), pp. 11, 27-29, 73-74.

'Actresses' Husbands', *Athenaeum* no. 2423 (4 April 1874), pp. 469-70.

'Advice to the Ladies', *Eliza Cook's Journal* 3 (1850), pp. 10-11.

Alford, Lady Marian, 'Art Needlework', *Nineteenth Century* 9 (1881), pp. 439-50.

'Appalling Disclosure for the Lord Chamberlain', *All The Year Round* 1 (1859), pp. 261-64.

A.R., 'The Royal Academy', *Athenaeum* no. 1637 (12 March 1859), pp. 361-62.

A.R.L., 'Facts *Versus* Ideas', *English Woman's Journal* 7 (1861), pp. 73-84.

——, 'The Portrait', *English Woman's Journal* 7 (1861), pp. 104-16, 180-91, 245-58, 318-27, 386-95.

'The Army and the Stage', *Saturday Review* 13 (1862), pp. 321-22.

Art Circular no. 2 (23 Jan. 1851), p. 10.

'Art in the House', *Artist* 1 (1880), p. 85.

'The Art of the Stage', *Art Journal* 19 (1867), pp. 20-21.

'Art Publications', *Art Journal* 30 (1878), p. 144.

'Art Work for Women', *Artist* 4 (1883), pp. 38-39.

Athenaeum, no. 1149 (3 Nov. 1849), p. 1107.

Atkinson, Agnes D., 'Modern Art Needlework', *Portfolio: An Artistic Periodical* 16 (1886), pp. 129-33.

[Austin, Alfred], 'The Present State of the English Stage', *Temple Bar* 33 (1871), pp. 456-68.

'Authoresses', *Saturday Review* 16 (1863), pp. 483-84.

[Baker, H.B.], 'The Theatres', *Temple Bar* 39 (1873), pp. 547-52.

——, 'Our Old Actors: Mrs. Jordan', *Temple Bar* 51 (1877), pp. 174-88.

Barlee, Ellen, 'The Needlewomen', *The Times* (8 Dec. 1866), p. 10.

'Beauty Natural to Woman', *Quarterly Review* (1851), rpt. in *Eliza Cook's Journal* 6 (1852), p. 255.

Becker, Lydia, 'Is There Any Specific Distinction Between Male and Female Intellect?' *Englishwoman's Gazette* 1 (1868), pp. 483-91.

'Bishop Fraser on Stage Decorum', *The Times* (3 Feb. 1877), p. 9.

Blackburn, Henry, 'Artistic Employment for Women', *Women and Work* no. 5 (4 June 1874), p. 2.

'The Blackburn Sewing-Schools', *Temple Bar* 7 (1873), pp. 339-48.

Booth, Charles, ed., *Life and Labour of the People in London*, 9 vols (London: Macmillan, 1892-97).

Brontë, Charlotte, *The Letters of Charlotte Brontë, 1827-1847*, Margaret Smith, ed., 2 vols (Oxford: Clarendon Press, 1995).

Butler, Josephine, *The Education and Employment of Women* (Liverpool: T. Brakell, 1868).

'Cameo-Cutting by Lady Artists', *Builder*, rpt. in *Women and Work* no. 27 (5 Dec. 1874), p. 4.

Carlyle, Thomas, *Lectures on Heroes* (London: Chapman & Hall, n.d.).

——, *Past and Present* (London: Chapman and Hall, 1897).

[Carr, J. Comyns], 'English Actors: – Yesterday and Today', *Fortnightly Review* 39 (1883), pp. 221-32.

C.E.B., *Athenaeum* no. 1863 (19 March 1859), p. 394.

'A Celebrated Needlewoman', *Melbourne Paper*, rpt. in *Women and Work* no. 86 (22 Jan. 1876), p. 5.

Chatterton, F.B., 'The Church and the Stage', *The Times* (5 Oct. 1878), p. 6.

Chesney, Jane, 'A New Vocation for Women', *Macmillan's Magazine* 40 (1879), pp. 341-46.

[Chorley, Henry] '*No Name*', *Athenaeum* no. 1836 (3 Jan. 1863), pp. 10-11.

Collet, Clara E., *Women's Work* (London: Macmillan, 1893).

Conder, F.R., 'Women's Work in Austria', *Art Journal* 27 (1875), pp. 105-107.

Conway, Monoure, 'Women as Decorative Artists', *Harper's Magazine,* rpt. in *Women and Work* no. 22 (31 Oct. 1874), p. 3.

'Court Cards', *Punch* 80 (1881), p. 165.

Craik, Dinah, 'Merely Players', *Nineteenth Century* 20 (1886), pp. 416-22.

——, 'To Novelists – and a Novelist', *Macmillan's Magazine* 3 (1861), pp. 441-48.

——, *A Woman's Thoughts About Women,* (London: Hurst and Blackett, 1858).

Croly, Jennie June, 'An Author or a Dressmaker', *Women and Work* no. 23 (7 Nov. 1874), p. 2.

Crowest, Frederick J., 'Music as a Livelihood', *The Lady's World* (1887), p. 174.

Dafforne, James, 'British Artists: Their Style and Character, no. LXXV – Emily Mary Osborn', *Art Journal* 16 (1864), pp. 261-63.

——, 'British Artists: Their Style and Character, no. LXXVII – Henrietta Ward', *Art Journal* 16 (1864), pp. 357-59.

Davidson, A.T., 'The Clergy and the Theatre', *Macmillan's Magazine* 37 (1878), pp. 497-503.

[Doran, John], 'The Saints of the Stage', *Cornhill Magazine* 15 (1867), pp. 429-39.

'The Dressmaker's Life' *English Woman's Journal* 1 (1858), pp. 319-25.

Eastlake, Lady Elizabeth, '*Vanity Fair* – and *Jane Eyre*', *Quarterly Review* 84 (1848), pp. 153-85.

Eliot, George, 'Silly Novels by Lady Novelists', *Westminster Review* 66 (1856), pp. 442-61, rpt. in *Essays of George Eliot*, Thomas Pinney, ed. (London: Routledge and Kegan Paul, 1963), pp. 300-24.

——, *The George Eliot Letters*, G.S. Haight, ed., 9 vols (New Haven: Yale University Press, 1954-78).

'Employment for Educated Women', *Englishwoman's Review* 6 (1867), pp. 312-13.

'Employment for Women', *Birmingham Morning News*, rpt. in *Women and Work* no. 37 (13 Feb. 1875), p. 2.

'English Poetesses', *Englishwoman's Review* 15 (1884), pp. 371-72.

'English Women of Letters', *Saturday Review* 14 (1862), pp. 718-19.

'Etching As an Employment for Women', *Women and Work* no. 9 (1 Aug. 1874), p. 2.

'Exhibition of School Needlework', *Woman's Gazette* 1 (1876), p. 75.

Fearon, Daniel Rose, 'The Ladies Cry, Nothing To Do!', *Macmillan's Magazine* 19 (1869), pp. 451-54.

'The Female School of Art', *Art Journal* 23 (1871), p. 138.

'Female School of Design', *Art Journal* 3 (1851), pp. 121-22.

'Female Students at the Royal Academy', *Art Journal* 18 (1866), p. 94.

'Feminine Influence', *Saturday Review* 22 (1866), pp. 784-66.

'A Few Words About Actresses and the Profession of the Stage', *English Woman's Journal* 2 (1859), pp. 385-98.

'The Fifth Annual Exhibition of the Society of Female Artists', *English Woman's Journal* 7 (1861), pp. 56-60.

'The Flame Once Kendal'd', *Punch* 87 (25 Oct. 1884), p. 193.

Gann, Louisa, 'The Gower Street (Female) School of Art', *Art Journal* 12 (1860), p. 61.

Gaskell, Elizabeth, *The Letters of Mrs. Gaskell*, J.A.V. Chapple and Arthur Pollard, eds (Manchester: Manchester University Press, 1966).

'Going on the Stage', *Saturday Review* 22 (1866), pp. 602-604.

'The Goose and the Gander', *Saturday Review*, rpt. in *Englishwoman's Review* 1 (1868), pp. 437-41.

Grainger, R.D., 'Second Report of the Commissioners Inquiring into the Employment of Children in Trades and Manufactures', *Parliamentary Papers* 14 (1843).

[Greenwell, Dora], 'Our Single Women', *North British Review* 36 (1862), pp. 632-87.

Greg, W.R., 'Why Are Women Redundant?', *National Review* 14 (1862), pp. 434-60.

Hall, Anna Maria, 'Memories of Miss Jane Porter', *Art Journal* 2 (1850), pp. 221-23.

Hall, S.C. and Mrs. S.C. Hall, 'Memories of Authors of the Age: Letitia Elizabeth Landon', *Art Journal* 17 (1865), pp. 89-93.

——, 'Memories of Authors of the Age: Maria Edgeworth', *Art Journal* 18 (1866), pp. 345-49.

——, 'Memories of Authors of the Age: Mary Russell Mitford', *Art Journal* 18 (1866), pp. 117-21.

——, 'Memories of Authors of the Age: Mrs. Hemans', *Art Journal* 18 (1866), pp. 205-209.

Hazlitt, William, 'On Actors and Acting', *Examiner* (15 Jan. 1817), rpt. in George Rowell, ed., *Victorian Dramatic Criticism* (London: Methuen, 1971), pp. 3-8.

Heath, Fanny, 'Needlework in the German Schools', *Macmillan's Magazine* 40 (1879), pp. 405-13.

Herbert, Christopher, *Victorian Relativity: Radical Thought and Scientific Discovery* (Chicago: University of Chicago Press, 2001).

Hood, Thomas, 'The Song of the Shirt', *Punch* 5 (16 December 1843), p. 260.

'How Can the Young-Ladyhood of England Assist in Improving the Conditions of the Working Classes?', *The Sempstress* 1 (1855), 3-12.

[Hutton, R.H.], 'Novels by the Authoress of *John Halifax*', *North British Review* 29 (1858), pp. 466-81.

'Institute of Art', *Artist* 1 (1880), p. 358.

'Institution for the Employment of Needlewomen', *English Woman's Journal* 5 (1860), pp. 255-59.

James, Henry, 'Frances Anne Kemble', *Temple Bar* 97 (1893), pp. 503-25.

Jeaffreson, J. Cordy, 'Female Artists and Art Schools of England', *Art Pictorial and Industrial* 1 (1870), pp. 25-30, 50-52, 70-73.

Jewsbury, Geraldine, *Selections from the Letters of Geraldine Endsor Jewsbury to Jane Welsh Carlyle*, Mrs. A. Ireland, ed. (London: Longmans, 1892).

Jones, Henry A., 'Religion and the Stage', *Nineteenth Century* 17 (1885), pp. 154-69.

Kemble, Frances Anne, *Journal of a Young Actress* (1835), Monica Gough, ed. (New York: Columbia University Press, 1990).

——, *Journal of a Young Actress*, 2 vols (Philadelphia: Carey, Lea & Blanchard, 1835).

——, 'On the Stage', *Cornhill Magazine* 8 (1863), pp. 733-37.

[Kingsley, Charles], 'Recent Novels', *Fraser's Magazine* 39 (1849), pp. 417-32.

'Ladies as Dressmakers', *Labour News*, rpt. in *Women and Work* no. 12 (22 Aug. 1874), p. 3.

'Ladies' Dressmaking and Embroidery Association', *Woman's Gazette* 2 (1877), pp. 75-76.

'Ladies' Dressmaking and Embroidery Association', *Woman's Gazette* 4 (1879), p. 184.

'The Ladies' Guild', *Eliza Cook's Journal* 5 (1851), p. 277.

'Lady Marian Alford on Art Needlework', *Edinburgh Review* 164 (1886), pp. 137-65.

'Letter to the Editor', *English Woman's Journal* 8 (1861), pp. 139, 205-208, 356-58.

Lewes, G.H., *On Actors and the Art of Acting* (New York: Greenwood Press, 1968).

The Life of Marie-Eustelle Harpin, The Sempstress of Saint-Pallais (London: Burns, Oates, & Co., 1868).

Linton, Eliza Lynn, 'The Wild Women as Social Insurgents', *Nineteenth Century* 30 (1891), pp. 596-605.

'Literature Regarded as a Profession', *Work and Leisure* 6 (1881), pp. 40-43.

'Literary Women of the Nineteenth-Century', *English Woman's Domestic Magazine* 7 (1859), pp. 341-43.

[Ludlow, J.M.], 'Ruth', *North British Review* 19 (1853), pp. 151-74.

[Lytton, Edward Robert Bulwer], 'The Stage in Relation to Literature', *Fortnightly Review* 40 (1883), pp. 12-26, 215-26.

[Mackay, Charles], 'Stage Morality, and the Ballet', *Blackwood's Magazine* 105 (1869), pp. 354-60.

Macready, W.C., *The Times* (8 May 1860), p. 5.

Mademoiselle Rachel', *Art Journal* 10 (1858), p. 253.

'Mademoiselle Rosa Bonheur', *Art Journal* 7 (1855), p. 243.

[Mansel, H.L.], 'Sensation Novels', *Quarterly Review* 113 (1863), pp. 481-514.

[Martin, Theodore], 'The English Stage', *Quarterly Review* 155 (1883), pp. 354-88.

Martineau, Harriet, 'Female Industry', *Edinburgh Review* 109 (1859), pp. 293-334.

Maurice, F.D., 'Female School of Art; Mrs. Jameson', *Macmillan's Magazine* 2 (1860), pp. 227-35.

Mayhew, Henry, *London Labour and the London Poor*, 4 vols (New York: Dover Publications, 1968).

——, 'Slopworkers and Needlewomen', *The Unknown Mayhew: Selections from the* Morning Chronicle *1849-50*, E.PP. Thompson and Eileen Yeo, eds (London: Merlin Press, 1971), pp. 116-80.

Merrifield, Mrs., 'On Design as Applied to Ladies Work', *Art Journal* 7 (1855), pp. 37-39, 73-75, 133-37.

[Meteyard, Eliza], *Lucy Dean; The Noble Needlewoman, Eliza Cook's Journal* 3 (Jan. 1850-Jan. 1851).

——, 'A Woman's Pen', *English Woman's Journal* 1 (1858), pp. 246-59.

M.G., 'Industrial Art-Work', *Woman's Gazette* 1 (1875), pp. 11, 27-29, 73-74.

Michell, Nicholas, 'The Actress and the Concert Singer', *Ainsworth's Magazine* 16 (1849), pp. 326-40.

Mill, John Stuart, *The Subjection of Women* (Ontario: Broadview Press, 2000).

'Milliners and Dressmakers', *Women and Work* no. 19 (10 Oct. 1874), p. 2.

'Miss Louisa Hereford', *Art Journal* 23 (1871), p. 80.

Morris, Mowbray, 'On Some Recent Theatrical Criticisms', *Macmillan's Magazine* 48 (1883), pp. 321-27.

Morris, William, 'Textiles', *William Morris: Artist, Writer, Socialist*, May Morris, ed. (Oxford: Basil Blackwell, 1936), p. 244-51.

'Mosaic Working as an Employment for Women', *Women and Work* no. 8 (25 July 1874), p. 3.

Mowatt, Mrs., *Autobiography of an Actress*, rpt. in *Eliza Cook's Journal* 7 (1854), pp. 7-10, 361-64.

——, 'Ballet Girls', from *Autobiography of An Actress*, rpt. in *Eliza Cook's Journal* 7 (1854), pp. 186-87.

'Mr. Bell's New Novel', *Rambler: A Catholic Journal and Review* 3 (1848), pp. 65-66.

'Mrs. Barrett Browning – *Aurora Leigh*', *Blackwood's Magazine* 81 (1857), pp. 23-41.

Müntz, Eugéne, *A Short History of Tapestry from the Earliest Time to the End of the Eighteenth Century*, trans. by Louisa J. Davis (London: Cassell, 1885).

'The Music Hall', *The Cornhill Magazine* 13 (1889), pp. 68-79.

'Needlework', *Artist* 1 (1880), pp. 123-24.

'Needlework', *London Quarterly Review* 66 (1886), pp. 284-300.

'Needlework', *Macmillan's Magazine* 28 (1873), pp. 429-35.

Nos. 3014, 3015, 3016, *Catalogue of Films* (Warwick Trading Co. Ltd, 1897), pp. 59-60.

'Notes of an Exhibition of the School of Art Embroidery', *Art Journal* 28 (1876), pp. 173-74.

'A Novelty in Fancy-Work', *Art Journal* 8 (1856), pp. 139-40.

[Oliphant, Margaret], 'Novels', *Blackwood's Magazine* 94 (1863), pp. 168-83.

'On the Adoption of Professional Life by Women', *English Woman's Journal* 2 (1858), pp. 1-10.

'On the Best Means of Relieving the Needlewomen', *Eliza Cook's Journal* 5 (1851), pp. 189-91.

'Our Suffocated Sempstresses', *Punch* (4 July 1863), p. 46.

Palgrave, F.T., 'Women and the Fine Arts', *Macmillan's Magazine* 12 (1865), pp. 118-27, 209-21.

Palliser, Mrs. Bury, 'The School of Art-Needlework', *Art Journal* 29 (1877), p. 213.

[Patmore, Coventry], 'Mrs. Browning's Poems', *North British Review* 26 (1857), pp. 443-62.

'Peace and Good-Will: The Pulpit and the Stage', *Era* (27 Jan. 1867), p. 10.

Pearson, Karl, 'Woman and Labour', *Fortnightly Review* ns 55 (1894), pp. 561-77.

Pfeiffer, Emily, 'The English Stage' [a letter to the editor], *The Times* (8 Oct. 1879), p. 8.

——, *Women and Work, An Essay* (London: Trubner & Co., 1888).

Phillips, M.E., 'On the Necessity for Studying Practical Needlework', *Woman's Gazette* 1 (1876), p. 170.

'Photographic Colouring', *Women and Work* no. 13 (29 Aug. 1874), p. 2.

'Photography as an Employment for Women', *Englishwoman's Review* 1 (1867), pp. 219-23.

'A Plea for Players', *Saturday Review* 16 (1863), pp. 722-24.

Pollock, Juliet, 'For and Against the Play', *Nineteenth Century* 1 (1877), pp. 611-22.

Potter, Beatrice, "Pages From a Work-Girl's Diary," *Nineteenth Century* 24 (1888), 301-14.

'The Profession of the Teacher', *English Woman's Journal* 1 (1858), p. 8.

Rathbone, H.M., 'The Seamstress', *Working Man's Friend and Family Instructor* 1 (1850), pp. 306-308.

Reynolds, G.W.M., 'Warning to the Needlewomen and Slopworkers', *Reynolds's Political Instructor* 1 (1850), pp. 66-67, 74-75.

'Right Hon. A.J. Mundella, MP.', *Artist* 4 (1883), pp. 100-101.

[Ritchie, Anne], 'Arachne in Sloane Street', *Cornhill Magazine* 29 (1874), pp. 571-76.

Robertson, Eric, *English Poetesses: A Series of Critical Biographies* (London: Cassell, 1883).

'Romeo and Juliet at the Lyceum', *The Times* (9 Mar. 1882), p. 6.

'Rosa Bonheur', *English Woman's Journal* 1 (1858), pp. 227-43.

'The Royal Academy and Female Artists', *English Woman's Journal* 7 (1861), pp. 71-72.

'Royal Academy Exhibition', *Art Journal* 9 (1857), pp. 166-68.

'Rules of the Royal School of Art Needlework', *Woman's Gazette* 2 (1877), pp. 53-54.

Ruskin, John, *Sesame and Lilies* (London: Blackie & Son, n.d.).

'Ruth', *Eliza Cook's Journal* 8 (1853), pp. 277-80.

Sandby, William, *The History of the Royal Academy of Arts from its Foundation in 1768 to the Present Time*, 2 vols (London: Longman, Green, Longman, Roberts & Green, 1862).

Saward, B.C., 'Artistic Occupations for Ladies', *Lady's World* (1887), pp. 29-31, 138-39.

Scott, Miss, 'Art Embroidery I', *Woman's Gazette* 1 (1875), p. 40.

——, 'Art Embroidery II', *Woman's Gazette* 1 (1876), p. 59.

'The Seamstress', *Eliza Cook's Journal* 3 (1850), pp. 17-19.

'Seamstresses Again: A Story of Christmas Eve', *English Woman's Journal* 5 (1859), pp. 235-46.

The Sempstress 1 (1855).

The Sempstress and the Actress; or, The Power of Prayer (London: J.F. Shaw, 1859).

'A Sign of the Times', *Eliza Cook's Journal* 3 (1850), p. 408.

'The Singing Girl', *Eliza Cook's Journal* 2 (1850), pp. 289-91.

'Sir F. Grant at the Female School of Art', *Englishwoman's Review* 1 (1868), p. 396.

Smith, Alexander, 'Novels and Novelists of the Day', *North British Review* 38 (1863), pp. 168-90.

Smith, Barbara Leigh, 'Women and Work', rpt. in *The Exploited: Women and Work*, Marie Mulvey Roberts and Tamae Mizuta, eds (London: Routledge, 1995), pp. 5-49.

'Society for Promoting the Employment of Women', *English Woman's Journal* 5 (1860), pp. 388-96.

'The Society of Female Artists', *Art Journal* 9 (1857), pp. 215-16.

'The Society of Female Artists', *Art Journal* 24 (1872), pp. 89-90.

'The Society of Female Artists', *English Woman's Journal* 1 (1858), pp. 205-209.

'Society of Female Artists', *Englishwoman's Review* ns 1 (1871), pp. 149-50.

'Stage Decorum', *The Times* (7 Dec. 1874), p. 10.

'Stage Decorum', *The Times* (1 Feb. 1877), p. 9.

Stannard, Henrietta, 'Stage Effects', *Cornhill Magazine* 6 (1886), pp. 490-503.

Stewart, J., 'Art-Decoration: A Suitable Employment for Women', *Art Journal* 12 (1860), pp. 70-71.

'A Suggestion', *Macmillan's Magazine* 20 (1869), pp. 365-66.

Sunbeam, Silas, 'Church and Theatre', *Era* (13 Jan. 1867), p. 7.

Terry, Ellen, *The Story of My Life* (Woodbridge: Boydell Press, 1982).

'To Amateur Authors', *Work and Leisure* 6 (1881), pp. 362-64.

Toulmin, Camilla, 'The Orphan Milliners: A Story of the West End', *Illuminated Magazine* 2 (1844), pp. 279-85.

Turner, Godfrey, 'Amusements of the English People', *Nineteenth Century* 2 (1877), pp. 820-30.

'Unsigned review', *Christian Remembrancer* (1848), rpt. in *The Brontës: The Critical Heritage*, Miriam Allott, ed. (London: Routledge and Kegan Paul, 1974), pp. 88-92.

'Unsigned review', *Sharpe's London Magazine* 7 (1848), rpt. in *The Brontës: The Critical Heritage*, Miriam Allott, ed. (London: Routledge & Kegan Paul, 1974), pp. 263-65.

'Unsigned review', *Sharpe's London Magazine* n.s. 2 (1853), rpt. in *Elizabeth Gaskell: The Critical Heritage*, Angus Easson, ed. (London: Routledge, 1991), pp. 208-11.

'Unsigned review', *Spectator* 26 (1853), rpt. in *Elizabeth Gaskell: The Critical Heritage*, Angus Easson, ed. (London: Routledge, 1991), pp. 211-14.

Vincent, W.M., 'The Condition of the Stage', *The Times* (30 Sept. 1884), p. 12

'Warehouse Seamstresses. By One Who Has Worked With Them', *English Woman's Journal* 3 (1859), pp. 164-71.

Webb, Beatrice, *The Diary of Beatrice Webb, Volume One, 1873-1892,* Norman and Jeanne MacKenzie, eds (London: Virago, 1982).

'West-End Housekeepers', *English Woman's Journal* 8 (1861), pp. 249-54.

Willich, Charles M. and E.T. Scargill, 'Tables Relating to The State of The Population of Great Britain at The Census of 1851, with a Comparative View, at the Different Ages, of the Population of France; Also a Comparative Return of Births and Deaths, 1838-1854', *Journal of the Statistical Society of London* 21, no. 3 (1858), pp. 297-307.

'With Needle and Thread: The Work of Today', *Lady's World* (1887), pp. 32-33.

'Woman's Work in Public Amusements', *Work and Leisure* 6 (1881), pp. 129-32, 159-64.

'Women and the Stage', *Daily Telegraph*, rpt. in *Women and Work* no. 31 (2 Jan. 1875), p. 5.

Women and Work no. 37 (13 Feb. 1875), p. 4.

Women and Work no. 56 (26 June 1875), p. 4.

'Women and Work', *Work and Leisure* 5 (1880), pp. 1-7.

'Women's Industries', *Englishwoman's Review* 15 (1884), pp. 509-12.

Wordsworth, William, 'Preface to Lyrical Ballads (1802)', rpt. in *Romantic Poetry and Prose*, Harold Bloom and Lionel Trilling, eds (London: Oxford University Press, 1973), pp. 594-611.

Yonge, Charlotte M., *Beechcroft at Rockstone* (London: Macmillan and Co., 1893), p. 55.

Secondary Sources

Abrams, M.H., *The Mirror and the Lamp: Romantic Theory and the Critical Tradition* (London: Oxford University Press, 1953).

Alexander, Christine and Jane Sellars, *The Art of the Brontës* (Cambridge: Cambridge University Press, 1995).

Alexander, Lynn, *Women, Work, and Representation: Needlewomen in Victorian Art and Literature* (Athens: Ohio University Press, 2003).

——, 'Creating A Symbol: The Seamstress in Victorian Literature', *Tulsa Studies in Women's Literature* 18 (1999), pp. 29-38.

——, 'Following the Thread: Dickens and the Seamstress', *Victorian Newsletter* no. 80 (1991), pp. 1-7.

Anderson, Amanda, *Tainted Souls and Painted Faces: The Rhetoric of Fallenness in Victorian Culture* (Ithaca: Cornell University Press, 1993).

Andrew August, 'How Separate a Sphere? Poor Women and Paid Work in Late-Victorian London', *Journal of Family History* 19 (1994), pp. 285-309.

Ardis, Ann, *New Women, New Novels: Feminism and Early Modernism* (London: Rutgers University Press, 1990).

Armstrong, Isobel, *Victorian Poetry: Poetry, Poetics and Politics* (London: Routledge, 1993).

Auerbach, Nina, *Ellen Terry, Player in Her Time* (London: Phoenix House, 1987).

——, *Romantic Imprisonment: Women and Other Glorified Outcasts* (New York: Columbia University Press, 1986).

——, *Private Theatricals: The Lives of the Victorians* (Cambridge, MA: Harvard University Press, 1990).

Baker, Michael, *The Rise of the Victorian Actor* (London: Croom Helm, 1978).

Barstow, Susan Torrey, 'Ellen Terry and the Revolt of the Daughters', *Nineteenth Century Theatre* 25 (1997), pp. 5-32.

Beer, Gillian, *Meredith, A Change of Masks: A Study of the Novels* (London: Athlone Press, 1970).

——, '"Coming Wonders": Uses of Theatre in the Victorian Novel', *English Drama: Forms and Development* (Cambridge: Cambridge University Press, 1977), pp. 164-85.

——, *George Eliot* (Brighton: Harvester, 1986).

Beer, Patricia, *Reader, I Married Him: A Study of the Women Characters of Jane Austen, Charlotte Bronte, Elizabeth Gaskell, and George Eliot* (London: Macmillan, 1974).

Bick, Suzann, '"Take Her Up Tenderly": Elizabeth Gaskell's Treatment of the Fallen Woman', *Essays in Arts and Sciences* 18 (1989), pp. 17-27.

Birch, Dinah, 'Beauty and the Victorian Body', *Essays in Criticism* 44 (1994), pp. 102-16.

Black, Clementina, ed., *Married Women's Work: Being the Report of an Enquiry Undertaken by the Women's Industrial Council (1915)* (London: Virago, 1983).

Blake, Kathleen, 'Elizabeth Barrett Browning and Wordsworth: The Romantic Poet as a Woman', *Victorian Poetry* 24 (1986), pp. 387-98.

Blythell, Duncan, 'Women in the Workforce', *The Industrial Revolution and British Society*, Patrick K. O'Brien and Roland Quinault, eds (Cambridge: Cambridge University Press, 1993), pp. 31-53.

Boardman, Kay, 'The Ideology of Domesticity: The Regulation of the Household Economy in Victorian Women's Magazines', *Victorian Periodicals Review* 33 (2000), pp. 150-64.

Bodenheimer, Rosemarie, *The Politics of Story in Victorian Social Fiction* (Ithaca: Cornell University Press, 1988).

Booth, Alison, 'From Miranda to Prospero: The Works of Fanny Kemble', *Victorian Studies* 38 (1995), pp. 227-54.

——, 'Incomplete Stories: Womanhood and Artistic Ambition in *Daniel Deronda* and *Between the Acts*', *Writing the Woman Artist: Essays on Poetics, Politics, and Portraiture*, Suzanne W. Jones, ed. (Philadelphia: University of Pennsylvania Press, 1991), pp. 113-30.

Booth, Michael, 'Ellen Terry', *Bernhardt, Terry, Duse: The Actress in her Time*, John Stokes, Michael Booth and Susan Bassnett, eds (Cambridge: Cambridge University Press, 1988), pp. 65-181.

——, *Theatre in the Victorian Age* (Cambridge: Cambridge University Press, 1991).

——, *Victorian Spectacular Theatre, 1850-1910* (London: Routledge & Kegan Paul, 1981).

Borzello, Frances, *Seeing Ourselves: Women's Self-Portraits* (London: Thames and Hudson, 1998).

Bossche, Chris Vanden, 'The Queen in the Garden/The Woman of the Streets: The Separate Spheres and the Inscription of Gender', *Journal of Pre-Raphaelite Studies* 1 (1992), pp. 1-15.

Bossche, Chris Vanden, and Laura Haighwood, 'Revising the Prelude: Aurora Leigh as Laureate', *Studies in Browning and His Circle* 22 (1992), pp. 29-42.

Bradley, Harriet, *Men's Work, Women's Work: A Sociological History of the Sexual Division of Labour in Employment* (Cambridge: Polity Press, 1989).

Braithwaite, Brian, *Women's Magazines: The First 300 Years* (London: Peter Owen, 1995).

Branca, Patricia, *Silent Sisterhood: Middle-Class Women in the Victorian Home* (London: Croom Helm, 1975).

Bristow, Joseph, ed., *Victorian Women Poets: Emily Brontë, Elizabeth Barrett Browning, Christina Rossetti* (London: Macmillan, 1995).

Brownstein, Rachel M., *Tragic Muse: Rachel of the Comédie Française* (New York: Alfred A. Knopf, 1993).

Burgan, Mary, 'Heroines at the Piano: Women and Music in Nineteenth-Century Fiction', *Victorian Studies* 29 (1986), pp. 51-76.

Burlin, Katrin R., '"At the Crossroads": Sister Authors and the Sister Arts', *Fetter'd or Free? British Women Novelists, 1670-1815*, Mary Anne Schofield and Cecilia Macheski, eds (Athens: Ohio University Press, 1986), pp. 60-84.

Burman, Sandra, ed., *Fit Work for Women* (London: Croom Helm, 1979).

Callen, Anthea, *Angel in the Studio: Women in the Arts and Crafts Movement, 1870-1914* (London: Astragal Books, 1979).

——, 'Sexual Division of Labour in the Arts and Crafts Movement', *Oxford Art Journal* 3 (1980), pp. 22-27.

Carnell, Rachel K., 'Feminism and the Public Sphere in Anne Brontë's *The Tenant of Wildfell Hall*', *Nineteenth-Century Literature* 53 (1998), pp. 1-24.

Cary, Meredith, 'Geraldine Jewsbury and the Woman Question', *Research Studies* 42 (1974), pp. 201-14.

Case, Alison, *Plotting Women: Gender and Narration in the Eighteenth- and Nineteenth-Century British Novel* (Charlottesville: University of Virginia Press, 1999).

Casteras, Susan, *Images of Victorian Womanhood in English Art* (Rutherford, NJ: Farleigh Dickinson University Press, 1987).

——, '"The Necessity of a Name": Portrayals and Betrayals of Victorian Women Artists', *Gender and Discourse in Victorian Literature and Art*, Anthony H. Harrison and Barbara Taylor, eds (DeKalb: Northern Illinois University Press, 1992), pp. 207-32.

Casteras, Susan P. and Linda H. Peterson, *A Struggle for Fame: Victorian Women Artists and Authors* (New Haven: Yale Center for British Art, 1994).

Cerný, Lothar, '"Life in Death": Art in Dickens's *Our Mutual Friend*', *Dickens Quarterly* 17 (2000), pp. 22-36.

Chadwick, Whitney, *Women, Art, and Society* (London: Thames and Hudson, 1990).

Chalmers, F. Graeme, *Women in the Nineteenth-Century Art World: Schools of Art and Design for Women in London and Philadelphia* (London: Greenwood Press, 1998).

Chase, Karen, and Michael Levenson, *The Spectacle of Intimacy: A Public Life for the Victorian Family* (Princeton: Princeton University Press, 2000).

Chattman, Lauren, 'Actresses at Home and On the Stage: Spectacular Domesticity and the Victorian Theatrical Novel', *Novel* 28 (1994), pp. 72-88.

Cheadle, Brian, 'Work in *Our Mutual Friend*', *Essays in Criticism* 51 (2001), pp. 308-29.

Cherry, Deborah, *Painting Women: Victorian Women Artists* (London: Routledge, 1993).

——, 'Women Artists and the Politics of Feminism 1850-1900', *Women in the Victorian Art World*, Clarissa Campbell Orr, ed. (Manchester: Manchester University Press, 1995), pp. 49-69.

Cohen, Monica, *Professional Domesticity in the Victorian Novel: Women, Work, and Home* (Cambridge: Cambridge University Press, 1998).

Cole, Margaret, *Women of To-day* (London: Thomas Nelson, 1946).

Cook, Ruth McDowell, 'Women's Work as Paradigm for Autonomy in Gaskell's *My Lady Ludlow*', *Gaskell Society Journal* 11 (1997), pp. 68-76.

Corbett, Mary Jane, *Representing Femininity: Middle-Class Subjectivity in Victorian and Edwardian Women's Autobiographies* (Oxford: Oxford University Press, 1992).

Correa, Delia Da Sousa, '"The Music Vibrating in Her Still": Music and Memory in George Eliot's *The Mill on the Floss* and *Daniel Deronda*', *Nineteenth Century Contexts* 21 (2002), pp. 541-63.

Craig, Edward Gordon, *Ellen Terry and Her Secret Self* (London: Sampson, Low, Marston and Co., [nd.]).

David, Deirdre, *Intellectual Women and Victorian Patriarchy: Harriet Martineau, Elizabeth Barrett Browning, George Eliot* (Ithaca: Cornell University Press, 1987).

——, 'Rewriting the Male Plot in Wilkie Collins's *No Name* (1862): Captain Wragge Orders an Omelette and Mrs. Wragge Goes into Custody', *The New Nineteenth Century: Feminist Readings of Underread Victorian Fiction*, Barbara Leah Harman and Susan Meyer, eds (London: Garland, 1996), pp. 33-43.

Davidoff, Leonore, *Between Worlds: Historical Perspectives on Gender and Class* (Cambridge: Polity Press, 1995).

Davidoff, Leonore and Catherine Hall, *Family Fortunes: Men and Women of the English Middle Class, 1780-1850* (Chicago: University of Chicago Press, 1987).

Davies, Ross, *Women and Work* (London: Arrow Books, 1975).

Davis, Tracy, 'Actresses and Prostitutes in Victorian London', *Theatre Research International* 13 (1988), pp. 221-34.

——, *Actresses as Working Women: Their Social Identity in Victorian Culture* (London: Routledge, 1991).

Delamont, Sara, 'The Domestic Ideology and Women's Education', *The Nineteenth-Century Woman: Her Cultural and Physical World*, Sara Delamont and Lorna Duffin, eds (London: Croom Helm, 1978), pp. 164-87.

DeMaria, Joanne Long, 'The Wondrous Marriages of *Daniel Deronda*: Gender, Work, and Love', *Studies in the Novel* 22 (1990), pp. 403-17.

Denisoff, Dennis, 'Lady in Green with Novel: The Gendered Economics of the Visual Arts and Mid-Victorian Women's Writing', *Victorian Women Writers and the Woman Question*, Nicola Diane Thompson, ed. (Cambridge: Cambridge University Press, 1999), pp. 151-69.

Digby, Anne, 'Victorian Values and Women in Public and Private', *Proceedings of the British Academy* 78 (1992), pp. 195-215.

Doumato, Lamia, 'The Literature of Woman in Art', *Oxford Art Journal* 3 (1980), pp. 74-77.

Easley, Alexis, 'Authorship, Gender and Identity: George Eliot in the 1850s', *Women's Writing* 3 (1996), pp. 145-60.

——, 'Gendered Observations: Harriet Martineau and the Woman Question', *Victorian Women Writers and the Woman Question*, Nicola Diane Thompson, ed. (Cambridge: Cambridge University Press, 1999), pp. 80-98.

Easson, Angus, ed., *Elizabeth Gaskell. The Critical Heritage* (London: Routledge, 1991), pp. 200-39.

Edelstein, T.J., 'They Sang "The Song of the Shirt": The Visual Iconography of the Seamstress', *Victorian Studies* 23 (1980), 183-210.

Elam, Diane, '"We Pray to Be Defended from Her Cleverness": Conjugating Romance in George Meredith's *Diana of the Crossways*', *Genre* 21 (1988), pp. 179-201.

Elliott-Binns, L.E., *Religion in the Victorian Era* (London: Lutterworth Press, 1936).

Foster, Shirley, *Victorian Women's Fiction: Marriage, Freedom, and the Individual* (London: Croom Helm, 1985).

Fredeman, William, 'Emily Faithfull and the Victoria Press: An Experiment in Sociological Bibliography', *The Library* 29 (1974), pp. 139-64.

Fitzwilliam, Marie, 'The Needle and Not the Pen: Fabric (Auto)biography in *Cranford*, *Ruth*, and *Wives and Daughters*', *Gaskell Society Journal* 14 (2000), pp. 1-13.

Gallagher, Catherine, 'George Eliot and *Daniel Deronda*: The Prostitute and the Jewish Question', *Sex, Politics, and Science in the Nineteenth-Century Novel*, Ruth Bernard Yeazell, ed. (Baltimore: The Johns Hopkins University Press, 1986), pp. 39-62.

——, *The Industrial Reformation of English Fiction, 1832-1867* (Chicago: University of Chicago Press, 1985).

——, *Nobody's Story: The Vanishing Acts of Women Writers in the Marketplace, 1670-1820* (Berkeley: University of California Press, 1994).

Gallagher, Catherine and Thomas Laqueur, eds, *The Making of the Modern Body: Sexuality and Society in the Nineteenth Century* (Berkeley: University of California Press, 1987).

Garb, Tamar, *Sisters of the Brush: Women's Artistic Culture in Late Nineteenth-Century Paris* (New Haven: Yale University Press, 1994).

Gilbert, Alan D., *Religion and Society in Industrial England: Church, Chapel and Social Change, 1790-1914* (London: Longman, 1976).

Gilbert, Sandra and Susan Gubar, *The Madwoman in the Attic: The Woman Writer and the Nineteenth-Century Literary Imagination*, 2nd ed. (New Haven: Yale University Press, 2000).

Gillett, Paula, *Worlds of Art: Painters in Victorian Society* (New Brunswick, NJ: Rutgers University Press, 1990).

Gordon, Jan B., 'Gossip, Diary, Letter, Text: Anne Brontë's Narrative *Tenant* and the Problematic of the Gothic Sequel', *ELH* 51 (1984), pp. 719-45.

Gottlieb, Stacey, '"And God Will Teach Her": Consciousness and Character in *Ruth* and *Aurora Leigh*', *Victorians Institute Journal* 24 (1996), pp. 57-85.

Graham, Kenneth, *English Criticism of the Novel: 1865-1900* (Oxford: Clarendon Press, 1965).

Gray, Janet, 'The Sewing Contest: Christina Rossetti and the Other Women', *a/b: Auto/biography Studies* 8 (1993), pp. 233-57.

Green, Laura Morgan, *Educating Women: Cultural Conflict and Victorian Literature* (Athens: Ohio University Press, 2001).

Guy, Josephine, 'Aesthetics, Economics and Commodity Culture: Theorizing Value in Late Nineteenth-Century Britain', *ELT* 42 (1999), pp. 143-71.

Haining, Peter, *The Penny Dreadful, or, Strange, Horrid, & Sensational Tales!* (London: Victor Gollancz, 1975).

Hall, Catherine, 'The History of the Housewife', *The Politics of Housework*, E. Malos, ed. (London: Allison and Busby, 1980).

——, 'Private Persons versus Public Someones: Class, Gender and Politics in England, 1780-1850', *British Feminist Thought: A Reader*, Terry Lovell, ed. (Oxford: Basil Blackwell, 1990).

Hankey, Julie, 'Body Language, the Idea of the Actress, and Some Nineteenth-Century Actress-Heroines', *New Theatre Quarterly* 8 (1992), pp. 226-40.

Hapke, Laura, 'He Stoops to Conquer: Redeeming the Fallen Woman in the Fiction of Dickens, Gaskell and Their Contemporaries', *Victorian Newsletter* no 69 (1986), pp. 16-22.

Harman, Barbara Leah, and Susan Meyers, eds, *The New Nineteenth Century: Feminist Readings of Underread Victorian Fiction* (London: Garland Publishing, 1996).

Hartley, J.M., 'Geraldine Jewsbury and the Problems of the Woman Novelist', *Women's Studies International Quarterly* 2 (1979), pp. 137-53.

Hartman, Kabi, '"An Artist in her Way": Representations of the Woman Artist in Margaret Oliphant's *Kirsteen*', *Schuykill: A Creative and Critical Review from Temple University* 2 (1999), pp. 74-84.

Heilmann, Ann, 'Mrs. Grundy's Rebellion: Margaret Oliphant Between Orthodoxy and the New Woman', *Women's Writing* 6 (1999), pp. 215-34.

Helsinger, Elizabeth K., Robin Lauterbach Sheets and William Veeder, *The Woman Question*, 3 vols (London: Garland Publishing, 1983).

Herbert, Christopher, *Victorian Relativity: Radical Thought and Scientific Discovery* (Chicago: University of Chicago Press, 2001).

Hesketh, Sally, 'Needlework in the Lives and Novels of the Brontë Sisters', *Brontë Society Transactions* 22 (1997), pp. 72-85.

Hewitt, Margaret, *Wives and Mothers in Victorian Industry* (Westport, CT: Greenwood Press, 1958).

Higgs, Edward, 'Women, Occupations and Work in the Nineteenth-Century Censuses', *History Workshop* 23 (1987), pp. 59-80.

Hill, Bridget, *Women, Work, and Sexual Politics in Eighteenth-Century England* (Oxford: Basil Blackwell, 1989).

Hirsch, Pam, 'Barbara Leigh Smith Bodichon: Artist and Activist', *Women in the Victorian Art World*, Clarissa Campbell Orr, ed. (Manchester: Manchester University Press, 1995) pp. 167-86.

——, *Barbara Leigh Smith Bodichon, 1827-1891: Feminist, Artist and Rebel* (London: Pimlico, 1999).

Holcombe, Lee, *Victorian Ladies at Work* (Newton Abbot: David & Charles, 1973).

——, 'Victorian Wives and Property: Reform of the Married Women's Property Law, 1857-1882', *A Widening Sphere: Changing Roles of Victorian Women*, Martha Vicinus, ed. (Bloomington: Indiana University Press, 1977), pp. 3-29.

Hollis, Patricia, *Women in Public, The Women's Movement, 1850-1900: Documents of the Victorian Women's Movement* (London: George Allen & Unwin, 1979).

Homans, Margaret, *Bearing the Word: Language and Female Experience in Nineteenth-Century Women's Writing* (Chicago: University of Chicago Press, 1986).

——, 'Victoria's Sovereign Obedience: Portraits of the Queen as Wife and Mother', *Victorian Literature and the Victorian Visual Imagination*, Carol T. Christ and John O. Jordan, eds (Berkeley: University of California Press, 1995), pp. 167-97.

Houston, Gail Turley, *Royalties: The Queen and Victorian Writers* (Charlottesville: University of Virginia Press, 1999).

Humphries, Jane, 'Women and Paid Work', *Women's History: Britain, 1850-1945*, June Purvis, ed. (London: UCL Press, 1995), pp. 85-107.

Jacobs, N.M., 'Gender and Layered Narrative in *Wuthering Heights* and *The Tenant of Wildfell Hall*', *Journal of Narrative Technique* 16 (1986), pp. 204-19.

John, Angela V., ed. *Unequal Opportunities: Women's Employment in England 1800-1918* (Oxford: Basil Blackwell, 1986).

Johnston, Judith, *Anna Jameson: Victorian, Feminist, Woman of Letters* (Aldershot: Scholar Press, 1997).

Jones, Kathleen, *Learning Not to Be First: The Life of Christina Rossetti* (Oxford: Oxford University Press, 1991).

Jordan, Ellen, 'The Exclusion of Women from Industry in Nineteenth-Century Britain', *Comparative Studies in Society and History: An International Quarterly* 31 (1989), pp. 273-96.

——, *The Women's Movement and Women's Employment in Nineteenth Century Britain* (London: Routledge, 1999).

Kaplan, Cora, *Sea Changes: Culture and Feminism* (London: Verso, 1986).

Kaplan, E. Ann, *Motherhood and Representation: The Mother in Popular Culture and Melodrama* (London: Routledge, 1992).

Keener, Frederick M. and Susan E. Lorsch, eds, *Eighteenth-Century Women and the Arts* (London: Greenwood Press, 1988).

Kelly, Gary, *Women Writing, and Revolution: 1790-1827* (Oxford: Clarendon Press, 1993).

Kent, Christopher, 'Image and Reality: The Actress and Society', *A Widening Sphere: Changing Roles of Victorian Women*, Martha Vicinus, ed. (Bloomington: Indiana University Press, 1977), pp. 94-116.

Kemp, Melody J., 'Helen's Diary and the Method(ism) of Character Formation in *The Tenant of Wildfell Hall*', *New Approaches to the Literary Art of Anne Brontë*, Julie Nash and Barbara A Suess, eds (Aldershot: Ashgate, 2001), pp. 195-211.

Kestner, Joseph, *Protest and Reform: The British Social Narrative by Women* (London: Methuen, 1985).

Kovacevic, Ivanka, *Fact into Fiction: English Literature and the Industrial Scene, 1750-1850* (Leicester: Leicester University Press, 1975).

Kranidis, Rita S., *Subversive Discourse: The Cultural Production of Late Victorian Feminist Novels* (London: Macmillan, 1995).

Langland, Elizabeth, *Nobody's Angels: Middle-Class Women and Domestic Ideology in Victorian Culture* (Ithaca: Cornell University Press, 1995).

——, 'The Voicing of Feminine Desire in Anne Brontë's *The Tenant of Wildfell Hall*', *Gender and Discourse in Victorian Literature and Art*, Anthony H. Harrison and Barbara Taylor, eds (DeKalb: Northern Illinois University Press, 1992), pp. 111-23.

Ledger, Sally, *The New Woman: Fiction and Feminism at the Fin-de-Siècle* (Manchester: Manchester University Press, 1997).

Leighton, Angela, *Victorian Women Poets: Writing Against the Heart* (London: Harvester Wheatsheaf, 1992).

Leonardi, Susan J. and Rebecca Pope, *The Diva's Mouth: Body, Voice, Prima Donna Politics* (New Brunswick: Rutgers University Press, 1996).

Levine, Philippa, *Victorian Feminism, 1850-1900* (London: Hutchinson, 1987).

Lewis, Jane, ed., *Labour & Love: Women's Experience of Home and Family, 1850-1940* (Oxford: Basil Blackwell, 1986).

Lewis, Linda M., 'The Artist's Quest in Elizabeth Barrett Browning's *Aurora Leigh*', *Images of the Self as Female: The Achievement of Women Artists in Re-envisioning Feminine Identity*, Kathryn M. Benzel and Laura Pringle De La Vars, eds (Lewiston, NY: The Edwin Mellor Press, 1992), pp. 77-88.

Logan, Deborah Ann, *Fallenness in Victorian Women's Writing: Marry, Stitch, Die, or Do Worse* (Columbia, MO: University of Missouri Press, 1998).

Lohrli, Anne, 'Women in British Periodicals', *Victorian Periodicals Review* 9 (1976), pp. 128-30.

Lown, Judy, *Women and Industrialization: Gender at Work in Nineteenth-Century England* (Cambridge: Polity Press, 1990).

Macheski, Cecilia, 'Penelope's Daughters: Images of Needlework in Eighteenth-Century Literature', *Fetter'd or Free? British Women Novelists, 1670-1815*, Mary Anne Schofield and Cecilia Macheski, eds (Athens: Ohio University Press, 1986), pp. 85-100.

Marsh, Jan, 'Art, Ambition and Sisterhood in the 1850s', *Women in the Victorian Art World*, Clarissa Campbell Orr, ed. (Manchester: Manchester University Press, 1995), pp. 33-48.

Marsh, Jan and Pamela Gerrish Nunn, *Pre-Raphaelite Women Artists* (Manchester: Manchester City Art Galleries, 1997).

Marshall, Gail, *Actresses on the Victorian Stage: Feminine Performance and the Galatea Myth* (Cambridge: Cambridge University Press, 1998).

——, 'Actresses, Statues and Speculation in *Daniel Deronda*', *Essays in Criticism* 44 (1994), pp. 117-39.

Martin, Bruce, 'Music and Fiction: The Perils of Populism', *Mosaic* 31 (1998), pp. 21-39.

Martinez, Michele, 'Sister Art and Artists: Elizabeth Barrett Browning's *Aurora Leigh* and the Life of Harriet Hosmer', *Forum for Modern Language Studies* 39 (2002), pp. 214-26.

McDonald, Jan, 'Lesser Ladies of the Victorian Stage', *Theatre Research International* 13 (1988), pp. 234-49.

McMaster, R.D., 'Women in *The Way We Live Now*' *English Studies in Canada* 7 (1981), pp. 68-80.

Messer-Davidow, Ellen, '"For Softness She": Gender Ideology and Aesthetics in Eighteenth-Century England', *Eighteenth-Century Women and the Arts*, Frederick M. Keener and Susan E. Lorsch, eds (London: Greenwood Press, 1988), pp. 45-55.

Metz, Nancy Aycock, 'The Artistic Reclamation of Waste in *Our Mutual Friend*', *Nineteenth-Century Fiction* 34 (1979), pp. 59-72.

Michie, Elsie, *Outside the Pale: Cultural Exclusion, Gender Difference, and the Victorian Woman Writer* (Ithaca: Cornell University Press, 1993).

Michie, Helena, *The Flesh Made Word: Female Figures and Women's Bodies* (Oxford: Oxford University Press, 1989).

——, '"There is no Friend Like a Sister": Sisterhood as Sexual Difference', *ELH* 56 (1989), pp. 401-21.

——, '"Who is this in Pain?" Scarring, Disfigurement, and Female Identity in *Bleak House* and *Our Mutual Friend*', *Novel: A Forum on Fiction* 22 (1989), pp. 199-212.

Miesel, Martin, *Realizations: Narrative, Pictorial and Theatrical Arts in Nineteenth-Century England* (Princeton: Princeton University Press, 1983).

Miller, Jane Eldridge, *Rebel Women: Feminism, Modernism and the Edwardian Novel* (London: Virago, 1994).

Mitchell, Rosemary, '"The Busy Daughters of Clio": Women Writers of History from 1820-1880', *Women's History Review* 7 (1998), pp. 107-34.

——, 'A Stitch in Time?: Women, Needlework, and the Making of History in Victorian Britain', *Journal of Victorian Culture* 1 (1996), 185-202.

Mitchell, Sally, *The New Girl: Girl's Culture in England, 1880-1915* (New York: Columbia University Press, 1995).

Morgan, H.C., 'The Lost Opportunity of the Royal Academy: An Assessment of its Position in the Nineteenth Century', *Journal of the Warburg and Courtauld Institutes* 32 (1969), p. 415.

Morris, Debra, 'Maternal Roles and the Production of Name in Wilkie Collins's *No Name*', *Dickens Studies Annual* 27 (1998), pp. 271-86.

Morse, Deborah Deneholz, '"I speak of those I do know": Witnessing as Radical Gesture in *The Tenant of Wildfell Hall*', *New Approaches to the Literary Art of Anne Brontë*, Julie Nash and Barbara A. Suess, eds (Aldershot: Ashgate, 2001), pp. 103-26.

——, 'Stitching Repentance, Sewing Rebellion: Seamstresses and Fallen Women in Elizabeth Gaskell's Fiction', *Keeping the Victorian House: A Collection of Essays*, Vanessa D. Dickerson, ed. (New York: Garland, 1995), pp. 27-73.

Murphy, Patricia, 'Reconceiving the Mother: Deconstructing the Madonna in *Aurora Leigh*', *Victorian Newsletter* no 91 (1997), pp. 21-27.

Murray, Janet, *Strong Minded Women & Other Lost Voices* (New York: Pantheon Books, 1982).

Nead, Lynda, *Myths of Sexuality: Representations of Women in Victorian Britain* (Oxford: Basil Blackwell, 1988).

Neff, Wanda, *Victorian Working Women: A Historical and Literary Study of Women in British Industries and Professions 1832-1850* (London: Frank Cass & Co., 1966).

Nestor, Pauline A., 'A New Departure in Women's Publishing: *The English Woman's Journal* and *The Victoria Magazine*', *Victorian Periodicals Review* 15 (1982), pp. 93-106.

Newton, Judith Lowder, *Women, Power, and Subversion: Social Strategies in British Fiction 1778-1860* (Athens: University of Georgia Press, 1981).

Nochlin, Linda, *Women, Art, and Power, and Other Essays* (London: Thames and Hudson, 1991).

Nunn, Pamela Gerrish, *Victorian Women Artists* (London: The Woman's Press, 1981).

Onslow, Barbara, 'Deceiving Images, Revealing Images: The Portrait in Victorian Women's Writing', *Victorian Poetry* 33 (1995), pp. 450-75.

Orr, Clarissa Campbell, ed., *Women in the Victorian Art World* (Manchester: Manchester University Press, 1995).

Paige, Lori A., 'Helen's Diary Freshly Considered', *Brontë Society Transactions* 20 (1991), pp. 225-27.

Palmegiano, E.M., 'Mid-Victorian Periodicals and Careers for Women', *Journal of Newspaper and Periodical History* 6:2 (1990), pp. 15-19.

Parker, Christopher, ed., *Gender Roles and Sexuality in Victorian Literature* (Aldershot: Scholar Press, 1995).

Parker, Rosie, 'The Word for Embroidery Was Work', *Spare Rib* no. 37 (1975), pp. 41-45.

Parker, Rozsika, *The Subversive Stitch: Embroidery and the Making of the Feminine* (London: The Women's Press, 1984).

Parker, Rozsika and Griselda Pollock, *Old Mistresses: Women, Art and Ideology* (London: Rivers Oram Press, 1981).

Parkin-Gounelas, Ruth, '"Speaking Likenesses" – And "Differences": The Prose Fantasies of Christina Rossetti', *Victorian Literature and Culture* 23 (1995), pp. 147-57.

Peterson, Linda, 'The Female *Bildungsroman*: Tradition and Revision in Oliphant's Fiction', *Margaret Oliphant: Critical Essays on a Gentle Subversive*, pp. 66-89.

Pinchbeck, Ivy, *Women Workers and the Industrial Revolution* (London: Frank Cass & Co., 1969).

Pollock, Griselda, *Differencing the Canon: Feminist Desire and the Writing of Art's Histories* (London: Routledge, 1999).

——, *Vision and Difference: Femininity, Feminism and the Histories of Art* (London: Routledge, 1988).

Poovey, Mary, *Uneven Developments: The Ideological Work of Gender in Mid-Victorian Britain* (London: Virago, 1989).

Powell, Kerry, *Women and Victorian Theatre* (Cambridge: Cambridge University Press, 1997).

Prochaska, F., *Women and Philanthropy in Nineteenth-Century England* (Oxford: Clarendon Press, 1980).

Psomiades, Kathy Alexis, *Beauty's Body: Femininity and Representation in British Aestheticism* (Stanford: Stanford University Press, 1997).

Pykett, Lyn, *The Improper Feminine: The Women's Sensation Novel and the New Woman Writing* (London: Routledge, 1992).

——, 'Portraits of the Artist as a Young Woman: Representations of the Female Artist in New Woman Fiction of the 1890s', *Victorian Women Writers and the Woman Question*, Nicola Diane Thompson, ed. (Cambridge: Cambridge University Press, 1999), pp. 135-50.

——, *The Sensation Novel from The Woman in White to The Moonstone* (Plymouth: Northcote House, 1994).

Rance, Nicholas, *Wilkie Collins and Other Sensation Novelists* (Rutherford: Fairleigh Dickinson University Press, 1991).

Redinger, Ruby, *George Eliot: The Emergent Self* (New York: Alfred A. Knopf, 1975).

Rendall, Jane, *Women in an Industrializing Society: England 1750-1880* (Oxford: Basil Blackwell, 1990).

Rennie, Mairi Calcraft, 'Maternity in the Poetic Margins', *Studies in Browning and His Circle* 19 (1991), pp. 7-18.

Reynolds, Kimberley and Nicola Humble, *Victorian Heroines: Representations of Femininity in Nineteenth-Century Literature and Art* (New York: New York University Press, 1993).

Richards, Sandra, *The Rise of the English Actress* (London: Macmillan, 1993).

Rinehart, Nana, '"The Girl of the Period" Controversy', *Victorian Periodicals Review* 13 (1980), pp. 3-9.

Roberts, Elizabeth, *Women's Work 1840-1940* (London: Macmillan Education, 1988).

Roberts, Neil, *Meredith and the Novel* (Basingstoke: Macmillan Press, 1997).

Rogers, Helen, '"The Good Are Not Always Powerful, Nor The Powerful Always Good": The Politics of Women's Needlework in Mid-Victorian London', *Victorian Studies* 40 (1997), pp. 589-623.

Rose, Sonya, *Limited Livelihoods: Gender and Class in Nineteenth-Century England* (Berkeley: University of California Press, 1992).

Rosen, Judith, 'At Home Upon a Stage: Domesticity and Genius in Geraldine Jewsbury's *The Half Sisters*', *The New Nineteenth Century: Feminist Reading of Underread Victorian Fiction*, Barbara Leah Harman and Susan Meyers, eds (London: Garland Publishing, 1996), pp. 17-31.

Rosenman, Ellen Bayuk, 'Spectacular Women: *The Mysteries of London* and the Female Body', *Victorian Studies* 40 (1996), pp. 31-64.

—— 'Women's Speech and the Roles of the Sexes in *Daniel Deronda*', *Texas Studies in Literature and Language* 31 (1989), pp. 237-56.

Rowell, George, *Theatre in the Age of Irving* (Oxford: Basil Blackwell, 1981).

——, *Victorian Dramatic Criticism* (London: Methuen, 1971).

Sanders, Valerie, *Eve's Renegades: Victorian Anti-Feminist Women Novelists* (London: Macmillan, 1996).

——, *The Private Lives of Victorian Women: Autobiography in Nineteenth-Century England* (London: Harvester Wheatsheaf, 1989).

Sarad, Kay, 'Emily Faithfull and the Victoria Press: Women, Culture and Work, 1850-1880', *Studies in the History of Feminism (1850s-1930s)*, Sally Alexander, ed. (London: University of London Press, 1984), pp. 18-31.

Seeley, Tracy, 'Victorian Women's Essays and Dinah Mulock's *Thoughts*: Creating an *Ethos* for Argument', *Prose Studies* 19 (1996), pp. 93-109.

Shannon, E., 'Poetry as Vision: Sight and Insight in the Lady of Shalott', *Victorian Poetry* 19 (1981), pp. 207-23.

Shaw, Karen, '*Wildfell Hall* and the Artist as a Young Woman', *West Virginia University Philosophical Papers* 48 (2001-2002), pp. 9-17.

Shires, Linda M., 'The Author as Spectacle and Commodity: Elizabeth Barrett Browning and Thomas Hardy', *Victorian Literature and the Victorian Imagination*, Carol T. Christ and John O. Jordan, eds (Berkeley: University of California Press, 1995), pp. 198-212.

Showalter, Elaine, *A Literature of Their Own: From Charlotte Brontë to Doris Lessing*, rev. ed. (London: Virago Press, 1999).

Shumaker, Jeanette, 'The Alcharisi and Gwendolen: Confession Rebellion', *George Eliot George Henry Lewes Studies* 18-19 (1991), pp. 55-62.

Shuttleworth, Sally, 'Demonic Mothers: Ideologies of Bourgeois Motherhood in the Mid-Victorian Era', *Rewriting the Victorian: Theory, History and the Politics of Gender*, Linda Shires, ed. (London: Routledge, 1992), pp. 31-51.

Siefert, Susan, *The Dilemma of the Talented Heroine: A Study in Nineteenth Century Fiction* (Montreal: Eden Press, 1977).

Signorotti, Elizabeth, '"A Frame Perfect and Glorious": Narrative Structure in Anne Brontë's *The Tenant of Wildfell Hall*', *Victorian Newsletter* no 87 (1995), pp. 20-25.

Smart, Carol, ed., *Regulating Womanhood: Historical Essays on Marriage, Motherhood, and Sexuality* (London: Routledge, 1992).

Smith, Peter, 'The Aestheticist Argument of *Our Mutual Friend*', *The Cambridge Quarterly* 18 (1989), pp. 362-82.

Steinmetz, Virginia V., 'Images of "Mother-Want" in Elizabeth Barrett Browning's *Aurora Leigh*', *Victorian Poetry* 21 (1983), pp. 35-48.

Stern, Rebecca, 'Moving Parts and Speaking Parts: Situating Victorian Antitheatricality', *ELH* 65 (1998), pp. 423-44.

Stokes, John, 'Rachel's "Terrible Beauty": An Actress Among the Novelists', *ELH* 51 (1984), pp. 771-93.

Stokes, John, Michael Booth, and Susan Bassnett, eds, *Bernhardt, Terry, Duse: The Actress in her Time* (Cambridge: Cambridge University Press, 1988).

Stubbs, Patricia, *Women & Fiction: Feminism and the Novel 1880-1920* (London: Methuen, 1981).

Sturrock, June, 'Literary Women of the 1850s and Charlotte Mary Yonge's *Dynevor Terrace*', *Victorian Women Writers and the Woman Question*, Nicola Diane Thompson, ed. (Cambridge: Cambridge University Press, 1999), pp. 116-34.

Surridge, Lisa, 'Madame de Staël Meets Mrs. Ellis: Geraldine Jewsbury's *The Half Sisters*', *Carlyle Studies Annual* 15 (1995), pp. 81-95.

——, 'Representing the "Latent Vashti": Theatricality in Charlotte Brontë's *Villette*', *The Victorian Newsletter* no. 87 (1995), pp. 4-14.

Sutherland, John, *Victorian Fiction: Writers, Publishers, Readers* (London: Macmillan, 1995).

Swenson, Kristine, 'Protection or Restriction? Women's Labour in *Mary Barton*', *Gaskell Society Journal* 7 (1993), pp. 50-66.

Swindells, Julia, *Victorian Writing and Working Women* (Cambridge: Polity Press, 1985).

Tasker, Meg, '*Aurora Leigh*: Elizabeth Barrett Browning's Novel Approach to the Woman Poet', *Tradition and Poetic of Self in Nineteenth-Century Women's Poetry*, Barbara Garlick, ed. (Amsterdam: Rodopi, 2002), pp. 23-41.

Taylor, Jenny Bourne, *In the Secret Theatre of Home: Wilkie Collins, Sensation Narrative and Nineteenth-Century Psychology* (London: Routledge, 1988).

Thompson, Dorothy, 'Women, Work and Politics in Nineteenth-Century England: The Problem of Authority', *Equal or Different: Women's Politics 1800-1914*, Jane Rendall, ed. (Oxford: Basil Blackwell, 1987), pp. 57-81.

Thompson, F.M.L., *The Rise of Respectable Society: A Social History of Victorian Britain 1830-1900* (Cambridge, MA: Harvard University Press, 1988).

Thompson, Nicola Diane, 'Responding to the Woman Questions: Rereading Noncanonical Victorian Women Novelists', *Victorian Women Writers and the Woman Question*, Nicola Diane Thompson, ed. (Cambridge: Cambridge University Press, 1999), pp. 1-23.

——, *Reviewing Sex: Gender and the Reception of Victorian Novels* (London: Macmillan, 1996).

——, ed., *Victorian Women Writers and the Woman Question* (Cambridge: Cambridge University Press, 1999).

Thompson, Patricia, *The Victorian Heroine: A Changing Ideal, 1837-1873* (Westport, CT: Greenwood Press, 1978).

Tuchman, Gaye with Nina Fortini, *Edging Women Out: Victorian Novelists, Publishers, and Social Change* (New Haven: Yale University Press, 1989).

Turner, Charlotte, *Living By the Pen: Women Writers in the Eighteenth Century* (London: Routledge, 1992).

Turner, Mark W., *Trollope and the Magazines: Gendered Issues in Mid-Victorian Britain* (London: Macmillan, 2000).

Uglow, Jennifer, *George Eliot* (London: Virago, 1987).

Vann, J. Don and Rosemary T. Van Arsdel, eds, *Victorian Periodicals and Victorian Society* (Aldershot: Scholar Press, 1994).

Vicinus, Martha, *Independent Women: Work and Community for Single Women, 1850-1920* (London: Virago Press, 1985).

——, *A Widening Sphere: Changing Roles of Victorian Women* (Bloomington: Indiana University Press, 1972).

Victor, Carol de Saint, 'Acting and Action: Sexual Distinctions in *Daniel Deronda*', *Cahiers Victoriens et Edouardiens* 26 (1987), pp. 77-88.

Walker, Linda, 'Party Political Women: A Comparative Study of Liberal Women and the Primrose League, 1890-1914', *Equal or Different: Women's Politics 1800-1914*, Jane Rendall, ed. (Oxford: Basil Blackwell, 1987), pp. 165-91.

Walkley, Christina, *The Ghost in the Looking Glass: The Victorian Seamstress* (London: Peter Owen, 1981).

Walkowitz, Judith, *City of Dreadful Delight: Narratives of Sexual Danger in Late-Victorian London* (London: Virago, 1992).

——, *Prostitution and Victorian Society: Women, Class, and the State* (Cambridge: Cambridge University Press, 1980).

Wallace, Anne D., '"Nor in Fading Silks Compose": Sewing, Walking, and Poetic Labor in *Aurora Leigh*', *ELH* 64 (1997), pp. 223-56.

Weliver, Phyllis, *Women Musicians in Victorian Fiction, 1860-1900: Representations of Music, Science and Gender in the Leisured Home* (Aldershot: Ashgate, 2000).

Wheatley, Kim, 'Death and Domestication in Charlotte M. Yonge's *The Clever Woman of the Family*', *SEL* 36 (1996), pp. 895-915.

White, Allon, *The Uses of Obscurity: The Fiction of Early Modernism* (London: Routledge and Kegan Paul, 1981).

Whitehead, John, ed., 'A Grain of Sand: Ellen Terry's Letters to Amey Stansfield', *Theatre Research International* 13 (1988), pp. 191-220.

Williams, Merryn, 'Feminist or Antifeminist? Oliphant and the Woman Question', *Margaret Oliphant: Critical Essays on a Gentle Subversive*, D.J. Trela, ed. (Selingsgrove: Susquehanna University Press, 1995), pp. 165-80.

——, *Women in the English Novel: 1800-1900* (London: Macmillan Press, 1984).

Wilson, Anita C., 'Elizabeth Gaskell's Subversive Icon: Motherhood and Childhood in *Ruth*', *Gaskell Society Journal* 16 (2002), pp. 85-111.

Wilson, Carol Shiner, 'Lost Needles, Tangled Thread: Stitchery, Domesticity, and the Artistic Enterprise in Barbauld, Edgeworth, Taylor, and Lamb', *Revisioning Romanticism: British Women Writers, 1776-1837*, Carol Shiner Wilson, ed. (Philadelphia: University of Pennsylvania Press, 1994), pp. 167-90.

Wolff, Janet, *Feminine Sentences: Essays on Women and Culture* (Oxford: Polity Press, 1990).

Winston, Elizabeth 'Revising Miss Marjoribanks', *Nineteenth-Century Studies* 9 (1995), p. 89.

Wood, Christopher, *Victorian Panorama* (London: Faber and Faber, 1976).

Wright, Terence, *Elizabeth Gaskell: 'We are Not Angels': Realism, Gender, Values* (London: Macmillan, 1995).

Yeldham, Charlotte, *Women Artists in Nineteenth Century France and England*, 2 vols (London: Garland Publishing, 1984).

Young, Arlene, *Culture, Class and Gender in the Victorian Novel* (London: Macmillan, 1999).

Index